Praise for Jane Doherty

"Come along with Jane Doherty on this beautifully written journey of her search for her inner psychic abilities. Jane helps the reader find his or her own center to better listen to the internal energy we each have. Jane's strong sense of spirituality as it relates to psychic ability make this book a refreshing , unique must-read!"

Melanie Rigney ~ Editor, *Writer's Digest* magazine

"Jane's quest for the truth, and her search into the world of the paranormal, reads like a good detective story."

Marilyn McGuire ~ NAPRA, Founder

"Jane's psychic gift will leave you surprised, astonished and even amazed. The one thing that stands out is the way her outpouring of love and kindness, inspire listeners to believe miracles can happen everyday. And now her book, *Awakening the Mystic Gift*, will inspire her readers to believe the same."

Ted Efaw ~ Radio host

"This is a book for those readers hungry for new spiritual revelations! No other psychic has given us this much detail about the gift. You go inside Jane Doherty's mind and into the psychic development process as she goes through it. Incredible!"

Dennis Nagy ~ Remote viewer and author of
The Ultimate Guide to Dating 911: Internet Dating Safety

"Beautifully written, *Awakening the Mystic Gift*, is a groundbreaking story that takes psychic abilities apart, sees what makes them tick and uncovers why God bestows the gift. Fascinating and powerful!"

Anna M. Lascurain ~ Co-author of
Shopping for Miracles: A guide to psychics and psychic powers and
author of a children's book, *The Moonboy*.

"*Awakening the Mystic Gift* emits an amazing amount of energy generated by Jane's words and the story she tells. It has certainly had an effect on me. I read as far as chapter five – *Where the Dream Begins* – and was visited by my deceased grandfather during a dream. I also witnessed my first aura. Brilliant! The book really draws you in. Better brace yourself, this book is going to knock your psychic socks off!"

Leeza Hernandez ~ Designer, *Awakening the Mystic Gift*.

"Time after time, Jane has displayed an uncanny ability to predict the things that happen in my future. Her accuracy with names, situations and events amazes me."

Joanne M.

"I had been looking for my lost engagement ring for over a month without success. I called Jane during her psychic call-in show to ask for her guidance in helping me locate the ring. Within five minutes after talking to her I located the ring in the exact spot she told me to look – in a shoe hidden by clothes that had fallen in my closet. My husband and I were so grateful to her."

Susan K.

"I have seen Jane help a countless number of people at my center and always with a great deal of warmth and love for her client. Personally, I have gone through a huge transformation since meeting her. She is blessed with an awesome psychic gift and a tremendous ability to exhibit love to all those she guides."

Denise B. ~ Unlimited Horizons

"Jane refused to let me accept a job offer in a company located at the World Trade Center. She had an uncomfortable feeling about the company and predicted it was going to collapse in some way. Her unusual feeling seemed odd to me since she had never reacted that strongly in the eight years I had been seeking her guidance, so I listened to her. Fortunately, the day after 9-11 I was able to thank God and Jane for the guidance."

Marybeth T.

"I was a total skeptic and came to Jane as a joke, but left the reading a believer. There is one prediction that still blows my mind! Jane told me that a friend's husband would make his transition within two years and that his mother would die a few month's after his death. That's exactly what happened right to the exact timing."

Pat H.

"Everyone who comes to the center for a reading just raves about Jane. Jane's seances never cease to amaze us and her workshops are packed with information. She is just as much a natural born teacher as she is a psychic. She is the best!"

Jack and Shirley ~ Yoga West Holistic Center

"I called Jane on a psychic call-in show to ask about my son who was going to be operated on for a brain tumor that could be cancerous. The doctor's expected complications. However, Jane predicted there would be no complications or cancer. That's exactly what happened, which puzzled the doctors. I feel Jane's psychic gift and good vibrations helped in some way."

Joann W.

"For several weeks after Jane's presentation at the center, the senior citizens were still practicing the psychic development exercises she taught them. She opened our minds and helped us to realize our connection to the hereafter. Jane is inspiring and insightful to all who come in contact with her positive energy, psychic gift and wisdom. We can't wait to have her back!"

Michele ~ Program director of a senior citizen facility

"God has blessed Jane with a spiritual gift that she freely shares with others. She has helped me to grow emotionally and spiritually by teaching me to pay attention to God's guidance in everyday life. Whenever I look and feel her energy, I can see God's love in her accomplishments."

Evie F.

"An angelic channel in Ohio told us about Jane and how to find her in New Jersey. What a blessing in our lives! We now travel to New Jersey several times a year just to have readings with her. Jane is a great psychic and truly a servant of God. She has greatly enriched our lives."

Pilot and wife ~ Ohio

"Jane is a beautiful spirit. She grows closer to her angels. And I am growing closer to her."

Dr. James Peebles ~2004

AWAKENING THE MYSTIC GIFT

The Surprising Truth About
What It Means To Be Psychic

Jane Doherty

For information address Hummel & Solvarr Publishing,
P.O. Box 10086, New Brunswick, New Jersey 08899.

Hummel & Solvarr books are available at special quantity discounts for bulk purchases for sales promotions, premiums, fund-raising, or educational use. Special books, or book excerpts, can also be created to fit specific needs.

For details, write: Special Markets: Hummel & Solvarr Publishing, P.O. Box 10086, New Brunswick, New Jersey 08899.

Hummel & Solvarr Web site: www.hummelsolvarr.com

FIRST EDITION
ISBN: 0-9746659-6-7

Interior design by Leeza Hernandez-Stelzer
Book cover writing by Susan Kendrick Writing

Library of Congress Control Number:
2 0 0 3 1 1 6 9 0 1

The individual experiences recounted in this book are true. However, in some instances, names and other descriptive details have been altered to protect the identities of the people involved.

This book is printed on acid-free paper.

Publisher's Cataloging-In-Publication Data
(Prepared by The Donohue Group, Inc.)
Doherty, Jane.
   Awakening the mystic gift : the surprising truth about what it means to be psychic / Jane Doherty. – 1st ed.
      p. ; cm.
   Includes bibliographical references.
   ISBN: 0-9746659-6-7
1. Psychics--United States. 2. Parapsychology. 3. Psychic ability. I. Title.

BF1027.D64 D64 2004
133.8/092   2003116901

With heartfelt gratitude, respect and unlimited love I dedicate this book to my parents, Walter and Teresa Malec, and to my children, Jimmy and Teri Ann Doherty.

TABLE OF CONTENTS

ACKNOWLEDGMENTS

There have been many people who have encouraged me to write this book, because they believed my message was important enough to tell. I am grateful to all of them for their support. Although it's impossible to acknowledge each one individually, there are a few I would like to mention.

To Dad and Mom, Walter and Teresa Malec ~ Your years of love, guidance and example have shaped me into who I am. Thank you for teaching me to love others and instilling in me that same love for God. I am also grateful to you for recognizing the importance of an education and the sacrifices you both made to put me and my siblings through college so that we could have the education you were not able to have. Without that education I could not have written this book. I am so blessed that at 88 and 93 you are here to see this book published. God Bless.

To my Son and Daughter, Jimmy and Teri Ann Doherty ~ You are my pride, my joy and my best friends. From the bottom of my heart I want to thank you for your support and never-ending encouragement, as well as for our mutual bonds of love,

i

respect and friendship. I am so blessed to have such caring and uniquely talented children who are also dedicated to helping me get my message told.

To Teri Ann Doherty ~ Without you being there to do things for me whenever I needed help, I couldn't have completed this book. I am also grateful to you for being my stylist and helping me to look my best with your awesome fashion sense and make-up expertise. Thank you for also providing me with some creative marketing ideas for my book's success.

To Jimmy Doherty ~ Thank you for designing my Website and my other informational materials with your incredible creative, technical and organizational skills. I am so grateful to you for using so much of your time to help me complete this book and for your endless dedication to direct this project. Without your managing me- despite my objections at times – this book would be still be a manuscript.

To Pat and Jack Kudrick, my sister and brother-in-law; **Anthony Malec,** my brother; **John and Jen Kudrick;** my nephew and his wife and their children, **Taylor Paige and Jack Robert** ~ Thank you for being there for me whenever I needed support. Our close family bond is one of the biggest joys of my life.

To Anna Lario ~ Without you I wouldn't be me. I am honored that God chose you to guide me to my truth. You were the instrument the otherside used to set me on this path and the earthly guide who helped me to get there. My heartfelt thanks for the years of inspiration, psychic guidance, and unconditional love you have given me and the many others you have guided. Your example has been my greatest teacher.

To Ron Hummel ~ You were the wind beneath my wings that took me to these heights. No words could ever express my gratitude for your unconditional love, friendship and never-ending support. You are the "model" that exemplifies the true meaning of friendship. Thank you for believing enough in me to be an incredible friend and for being my publisher. This book could not have happened without your support. And I thank God for sending you to me.

To Pat Kudrick ~ Thank you for helping me get things done even when it seemed impossible. I couldn't have completed this book without your help. My wish is for all sisters to have our same closeness and willingness to help each other.

To Rachele Starr ~ You believed in me when I hadn't even begun to believe in myself. Our mutual interest took us through many adventures, including you coming with me on my first ghost investigation. Thank you for the years of encouragement, support and friendship.

To Peter and Clare Montagna ~ Our friendship began in the NBC make-up room during my first national television appearance. And it soon developed into a bond that felt like family and has been cherished ever since. Thank you for your years of encouragement and support and for inspiring me to believe in my dream.

To Ruth Sklar ~ It started with a consultation and became an endearing friendship. Thank you for always being there for me and inspiring me to reach my goal – even when I had doubts. Your dedicated support and belief in me helped to make this book happen. I want to also thank your son, Jason, and the other members of your family for their friendship and support.

To Donna Pedota ~ You typed the first draft of the book and have been there ever since as my friend and part of my cheerleading team. Thank you for your unwavering support, encouragement and belief in my mission, especially at crucial moments during the writing process. I also want to thank your mom and dad, Joan and Ben, for their encouragement.

To Melba Delfino ~ You have been my angel on earth, always willing to help me in whatever way you could so this project could go forward. Your belief in my mission strengthened my resolve to finish the book. And I also want to thank your husband, Ken for always encouraging you to be there for me – even if it meant flying all the way from California to New Jersey.

To Denise Bruccato and Liz Stoia ~ Thank you for being my number one and number two fans and for turning that admiration into a lasting friendship. Your support and enthusiasm for my work always uplifted me, especially during difficult moments. And your encouragement helped me to complete this book.

To Shirley and Jack Scisko ~ Thank you for your friendship, your years of support and for the opportunity to guide so many wonderful clients of Yoga West Holistic Center. Your enthusiasm for my work helped me to reach my dream.

To Nick Salerno and Nick Ficocello ~ I am grateful for your belief in me, your encouragement and your friendship. Thank you for your support and for proving long distance friendship can feel like family, too.

To Ross and Valerie Gwynn ~ Your faith in me and in my guides gave me strength when I needed it. Thank you for the many times you have supported and assisted me, especially at crucial moments when the progress of the book was essential. I am also grateful to you for being my prayer warriors and for keeping me and the fulfillment of God's plan in your prayers.

To Anna Lascurain ~ It started with an interview on the Spy House and turned into years of friendship. You have always been there to help me in whatever way you could – sometimes at a moments notice. With heartfelt gratitude I am so thankful for all your support and encouragement.

To Sandra Jimenez and Sylvia Morales ~ You were the

first to offer me your support. Your kindness and generosity touched my heart and gave me the confidence to start writing this book.

To Dennis and Diane Nagy ~ Thank you for being two of my biggest fans. I am grateful for your friendship, boundless enthusiasm and support for me. You were always there when I needed you and at other times when I didn't think I needed support, but did. Keep listening to your intuition!

To Carol Russo ~ When I needed to get organized, you were there to help me recapture my sanity so I could continue writing. Thank you for your friendship and support throughout the years.

To Jeff Williamson ~ "The pirate" ~ You helped me in the very beginning stages of this book , which motivated me to do it. A great big thank you.

To Florence Cohen ~ Thank you for your friendship and for putting Hollywood Duke into our lives. Your prayers and belief in me inspired me to believe that I could achieve this goal. You're one special lady.

To David Stahl ~ Your insightful comments were helpful in my deciding to change the direction of this book. I am grateful to you for proving there are strangers out there willing to help another person in need. Your kindness will never be forgotten.

To Meredith Stark ~ You encouraged me to tell my message and to live my dream. Our lives touched for just a short time, but that inspiration will always stay with me. Thank you for that gift.

To Rhonda Rich ~ Without your kind gesture of passing my manuscript on to an agent and your support for this project, this book would still be a manuscript. You are one of Georgia's gems and a wonderful example of southern friendship.

To Melanie Rigney ~ Your support and encouragement will always be remembered. And I thank God for putting you in my path.

To Dr. Araceli Ziemba ~ Your kindness gave me the hope I needed to continue and it will always be remembered. You are one special lady!

To Richard Curtis ~ Without your belief in my ability I could never have completed this book. Thank you for your support and for being my agent. Here's hoping there are many more years of working together.

To Bob Aaronson ~ You believed enough in my sincerity to trust your intuition – even though you had no belief in psychic ability. I am so grateful to you for starting my career as a radio psychic on your show and for helping me gain recognition.

To Ted Efaw ~ Thank you for your years of support, encouragement, friendship and for the fun I had doing a bi-weekly psychic call-in segment on your radio show. You helped me to become known as "Central Jersey's favorite clairvoyant," which helped to pave the way for my success.

To Julie Briggs and Jesse Frees ~ Your enthusiasm and support for my work always encouraged me to follow my dream. Thank you for inviting me to be a frequent guest on your radio show and for helping me gain recognition.

To Kathi Dunn, Susan Kendrick, Leeza Hernandez-Stelzer, Kathleen Marusak, Alastair Sergedahl ~ Thank you for the awesome job all of you have done as part of my production team. It felt-like you were long-time friends who cared enough about me and my project to make it perfect. You are incredibly talented people. **Susan** ~ I appreciate your spiritual guidance and resolve to get the words on the copy absolutely perfect. **Kathleen** ~ Your comments encouraged and excited me because I knew I had succeeded in expressing my message. **Kathi** ~ You expressed your heavenly guidance so well in your awesome design work. **Leeza** ~ It seemed like we were friends for years when we met – but it was a hint of the years of friendship ahead of us. You are one talented and special lady. Thank you for your incredible support and enthusiasm for my book.

A special thank you to four wonderful people who have helped me, but crossed-over before the completion of this book.

To Christopher Kapsak ~ You were my young cousin who only had twenty-eight short years on this earth, yet you touched the hearts and minds of so many people. Your kindness, honesty, enthusiasm and faith in God will live on in our memories and continue to inspire all of us who loved you. Thank you for your enthusiastic response when I told you I was writing a book. Your comment, "Now you will go down in history because you are an author," inspired me to keep writing especially during those frustrating moments when I thought about quitting.

To Jane Martin ~ You were known to many as the "angel lady," but to me you were that and so much more: an incredible friend, a loving mother to your children and a talented artist. Your incredible courage and faith in God in the face of illness inspired me and so many others. Thank you for being there for me for so many years, tirelessly supporting and encouraging me to succeed. Without your help I would not be where I am today. You designed my first brochure and business card, which helped to launch my career. And I know you are there in spirit still helping me.

To Marlene Heacock ~ You were loved by many and bought joy to all that knew you and Ted E. Bear, your standard poodle

That joy will live on in the hearts of all those that loved you. Thank you for your encouragement and support.

To Mary MacArthur ~ Our "spiritual messenger" gave us the wisdom to grow spiritually and to understand our part of the greater plan. If it weren't for your hospitality all those years, I would not have had the "push" from the otherside to complete this task. Thank you for all your support. You will never be forgotten.

I want to thank the following people from the various media venues for helping me to gain recognition: Ted Efaw, Steve Doucey, Bill Roller, Paige Hopkins, Jodi Applegate, Emily Frances, Jenny Jones, Nancy Wegard, Jacqueline Urgo, Bob Aaronson, Dan Flatt, Andy Santoro, Dr. Hans Holzer, Antoinette Rainone, Jane Dornick, Nancy Grennier, Bob Makin, Bill Kent, Patrick Jenkins, Bernice Paglia, Todd Venezia, Ralph Soriano, Judith Leiblein, Eddie Davis, Sylvie Mulvaney, Lorraine Ash, Michael Casey, Ray Blanco, Joe Silvestri, Edge Entertainment, Maurice Fitzgibbons, Barbara Hoffman, Alfredo Travieso, Dick and Debra Miller, Sam D'Amico, Anita Stratos, Bill Hine, Randi Jones, Redline studios, Clyde Lewis, Ground Zero radio show, Jon Stewart Show, Stephanie Todd, Linda Vaccaro, Alicia Gray, John Granelli, Eric Stenson, John A. Harnes, Kelly-Jane Cotter, Philip Hosmer, Angela Cody, David Ross, Steven Hart, Anne Levin, David Bergeland, Mark Sullivan, Kenny Pang, John Bell and Carmine Galasso.

No life is complete without friends or the people who touch

our lives. And I have been blessed with many. I want to thank the following for their support: Midge Bortone – my friend from high school, Michael O'Brien, Peg and John Moravak, Stephanie Corbo, Gregg Hennessy, Ralph and Sandi Fech, Michael Smolinsky, Daniela Dicarlo, Hollywood Duke, Beth Paynter, Elizabeth and Ted Dolch, Ellie Crystal, Evie Fitzgerald, Bea Palumbo, Gail Marshak, Nan Wheeler, Ken and Berta Cohen, Frank Michele, Marlene Tonjes, Donna Howard, Ann Card, Bob Zalusky, Norm Hacker, Lilla Redmond, Jerry Weiss, Betty Pellerito, Claudette Lockhart, Mary Swarbrick, June Sadlowski, Don Peck, Ann Farahi, members of the Jersey Society of Parapsychology, Maxine Henderschott, Ursula McDonald, Milfred Duffy, Lew Ross, Watchung Mountain Poodle Club, Dorothy Griffin, Carolyn O'Rourke, Poodle Obedience Training Club, Dr. Andrew Boyarsky, Dr. Jane Rosenfeld, Dr. Henry Taylor, Dr. Francine Sinofsky, Dr. Kurt Blaicher, Father John Skwara, J.D.'s of Edison, Menlo Park Nordstrom Cosmetic Department, the Metlar-Bodine House Association, the Proprietary House Association, James La Sala, Esq., John Colasanti, Rich Pagini, Roxanne Cortese, Gertrude Neidlinger and the Spy House.

I want to thank all my aunts, uncles and cousins – who enriched my life as a result of their love and our close family bonds. And to my present and past pets that have all nurtured my soul and my creativity with their love.

And a special thanks to my clients, and to my faithful radio listeners, who have supported me throughout the years. Without your support and belief in me I would not be where I am today.

I would like to thank my guides for leading me to my path

and keeping me on it. And a great big thank you to anyone I may not have mentioned, but should have.

I would like to thank the "spiritual messenger" I know only as Anne, who came mysteriously into my life and left it just as mysteriously. During those five years, you gave me wisdom, and supported, encouraged and prepared me for the years yet to come. Wherever you are now, I know you are pleased the book and this part of the task are done.

Lastly, but most importantly – I want to thank God for my many blessings. May God bless everyone holding this book, doing God's work and all those who have helped me throughout the years in one way or another.

FOREWORD

With the hasty pace of day-to-day living, little time is often available for the exploration of spirituality. Modern society is task oriented, whether that task is the pursuit of material wealth or the more desperate need to survive day-to-day life.

So where does this leave the quest for one's own spiritual development? In a word: nowhere. Unless a conscious choice is made by an individual to travel down a mystical path, a person simply moves through life untouched by the deeper world surrounding him or her.

Many seeking spirituality turn to religion, become agnostics, or turn to the world of the metaphysical – the world of psychics and psychic phenomenon. While parapsychologists study the science of psychic phenomenon, more often than not, the psychic becomes the tool for interpretation of the psychic experience for the scientist.

But one question has often gone largely unanswered: Why and how does one become psychic?

Awakening the Mystic Gift: The Surprising Truth About What It Means to be Psychic is a fascinating story that lays out the path of how one special woman, Jane Doherty, started down a road untraveled by many and understood by few – the world of the psychic researcher. She will take you through her personal journeys and her emotional and philosophical challenges and inspire you to believe in your own possibilities. Her book is an interesting and unique examination of spirituality and mysticism that reads like an adventure story.

From her first encounters with psychics to her own psychic moments, then to an out-of-body experience that puts her on the other side, and finally to a Catholic priest asking her to read him, these are just some of the experiences that will fascinate and keep you reading.

Take the journey with her ... whether you believe or not.

Anna M. Lascurain ~
Co-author of *Shopping for Miracles: A guide to psychics and psychic powers*
and author of a children's book, *The Moonboy*.

Jane's words reflect the light in her soul
which is full of truth and love.
She was sent to us by a Supreme Being
and is an inspiration to us all.
She will touch your heart and soul
as you seek your own truth.

Anna Lario

INTRODUCTION

No two people have become psychic in the same way or for the same purpose. All psychics have a story to tell that reveals the experiences and circumstances that put them on this path. For me, it started with a psychic's prediction. The book you are about to read is a story on how a person with no apparent psychic ability became extraordinarily psychic – and it can happen to anyone.

It seems like it was just yesterday that I was looking for ways to find answers for my life. What is the purpose for my being? Is it possible to know God in everyday life? Why are some people more aware of a sixth sense and others are not? Is it really possible to see into the future? Can I experience a psychic moment or develop psychic ability? What do the mysteries of the unknown really portend for humanity?

I began my search for the answers by visiting a psychic for a glimpse of my future – but I wasn't prepared for what happened. My disbelief in the pyschic's shocking prediction took me on an astonishing adventure to prove or disprove psychic ability. With my curious mind and tenacity for information I encountered each experience,

1

and then scrutinized it for the truth. Before long, the mysterious pos-sibilities enticed me to look deeper in search of the secrets I believed the unknown held about life. I didn't think this quest would trans-form me – but it did.

With that in mind, I wrote this book to share my experiences and the nuggets of truths I discovered to inspire you, the reader, to believe you can do what I do. I do not profess to know all the secrets. However, what I learned from my experiences and uncovered in my quest will help you to find your own answers, so you , too, can dis-cover your own truth for a more meaningful life.

For many years, I have guided those seeking answers for their lives by encouraging them to take action toward their future or by helping them to avoid it. And those clients have confirmed my abili-ty to accurately predict the future. But the focus of this book is not on those experiences. There are already plenty of wonderful books written by psychics highlighting the talent.

Instead, I wanted to give you a fresh new perspective of the gift – an inside look into the development process and why the ability exists. It is my greatest desire that you too, will be inspired to believe in the divine spark within you and the guidance around you.

The book you are about to read chronicles the experiences that pushed me toward my destiny. The thirteen chapters of narrative con-tained within are deeply layered with the truth, which completely demystifies prophecy. I take psychic abilities apart to see what makes them tick, how they work, what makes a person psychic and why God bestows the gift. The insights presented throughout the story are summarized and provided at the end of each chapter for easy refer-ence. A hypno-meditation is included in the appendix for those read-ers who want to begin the psychic process .

Take the journey ... and discover your own truth.

FROM SKEPTIC
TO SEEKER

I always accepted the visual imagery that flashed through my mind as just part of my thought processes. These mental movies usually occurred during moments of intense concentration or deep thought, especially when I stared aimlessly through my window enjoying the beauty of nature. I had no real purpose to my focus, yet images automatically appeared without effort.

These rapidly moving images were mostly unrecognizable. At times, these mental pictures slowed enough for me to get a closer glimpse of the image, but I was still not able to interpret their meaning. The visual pictures were catalogued in my memory as day-dreams or simply a vivid imagination, which I considered the normal workings of the mind. I didn't identify these mental movies as psychic ability, because at the time I wasn't knowledgeable in psychic phenomena. I thought psychic or paranormal insight revealed itself dramatically to a person. And I also thought God's guidance came to a person in a dramatic and undeniable way. Nevertheless, I certainly didn't think either experience would become an integral part of my life.

To me a psychic reading was simply a fun experience, something I didn't take seriously. When I thought of someone predicting my future, I visualized the penny arcade on the Seaside Heights boardwalk and a mechanical fortune-teller spitting out predictions on a white card for every five cents deposited in the slot. Being there was a fun time in my childhood and the fortunes gave me dreams of wealth, romance and adventure. So going to a psychic, for me, evoked feelings of fun and entertainment, not thoughts of guidance or insight for the future. However, on one fateful day more than sixteen years ago, my life changed dramatically when a psychic predicted my future. I still remember that day vividly.

It was a cool, crisp autumn day and the scent of morning dew invigorated me. I arrived at the Menlo Park Mall with a specific shopping goal. I needed to purchase a present for my sister's birthday. As I walked through the doors, I saw people gathered in the center court. It was odd to see so many people in such a flurry of activity. At first glance, I thought there was an accident, but then realized a psychic fair in progress had attracted the crowd. I walked around the crowd and then into the Nordstrom store.

Two hours later, the center court at the Menlo Park Mall was even more packed than when I first entered it. People were still waiting for a psychic consultation. My curiosity nagged at me, so I approached an area closer to the registration table to take a better look. There were more than twenty-five psychics giving readings. All of them had people waiting for an appointment and my interest was piqued. I had never had a psychic reading before, so I debated whether I should register for a reading or not. What if the psychic frightened me or told me something I didn't want to hear? Each negative reason met with an affirmatively countered thought until I couldn't think of any more reasons not to have a psychic reading. Finally, I decided to register my name with a psychic named Joseph Sinclair for his next consultation.

As I waited for my appointment, I scrutinized Joseph's countenance. He looked normal, despite his supposed mystical powers. I observed his physical characteristics for clues as to what made him different from other people who didn't have his powers. A raven-colored beard outlined his square jaw. His broad shoulders and portly body distinguished him from the other male psychics. His confidence commanded the attention of those seeking his services, and he didn't appear mysterious.

Joseph's client finished his appointment and now it was my turn to be read. A bit shaky, I approached Joseph not knowing what to expect. I sat across from him, never taking my eyes off of his person. He held my hands, closed his eyes for a few moments, then began scribbling symbols, numbers and words on a piece of paper before he spoke.

His predictions shocked me. "Your whole life is going to change. Your awareness and thinking processes are going to expand. You are psychic and you will soon allow your psychic ability to surface. Let go of your conservative thinking and just let it happen. Don't be afraid. You are destined to be a prominent psychic in this life."

With a blank stare, I thanked him and nodded my head. Sensing my shock, he reached for a piece of paper and quickly scribbled something. I glanced at what he had written as Joseph verbalized the names of two books he suggested I read. One was *The Handbook To Higher Consciousness* by Ken Keyes and the other book was *The Magic of Believing* by Claude M. Bristol. I graciously accepted his suggestion while I focused my thoughts on what had just happened.

After a half-hour of similar predictions, the reading ended. And I walked away in disbelief, feeling that none of what he said could be the truth. His predictions were too far-fetched to be valid. How could I become a prominent psychic? I was simply a house-wife and mother and I certainly didn't think I had any psychic ability. To think of me as famous was even more absurd. I simply shrugged my shoulders and refused to believe there was validity in predictions or psychics.

I stayed awake that next night, tossing and turning. The encounter haunted me. The image of his confident demeanor flashed repeatedly in my mind's eye and his predictions gnawed at me. Disagreeing with him had not changed his interpretation of my future. In fact, his voice had developed an adamant quality when I questioned his predictions. He answered every one of my doubts with a forceful tone of voice and the repeated phrase: "This is your destiny. Your psychic ability will develop whether you want it to or not!"

Those words repeatedly played in my mind as I analyzed the prediction and the possible reasons for the psychic's words. Did the psychic tell me those things to boost his ego or to fulfill a need to feel powerful? Could a psychic conjure this ability in response to a business scheme? Or could there really be a destiny we subconsciously fulfill by our choices?

I wondered whether anyone becomes a doctor, lawyer, teacher, laborer, farmer or some other profession because they are destined to achieve that particular occupation in life. Or, do they inherit aptitudes, family guidance and financial means which influence the achievement of their particular occupation? Could one be wealthy because he or she is destined to be so or did that person recognize an opportunity, risk and then achieve the wealth through his or her actions instead of divine will? If someone is born to a poor family does that mean he or she is destined to a lifetime of poverty without any hope of ever changing their status with hard work? Does a child become incorrigible because it is his or her fate? To know these answers I had to stop pondering and start actually exploring the paranormal. I started my journey with the two books the psychic had recommended in the hopes of proving his sincerity and discovering the secrets to destiny.

After reading those books, I realized that the psychic was sincere. In fact, the books were surprisingly informative and motivating. I still didn't believe in a psychic's ability to predict the future, but at least, I determined, there was some sincerity in the reading. I just didn't understand his interpretation of my future. However, the books helped me rekindle my belief in the power of the mind, especially the power of positive thought. I recalled moments in my early teenage years when I believed enough in the thoughts and ideas that popped into my mind to spur me into action. At age fourteen, I observed that positive thought fueled success and negative thought begot failure. The recollections of my own personal experiences opened me to the real possibility that there may be much more power to the mind than I previously acknowledged, perhaps even the ability to know the future.

The more I analyzed, the more my thoughts turned to the meaning of life and the role of fate. I believed in the power of positive thought, so why couldn't I believe in a psychic having a higher sense of perception with a talent to predict a circumstance before it happens? I didn't have to probe for answers long before I acknowledged that the seeds of my beliefs and actions were planted in my thoughts by the opinions of others. Unless we are forced to consciously identify why or why not a belief or action is right, we unconsciously accept the belief as fact and claim it as our own. Our lives, somehow, are governed by what society dictates

7

without us even realizing it. We are then conditioned to believe only what we can see, hear, touch, taste or smell. With that, my attitude shifted and I developed more of a willingness to explore, rather than emphatically deny what seemed impossible.

Within a short period of time, my perceptions changed from being pessimistic to accepting the idea that somehow we influence fate by our thoughts and actions. Therefore, I felt it was possible for a person to possess psychic gifts giving us insights into our future as a means of guidance. The "what will be, will be" philosophy no longer seemed as viable as I had previously thought. In fact, I now realized that being pessimistic deprived me of the desire to create a better life. Until reading these books and then recalling personal experiences, I thought the best course in life was to wait for what the hand of fate dealt me. If fate gave me a burden or challenge, then I thought I needed to learn how to cope with it without any hope of changing it. On the other hand, if fate sent me one of life's rewards, then I thought I could just coast for awhile, enjoying a reprieve from any potential problems while I hoped for the good fortune to last.

Again, I questioned my role in life as I pondered this question: Do I have any responsibility in creating my life? My answer was yes. How could I believe in God and the possibility of a miracle without thinking I am also responsible for what I attract as the circumstances of my life? Why would God put us on earth without the tools to survive or to create a better life? How could I initiate a change in my behavior if we have no responsibility in creating the circumstances of our lives?

It did not make sense to me for us to simply live out our supposed fate to struggle or to suffer. Certainly, we couldn't just be robots here to live a miserable life bound to our fate, which at times may seem like punishment. If we have no responsibility for what happens to us, why would we ever need to be charitable to another person? Without taking some responsibility for the circumstances of life, it would simply not be worth living. Could life have more meaning if we discovered we had a destiny? And could we have an obligation to find our path to fulfill our purpose in life? There had to be a key to this mystery and I was determined to discover it. Somehow, I knew the powers of the unknown held the key to this puzzle.

In order to find that key, I had to change the focus of my exploration from being philosophical and analytical to being experimental, relying upon my experiences. It was hard at first to change modes since I was a college graduate with an analytical background. I knew I was so analytical at times I became indecisive or overly cautious. My cautiousness, however, served as a shield as well as an excuse for those awkward moments when I couldn't make a decision even when life demanded one. However, for this exploration, being analytical was a bonus, since the study of psychic ability is a relatively unknown field with very little concrete or repeatable experiences to convince a skeptic or a scientist. The evidence only had to convince me so my approach didn't have to be scientific. This was a personal journey to discover the truth about psychic power, fate and anything else I could learn about life.

The next phase of my personal quest for answers included a plan to consult psychics for more predictions regarding my future. As a result of those predictions, I hoped I could learn some truths about prophecy. This task seemed simple, until I actually started to delve into it. In my early attempts, I encountered neon signs that flashed the words, psychic reader, or advisor with the addition of a promise to solve all problems. When I looked in the phone book directory, I located listings for spiritual mediums, astrologers and Tarot card readers. The nearby book store displayed flyers for upcoming psychic fairs at a local mall. With so many possibilities to choose from, I had no idea whom to seek for a psychic consultation. I decided to attend the psychic fair because I had been to one before, and if anything too weird happened, I would be in an area that was public and not alone in a room in someone's house.

I arrived at the Garden State mall all set for the psychic adventure, but I became mentally dizzy from all the choices available in the psychic services being offered. This fair was much bigger than the previous one. There were palm readers, Tarot card readers, aura readers, mediums, channelers and clairvoyant readers with whom I could choose to consult. At that time I didn't know the difference between the psychic talents, so I chose to sit with a Tarot card reader.

As I waited for my turn, I noticed the large number of people engaged in readings around me, as well as the number of seekers patiently waiting for their turn with the various psychics. Seeing the volume of people having their future predicted comforted me. There had to be some validity to this, or there wouldn't be so many people eager to spend their money. My heart raced with excitement as my appointment time neared. I sat at a table across from the Tarot card reader without either of us extending much more of a greeting than a simple hello and nod. He introduced himself as Claude and I gave him my name.

As I shuffled the cards according to his instructions, I observed his intense manner. Claude watched me closely as I shuffled the cards, which, at first, made me expect a critical comment on my card shuffling ability. The furrowed lines on his brow deepened as he observed me. The strong energy he projected at me with his focused stare made me pull back in my seat. Dangling from his neck were gold Egyptian symbols which added a mystique to the psychic experience. When I finished shuffling the Tarot cards, Claude retrieved the cards from my hands without a comment. One by one he placed the cards on the table in a pattern. While Claude studied the card placement for meaning, I studied his expressions for clues into his mystical powers.

As he proceeded with the reading, the psychic described my husband's personality in the context of my future. His description wasn't flattering. I listened skeptically.

"Your husband doesn't allow you any freedom. You live in a very restricted environment that prevents you from reaching your full potential. You do not like arguments so you try to avoid conflict by agreeing with everything he wants or plans to do. When you live in the shadow of another, you are prevented from discovering your soul's uniqueness. You need your own identity to fulfill your life's purpose. To fulfill your soul's purpose you need to develop your natural psychic ability."

Shocked by his words I just stared at him. He ended the reading with a final prediction for my future. He simply stated, "Someday, your marriage will end. You will be divorced. It is not now but in a few years. Do not be frightened. Just let it happen. You will be all right. It is your destiny."

I reacted very strongly to his words and said, "You are wrong! My husband and I are happily married. There is no way we would ever divorce. In fact, every time we hear of someone who we know is seeking a divorce, we usually reaffirm our promise of commitment to each other. We love each other. We love our children. We would never divorce and I am one hundred percent sure of that!"

"Then your relationship will end in some other way," retorted Claude. I was satisfied with the modification of his first

11

interpretation of my future. However, my curiosity didn't stop there. I became more determined than ever to discover the truth regarding psychic powers, especially since I thought the psychic's prediction about my marriage was completely absurd. Again, my mind entertained the thought that this couldn't be real. People must go to psychics simply for entertainment purposes, just as I did as a child when I visited the mechanical gypsy fortuneteller at the Penny Arcade. However, I failed to find any fun in the psychic's prediction of my future divorce. Perhaps I just went to the wrong psychic. As I recovered from the shock of his revelation, I realized that I could have an unpleasant experience by having a psychic reading. Predictions might not always be pleasant. I quieted my mind and tried to forget the prediction. I didn't want to remember it. When I arrived home, I immediately hugged my husband without a word of my experience.

For months, I couldn't accept the prediction of my future divorce as valid. In my quiet moments, I carefully observed my husband's demeanor as I tried to imagine my life with out him. How could the psychic be correct? I repeatedly told myself that the psychic must have made a mistake. When I thought of our marriage, mutual respect and love were the only words I thought that could describe our relationship. We were devoted to each other and to our kids. And I was sure the thought of divorce would never enter either of our minds. We were a typical married couple living in suburbia with hopes, dreams and plans. We loved our son and daughter and were focused on family values.

I questioned the concept of fate again. Do we really have a destiny? Is there an inexplicable fate governing our lives? Thoughts of my husband and our first introduction to each other raced through my mind. I had always considered the circumstances of our meeting to have been fate. Kevin was a cousin to my friend's roommate, whom she wanted to introduce to me before summer break. Karen, my friend, told Kevin she had the perfect date for him. When they compared notes, I was the girl Kevin had just seen in the newspaper and whom he had wished to meet. The introduction was arranged, but I wasn't able to meet him because of prior commitments. Karen never returned to college for the fall semester, so any future connection to this man was lost. Or so I thought.

I moved from my off-campus house about eight months later, but Donna Marie, one of my former roommates, delayed her departure just long enough to receive Kevin's surprise telephone call. She gave him my new address and telephone number. If Donna Marie had not been there at the time of his call, he would have never located me because my new number was unlisted.

One week before his telephone call, my mother blurted these words to me: "You are going to receive a telephone call from a guy you don't know." I questioned my mother's prediction by asking, "What do you mean by that? Why did you say that to me?"

She simply stated, "I don't know. The thought just popped into my mind." Now, I didn't consider my mother to be psychic so I didn't give it much credence. I knew from early childhood, however, that my mother made profound statements which later came true. But at that time I just thought it was coincidence.

After talking to Susan, my married neighbor, about how she met her husband on a blind date, I received a telephone call. I didn't like blind dates, but Susan tried to convince me to be open to the possibility of meeting someone that way. Just to end our conversation, I told her I would consider it in the future, knowing it would not likely happen. No sooner had I finished those words, when the telephone rang. It was the man I was supposed to meet eight months ago. Surprised by the call, I thought

13

of my recent words with Susan. How could this happen immediately following that conversation? Was this just a coincidence or was this fate? I recalled thinking those thoughts as I talked to Kevin. I ended the conversation by agreeing to meet him on a blind date. Recollections of our meeting reminded me of my belief our marriage was destined. With this in mind, I refused to accept the psychic's prediction. Why would a marriage that was supposedly fate end in divorce?

My route of exploration now turned in an intellectual direction. I read research books about parapsychology authored by people with doctorate degrees who studied extra-sensory perception. My search for truth accelerated as I devoured the research texts with a voracious appetite. I soon discovered that extra-sensory perception encompassed a wide range of abilities. Extra-sensory perception included telepathy, clairvoyance, clairaudience, clairsentience, retrocognition, precognition and psychokinesis.

Excited by the depth of research into the mind I found, I was sure I would soon unearth the truth regarding psychic powers. My reading had already provided an understanding of all the abilities inherent in the mind that a psychic could tap into during a reading. The exploration of the material fueled my expectations of discovering real definitive knowledge to prove psychic readings were reliable predictions of the future. My expectations, however, were soon dampened when I discovered parapsychologists couldn't prove psychic ability by the current scientific model. In order for the extra-sensory perception research to fit into the scientific model, the phenomenon had to be repeatedly demonstrated in the laboratory under controlled conditions. Individual experiences outside the clinical environment were not viable proof and couldn't be included in the scientific model. In addition, not all psychic faculties could be observed or recorded in a clinical laboratory at the moment of the scientific test. With this knowledge, my heart sank.

According to the research, telepathy, retrocognition and psychokinetic ability are more demonstrable in the laboratory and can be viewed, recorded and analyzed at the moment they occur. Precognitive data, which is information that pertains to the future, can't be measured or analyzed during the actual moment of demonstration. Therefore, precognition is more difficult to prove, since it involves data that cannot be proven until there is a significant lapse in time. Clairvoyance has been demonstrated in the laboratory as images of symbols or bits and pieces of scenes, which are clues to the future that also need to be applied and interpreted. Clairvoyant images in telepathy have proved measurable in the laboratory. However, the clairvoyant images in precognition were again subject to a significant lapse in time before any validity in the image could be measured.

The researchers have concluded that psychic ability can be demonstrated in the laboratory but cannot be repeated sufficiently to be proven. Boredom setting in from the necessary repetitive tasks interfered with the accuracy of all extra-sensory perception demonstrations. How do you stop a psychic from being bored in the laboratory? I had observed psychics exhibiting outgoing and confident personalities with a tendency to be spontaneous. Outgoing personality types have a tendency to get bored in environments that are not mentally stimulating. I also imagined psychic ability to be similar to the creative talents of artists and musicians who often need space and outside stimuli for inspiration. Can you just imagine what your test results would be if you had to repeat the same task over and over again, while you demonstrated a creative talent? Most of us are bored with executing our repetitive chores everyday. So certainly, I could understand how psychic ability could not be demonstrated repetitively in the laboratory for this reason. I decided that formal research would never reveal the proof I needed, unless the current scientific model changed.

As I researched psychic phenomena further, I also learned there is a segment of society who enjoy debunking psychics and creating situations to dupe the scientists who are conducting parapsychology research. These debunkers are professional magicians and masters of illusion who have added the art of mind reading to their stage performances. A lot of these magicians and illusionists try to prove that psychic powers do not exist. I decided that it would be interesting to explore their take on psychic ability. However, I soon realized magic is a business and their point of view has a hidden agenda. Magicians and illusionists entertain the public. And publicity, especially for a controversial issue, only adds to their fame. Magicians are in the entertainment business, so how could I accept their view on psychics as valid? Mind reading is telepathy, which is a part of extra-sensory perception or ESP as it is commonly called. For entertainment purposes illusionists create a spin on telepathy. Obviously, my quest for proof couldn't be found in entertainment. Predictions about my future were potentially life changing and not entertaining. I quickly dismissed their point of view. How could I learn about fate and psychic predictions from magicians and illusionists who relied on a form of trickery to entertain?

The only way to arrive at the truth was to seek the services of psychics and compare their predictions to the actual reality of my future life experiences. I now knew there was no way to arrive at the truth except to explore it on an experiential level. I would not know the truth at the moment of the reading, but as the events of the predictions unfolded, I would be able to compare the predictions to the eventual circumstance. If none of the predictions proved true, then I would know precognitive psychic ability wasn't valid, as they couldn't predict the future.

INSIGHTS

❧ Do not expect a psychic impression to dramatically reveal its message to you. Most impressions are received as subtle sensory information in the form of a feeling, image or thought and must be interpreted.

❧ Psychic readings are not just for entertainment purposes. Some consultations can offer helpful guidance and insight that can prove to be a life-altering experience for you.

❧ There are predetermined circumstances as well as circumstances that you create when you make a choice or take an action. Through increased awareness, observation and continued interpretation of psychic impressions, you can master your destiny and create a better life.

❧ The mind is much more powerful than most people acknowledge. It is the avenue for receiving psychic information and the hidden key to understanding how we create a part of destiny that we must then accept as fate.

❧ A psychic could reveal something you are not prepared to hear in order to alert you to a problem, so that you can take the necessary steps to deal with that problem. Psychic information can reveal an issue that could redirect you from self-denial to a more productive course.

❧ A non-believer will always be a non-believer, until he or she has a paranormal experience that changes their preconceived idea about extra-sensory perception. There are experiences in life that cannot be proven scientifically, especially extra-sensory perception, until the scientific model is changed to include people's personal experiences.

❧ If you have a pessimistic attitude, you could falsely accept most bad circumstances in your life as unchangeable fate. Without hope and a more optimistic attitude, you risk attracting more negative circumstances which you must then act upon, thus creating a cycle of despair.

❧ The world is destined to change for the good. There are many people incarnated now who are on a mission for God. Some people are already aware of this mission and some are not.

❧ You must reach a higher level of consciousness to discover your own psychic potential. To do this, you eliminate the fixed patterns in your life to become more flexible and open as you strive to exhibit unconditional love.

THE QUEST FOR DESTINY

A few months passed as I searched for advertisements for a psychic fair. I grew increasingly impatient to explore the world of psychic predictions again, so I bought a few newspapers from different parts of the state in the hopes of locating the place for my next reading. This led no-where, so I called the management at the two malls who had sponsored the previous psychic fairs to ask for their schedule of events. To my surprise, the voice at the other end of the telephone told me there would be a psychic fair on the July 4th weekend, just two weeks away.

I couldn't wait for the event. My excitement turned into expectation as I hoped to seek the services of several psychics this time. By having readings from more than one psychic on the same day, I would be able to compare the similarities or discrepancies of what each psychic told me. This, I determined, would be my best avenue of approach.

The July 4th weekend arrived and I had planned to leave my house around 10 a.m. to start my holiday celebration. Twenty minutes later, the mall was crowded and the registration roster for the readings indicated there was a long wait. However, I was determined to explore the validity of prophecy no matter how long I had to wait in line.

The first psychic I sat with was another Tarot card reader. Her name was Angela. She had long, dark hair that framed her finely-featured face in a dramatic way. She was a pretty woman, about forty years old with almond-shaped green eyes. Her long finger nails commanded my attention as I studied her hands. Long and slender, her hands were exotic, especially since Angela wore a ring on every finger. Could those rings increase her ability in some way or did they have some other special meaning?

As I observed the rings more carefully, I spotted Egyptian symbols carved into the gold metal. There were amethyst and citrine stones set into the design of most of the rings. My eyes could not stop focusing on her hands. Every hand movement hypnotized me into a state of deep concentration as I observed Angela place five cards horizontally and then another five cards vertically in what looked like a cross. I watched her turn the cards over as I tried to decipher how she assigned meaning to the symbols on the deck. I listened carefully as she started to speak.

"You will have an opportunity to eventually open a business. Later on in life, you will need to watch the throat area for thyroid problems."

I responded by nodding my head to indicate that I understood her warning. Shaking her head from side to side, she cautioned, "Money always slips through your husband's fingers. He needs to save money for a new business deal that will present itself to him." I didn't know how to respond to her interpretation. I had thought of my husband as a person who enjoyed spending money, but I didn't perceive his spending as reckless.

The psychic placed an unusual looking card onto another card that looked like a female image before she stated more predictions. I couldn't read the Tarot cards nor did I really know anything about them. They looked mysterious and intimidating.

Angela began speaking again. "You will make money on your own through new ideas. And I see your name as an author of a book."

She paused for a few minutes as she stared at the image of the Tarot card. I assumed she looked at the card in order to analyze the placement of it for an interpretation. In that short moment I thought about the time as a teenager when I told myself I would be a writer after the age of forty. I wondered if she had tapped into my thoughts in some way or if this really was my future.

The psychic continued turning the cards from face down to face up as she studied them. "You will have two marriages in this life. There will be many changes around you. Let it happen. Eventually, your psychic ability will open and you will then do what I do."

I tried to stay calm, although inside my heart raced. I didn't want to openly react to the psychic's predictions. Some of the same themes were repeated. Although it was hard for me to believe I would be a professional psychic and married to someone else, I decided to just wait and see what developed in my life.

Before I left her table she added, "When you start to open psychically you will see spirits and hear voices. Don't be frightened by these experiences. You can handle it."

As I walked away from the table, I thought of her last words. Could being psychic actually be frightening? I never observed any of these psychics at the fairs as being frightened or overwhelmed by their experiences. Most of them seemed to read the cards rather routinely with little expression. That lack of expression made it difficult to determine if the psychics experienced fear or any other emotion during the process. Nor were there any clues to determine the level of confidence each psychic had in his or her ability. Consequently, it was difficult to determine if the psychic was sincere in interpreting the meaning of the Tarot cards. This was another prediction I would have to wait to have confirmed.

I really didn't want to be a psychic. The thought of having frightening experiences didn't appeal to me. Imagine the responsibility of seeing someone's future and having to guide the person to or away from that future? It seemed to me to be an awesome responsibility whether there was truth or not in such predictions. So I didn't look forward to my future career. Supposedly, this was my destiny, so I guess I didn't have a choice. I dismissed the idea with the acknowledgement, what will be, will be. I would have to wait and see if predicting the future was valid or not.

The next psychic I engaged was a palm reader. His foreign accent indicated he had a different ethnic background than the other psychics at the fair. He had deep olive-toned skin. His soft voice and gentle mannerisms matched his small, thin build. His chocolate brown eyes gave me the feeling he had a gentle-mannered personality. He didn't look mysterious and he made me feel very comfortable. As I held out my palm for him to read, J.R. pointed out the marriage lines, which indicated I would be married twice in this life. He also revealed a long lifeline. However, there was a broken line in my palm that showed I would have a major health challenge around the age of fifty. He also stated I would immediately recover from the health problem.

J.R. then pointed to an unusual pattern which he referred

24

to as a mystic cross and a sure sign of my psychic ability. The most disturbing prediction was a line indicating I had an experience in which divine intervention saved my life. I didn't recall any such experience, so that prediction frightened me. If it hadn't happened, did it now mean it was something that was going to happen? This thought disturbed me. In order to release my fear I focused on the thought that a divine force would save me if I ever encountered danger.

The prediction soon faded from my memory, but it resurfaced a few months later as I faced a life-threatening situation. A period of ice and snowstorms during a bitter cold February ravaged the states of New Jersey and Pennsylvania. During this time, my sister, my mother and I drove to Pennsylvania to attend a baby shower. As we were leaving the party, one of the other guests offered us directions for a shorter route to the highway, so we wouldn't get lost.

As we navigated the winding, deserted roads, we encountered icy road conditions. The dark desolate area made it difficult for us to turn back to our original starting point. There were no road signs to guide us. Following the directions we were given, we reached the last hurdle before the highway. In order to continue we had to drive up a steep incline without any visibility to the other side of the hill. We maneuvered the icy hill successfully only to face worse conditions. At the bottom of the hill was a one-lane metal bridge built over a raging river without guardrails for safety. We knew we were in trouble because the bridge was a solid sheet of ice. We tried to back up, but the car skidded out of control on the snow-packed road. We had no choice but to drive over the sheet of ice on the bridge even though one skid could plunge us into the water.

With pounding hearts and fear lodged in our throats, we

slowly inched our way toward the bridge. The three of us fervently prayed as the car moved slowly across the bridge. We reached the other side safely, and burst into tears. Without hesitation we thanked God for our safety and then comforted each other.

During the remainder of the drive home, I could only think of that palm reader's interpretation about my future. I certainly felt there had been some kind of divine intervention. With the road a solid sheet of ice, the car should have skidded and hit the bridge or slipped off into the raging water below.

Now, the focus of my thoughts turned in the direction of the palm reader's original predictions. The palm reader interpreted the symbol as something that had already occurred, but it had actually been a future event. The psychic prediction proved true even though it was misinterpreted. Could the psychic's misinterpretation be a one-time mistake or a frequent flaw in all psychic readings?

I continued going to psychics to compare my predicted future to my actual life. Themes about my future were definitely repeated by the psychic readers. I wondered if psychics were just reading my mind. How could predictions be repeated if precognitive ability was not valid? Had I accepted a thought into my mind that was now being telepathically sent to the readers without my conscious knowledge?

At psychic fairs, I observed the other people being read. Usually, they wore a serious expression on their faces. This indicated they were engrossed in deep thought, probably evaluating the predictions. How could a psychic reading be only for entertainment purposes when no one left feeling particularly jolly? People must seek these services with some respect and belief or they would leave the reading exhibiting a more carefree demeanor.

Many times, I wished I could confront the people leaving the reader to ask, "Have you ever had a prediction come true?" Since I didn't have that opportunity, I simply continued my research, determined to find that one psychic who could convince me of the validity of predictions. Questions nagged at me. Again, I pondered: Is psychic ability real or not? Does anyone know if it is really a predictive tool for your future? With all these questions still unanswered, my thirst for knowledge became even greater. I needed to talk to a professional who studied the mind. I sought the expertise of a clinical psychologist. Certainly, I thought, a doctor of psychology must have a professional opinion on psychics.

Michael, a friend, referred me to a clinical psychologist who was a relative of a friend of his. According to Michael, this psychologist, Dr. Simpson, had done a lot of research on the mind when he graduated from school. In fact, Michael believed Dr. Simpson had done research on psychic ability. So I made an appointment with the doctor, hoping he could answer my questions and give me some insight into psychic powers.

Dr. Simpson greeted me with a warm, pleasant 'Hello.' He seemed friendly, but reserved. He was dressed impeccably and his mannerisms indicated that he was detail-oriented. Despite his reserve, Dr. Simpson's approachable demeanor made me feel comfortable in his presence. I knew his expertise would be a defining moment in my journey. I explained to him the reason for my appointment. I was researching psychic phenomena for personal reasons, and I wanted a professional's opinion on the subject.

"I would be delighted to answer your questions," he responded enthusiastically.

I asked him, "Have you ever had a psychic reading?"

"No, I have not had a personal reading from a psychic, but I have studied them while I was in graduate school at Duke

27

University."

I asked bluntly, "Do you believe in psychic ability?"

"Demonstrations of psychic ability in those studies were impressive. The tests indicated that psychic ability did exist. Psychics can predict the future, but we just do not know how they do it. The actual process experienced in the mind when the information is received is still a mystery."

Dr. Simpson directed a question to me. "Is there a personal reason why you want to know about psychic ability?"

"Yes, I have had several readings from psychics. Most of them repeat the same prediction. It is sometimes a bit confusing to me, especially since I can't compare the validity of it to anything I now know or have experienced, because it is for the future."

"Would you mind telling me those predictions? Perhaps I can help you with your struggle."

I explained to Dr. Simpson that there were two themes repeated. Most of them predicted the termination of my marriage and the psychics also said that I had psychic ability.

"What upsets you about the predictions?" questioned Dr. Simpson.

"There are no problems in my marriage and I am just a stay-at-home mother, so how can I be a professional psychic?"

Quite calmly but authoritatively, Dr. Simpson responded. "You can't relate to the predictions now, because they are in the future. We can't see into the future, but the mind of a psychic functions in a different capacity than most people. Psychics can see what we can't even perceive. Anything can happen in the future, even if we cannot perceive it or comprehend it, now."

Sheepishly I asked, "Do you think I should believe the psychic predictions?"

"It's enough to have one psychic tell you something, but since you have had so many tell you the same predictions I would believe them to be valid."

Dr. Simpson's answer lifted a burden off my shoulders. I had finally received an answer. Thrilled to have a professional's opinion that validated psychic predicitions, I now knew my quest was to determine which psychic was accurate, as well as determine the psychic process involved in prophecy. Before leaving Dr. Simpson's office I asked, "Could I call you to ask you more questions, if I need an explanation for what I uncover?"

"I would be happy to answer your questions. And I hope you uncover many secrets."

Driven by my desire to understand, I sought the expertise of more psychics. However, I was not prepared for what happened next. I had a vision of a man wearing a tweed overcoat and a hat, walking down a dirt road. A woman with long, dark hair, wearing a white dress made of gauzy fabric stared from a broken screen door and wiped tears from her eyes as she watched the man walk away. In that vision the man never turned back. I had no idea who the man or woman was in the repeated vision or why I experienced this. I could not stop the vision from occurring. It happened during quiet moments, or during the times I stared out the kitchen window.

These visions ocurred for almost six months before I had an answer. An announcement in the mail alerted me to the next scheduled date for the upcoming fair at the Bergen Mall. I marked my calendar with the same anticipation and excitement as I had had for the previous fair. When I arrived at the Bergen Mall, it didn't take me long to register or to get an appointment, since I was familiar with the procedure.

The next psychic reader I sat with was a male from Kearney,

29

New Jersey, named Jim. He was a Tarot card reader who had been reading cards for more than twenty years. There were no distinguishing characteristics about Jim that would indicate he had psychic ability. In fact, Jim looked more like my next-door neighbor than a person with mystical powers.

I told him what I was seeing and asked, "What is the meaning of this vision?"

He replied with, "Oh, you are tapping spontaneously into a past life. That man was your husband in a past life. He is someone you just recently met in this life. You were that woman during the 1800's. The setting was in England. You were sad because you lost a child. Do not worry. You will not lose a child in this life."

Startled, I thought, Past Life? That's a new concept I need to explore.

"Do you mean we have all lived before?" I asked.

Jim replied. "Yes, we have all had many lives in order to perfect our soul. We die, exist in another dimension for a while and then we incarnate again on the earth."

"Is that why some people seem familiar to us even though we have never talked to them?"

"We usually have a physical or emotional reaction to someone we knew in a previous life, but are not consciously aware of it in this life," explained Jim.

"If we have lived before, then why don't we remember it?" I challenged.

"If we remembered all of our past lives, we would not be able to accomplish the goal of our soul in this life. It would become too confusing because we would be remembering people, places and events all at once. This confusion would interrupt our spiritual growth."

I needed to change the subject. This information over-whelmed me. Now I needed to ask him another question that didn't pertain to past life information.

"Why am I having these visions?" I questioned.

"Your psychic ability is starting to open," Jim replied. "Just relax and let it happen. In fact, I see that in the future you will be prominent. You will be on television. I see the letters NBC. You will be on NBC television for your psychic ability."

I walked away from the psychic feeling a bit dazed. The psychologist said psychics can predict the future, but how could I be on television? I was just a housewife. I was not a psychic. My mind replayed these questions over and over again.

Two months later I heard two women in a store talking about a psychic in Union County. She was supposed to be very accurate. I interrupted their conversation to find out the psychic's name and telephone number. They gave it to me and when I returned home, I immediately dialed the number to request an appointment. She was unavailable for two weeks, but I didn't mind the wait. I was anxious to see what she was going to say about my life. Secretly, I hoped she would confirm some of the other psychics' predictions.

The appointment for the reading was at the psychic's house. This was the first time I had a reading in a home rather than a mall. When I parked in front of her house, I sensed she lived alone because the house needed some major repairs. I stepped inside the foyer and saw the inside was not much better, with worn and tattered furniture. Alicia invited me to have a cup of tea and socialize with her a bit. So I did. She was a quiet, frail woman, under five feet tall and over eighty years old.

When it finally became time for my reading, Alicia's per-sonality suddenly changed. It was almost as if she had to perform a role, so she forced a shift in her attitude. Her personality became gruff and mistrusting. Alicia sternly directed me to the kitchen table. She replaced her smile with a long look that now studied me and mumbled something about the betrayals she had experienced. I did not know how to respond, so I just let her complain.

The cards that she used were so worn from all the readings that some of the faces were not legible. I shuffled the cards in preparation for her to do the reading. As she threw the cards on the table, she began to predict my future.

"Your marriage will eventually end when your kids are grown. I see that you do not live out your life with this man. However, you will have the opportunity to marry again. The man will be older. You will have two home bases. California will be important to you. I see you will travel to Mexico and England. You will also be a professional psychic and you will be prominently known for your psychic ability."

Again, it was difficult for me to believe these predictions, so I questioned the degree of her accuracy as we continued to engage in friendly conversation. She responded by showing me a document stating that her abilities had been tested and verified to be accurate. She further explained that the same researchers who tested Jeanne Dixon, a prominently-known psychic, scientifically tested her too. Alicia was obviously an old timer in the field, and genuine.

I left the reading emotionally numb. Again, a psychic predicted my marriage would end and that I would become a psychic. Only she added travel to my destiny, which I knew could not be possible with my present husband, since he had a fear of flying. I started to wonder if there really is a destiny we must fulfill in life. Perhaps our destiny is just the completion of specific circumstances. But how do we receive the circumstances in our lives? If there really is such a thing as destiny, would I have ever learned what it is if I had not sought psychic readings? If we have a destiny then what happens to all those people who do not explore psychic readings? Maybe our purpose in life is to discover our unique path through soul searching and psychic readers. If psychics have a unique gift to tap into an individual destiny through some extra sense, then psychics must then be somehow connected to God's wisdom and are here to guide us to our ultimate purpose.

These thoughts opened my mind to the idea that psychics may have a unique perspective on life that others don't. My opinion of psychics changed and I became more open in my attitude than when I first started my exploration. Perhaps the world is in turmoil because not enough people know the true meaning of life and their part in the world. Maybe psychic ability is actually an avenue of communication for God to point us in the right direction of our destiny.

The most frustrating aspect of my paranormal exploration was that no one could actually tell me how psychic predictions were accurate glimpses into the future. No one really knew if there was any truth to a pre-determined destiny. The books I found didn't offer much insight on the subject. Some religions hinted there was a possibility of destiny and other religions claimed life was all predestined.

The Bible mentions prophets, mystics and seers, so in ancient days people who could warn about problems before they happened were a normal part of everyday life. World history, however, revealed a different view of people who were psychic. It is estimated that over 300,000 women with extra-sensory perception were labeled witches and were hanged, burned or persecuted in other ways during the Protestant Reformation. The thought made me shudder. I thought of the psychic readers I had encountered and how they would have been killed if we still had that same perception of people who are different.

I decided it was time to let go of the past. I embraced a new way of thinking. Psychics had some information to offer that could prove to be valuable to me in living my life with more meaning and purpose. I decided to continue my exploration.

With each reader I engaged in predicting my future, I determined who was gifted and who wasn't genuine. I analyzed the readings and compared the predictions to my actual life. Sometimes I wondered if those predictions were influencing my life. In my quest for knowledge and understanding, it was almost as if I were addicted to discovering the answers. Sometimes, I quieted the addiction by forcing myself not to go to another reader for long periods of time. However, the time span between readings never lasted more than about three months. As soon as the next psychic fair was announced in the newspaper, I made plans to attend.

After nearly exhausting the psychic fairs, I came across the name of a highly talented psychic.

My friend Rachele called and announced, "I just received the number of a psychic who is supposed to be incredible. She read for several people in the nail salon and everyone raved that she was just amazing. Here is the number. Her name is Anna. Call to make an appointment for us." I didn't waste any time. I ended the conversation with my girlfriend and telephoned the psychic for an appointment.

Anna told me her method of reading was not with Tarot or other cards. She explained that she was clairvoyant, which means she received impressions, images or symbols that had to be inter-preted. Until this appointment, I had only received readings from psychics who used some type of card as their divining method.

I asked her if she read at the psychic fairs in a mall. She said no and added that she received her clients through word of mouth. Our telephone conversation piqued my curiosity. I couldn't wait to meet Anna. The sound of her voice appealed to me. It was warm and inviting.

I was glad I now had Rachele for a friend, because we could discuss our readings with each other. The circumstances of our friendship defined an example of one of the moments in life usually called a coincidence. I knew her casually as an acquaintance of my sister's, but I did not know her well enough to call her a friend. After one of my jaunts to the mall I received a surprise telephone call from Rachele.

Teasingly, she said, "So you are interested in psychics?"

"How do you know?" I asked.

Giggling, she answered, "I had a reading from the same psychic you just had a reading with at the mall!"

"Uh Oh, now my secret is out! You have an interest in psychics, too?" I asked.

We chuckled aloud and then talked for hours comparing notes. Our common interest bonded our friendship. Our scheduled appointment with Anna arrived and we were more than eager to get there.

When Anna greeted us at the door, I noticed she didn't look like any of the previous psychics I consulted. Although she was pretty, the most distinguishing feature about Anna was the twinkle in her eyes as she spoke. She made me feel comfortable and confident, inviting us into her mystical world. Anna read Rachele first and then me.

As I sat down to be read, Anna quieted herself. I observed how she seemed to enter a psychic mode instead of looking at cards placed in a pattern. There was no conversation. Instead, there was a peaceful silence to facilitate her psychic ability. While in the psychic mode, she glanced off in the distance as though she was staring into space as she psychically tuned into vibrations to read my destiny. Anna turned her head slightly to the side as she listened for information.

"Jane, I see you talking in front of large groups of people. Your destiny is to be in front of people. You are now married, but in the future, your marriage will end. You have a mission to accomplish that cannot be completed with your present husband. Don't worry, there will always be a strong bond between the two of you. Later, another man will walk into your life. You have a destiny to complete with this other man."

"There is that mysterious word destiny again. I have a supposed destiny but how will I know what it is or how to achieve it?"

Anna answered cryptically, "For now you are not supposed to know the details because it isn't time for you to know. There are steps you must go through to get to your destiny. Developing your psychic ability is the first step."

Her answer ignited my curiosity and I asked, "Why do I have to be with another man?"

"The two of you are supposed to do God's work together. You were born into this life to accomplish a major mission."

"What is the mission I could possibly do for God with this other man?" I asked.

"Janie, I am sorry I can't give you all the answers. If I gave you all the answers now you would not grow emotionally and spiritually. This task cannot be completed without your personal growth."

I was frustrated and confused by her answer, yet I could

not disagree with her based on the lack of proof I had regarding psychic predictions.

Anna continued discussing my future and went on to predict, "The path in your life is now changing. You will develop your psychic ability in this life. In fact, your mind is very strong. In time this energy will be projected to large groups of people in order to affect them in a positive way. In addition, you will travel all over the country to do your work."

Too stunned to talk, I just sat smiling graciously at Anna as I tried to absorb her words. These predictions seemed so unreal to me, yet Anna was so obviously sincere. I had a hard time trying to decide whether to believe her words or not. Did I dare ask her how accurate she had been in the past with other clients? The thought raced through my mind without my ever verbalizing it. I really had no choice but to wait to see if I developed my psychic ability or not. If I developed it, then I could look forward to finding out exactly what God had planned for me. I didn't know if I felt either honored or bewildered by these predictions.

After my reading was over, Anna escorted me to the door but stopped before it to retrieve a stone displayed on her wall.

She directed me, "Put this stone in the palm of your hand and tell me what you feel."

I held the stone in my hand as I closed my eyes. I then verbalized my reaction.

"Wow. I feel a strong tingling feeling. My whole hand is vibrating as an energy seems to be traveling up my arm."

Anna replied, "That's exactly what I thought would happen! You are physically sensitive to energy. In the future you will also sense spirit and other subtle energy fields."

I had not heard of subtle energy fields but that didn't matter because there were many new concepts presented to me that day. As I walked towards the door, she gave me a hug and invited me to call her again for a social evening. Just as I opened the door Anna made one last statement, "Someday you will take over my work."

Like a broken record, I replayed her words in my mind. Spirit energy? A mission? Divorce? Another man? Take over her work? These were the thoughts racing through my mind as I tried to grasp the meaning of my future. Momentarily shocked, I admitted it was just too much to acknowledge. I slowly plodded to my car, deep in thought. I knew I couldn't drive until I absorbed some of her words. I leaned against the window of my car, replaying the experience. I didn't dare drive until I regained my composure.

Anna was different from the other psychics. She had an air of class and sophistication. She didn't just consider herself a psychic. Anna told me that she had tried to leave the psychic work several times, but something stopped her each time and she was redirected back into this work. She referred to herself as a meta-physical counselor and not just a psychic. She was so positive and upbeat. Her style and choice of words indicated that there was more to her readings than just predictions. Anna exuded a confidence in her readings that calmed me. She embraced the concept of God with a confidence I had not experienced with any other psychic. I sensed that she understood life a bit more than most psychics.

I now had more information and certainly more insight than before the beginning of my search for the truth. However, I still questioned my findings. I wondered if I was addicted to an unattainable quest. I needed to read to understand more. I read every book in the field that I could locate. Sometimes I read five different books a night. I read a few chapters in one book, then I would switch books to change the topic and refresh my mind. I began to believe there was indeed a greater purpose for our existence.

The idea of a mission to do God's work was an intriguing thought that piqued my curiosity. That concept had not been presented to me until now. However, I dismissed that idea almost as quickly as I thought of it. How could I really have a mission to do God's work? What could I do for God? I was an ordinary person. I didn't have any special talents. I was just a housewife with two wonderful children. My husband and I considered them the product of my talent as a mother. We were devoted to raising them and we were very proud of their uniqueness and the special joy we received from them.

But I still entertained the thought of a mission. Maybe the psychics were correct and I would develop my psychic ability. Somehow, being psychic was part of my mission to do God's work. I did not understand, but I decided I did not need to know everything now. My mind drifted to my mother. I recalled a religious experience my aunt, my grandmother, and my mother had just before the declaration of World War I. My grandmother, while churning butter on her front porch with her two daughters, saw an image in the sky. She saw a figure of Jesus walking a path in the clouds with his hands behind his back. As he paced back and forth with a worried look, the three dropped to the ground to pray. The image was clear to all three of them. Jesus' worry bothered my grandmother. Two weeks to the day after the three saw that image in the clouds, World War I was declared.

That mystical experience obviously affected my mother's life and her attitude towards God. She has always had an incredible devotion and belief in God's love and power. Every night of her life, my mother recited a prayer of protection for all of God's children. Her attitude instilled in me the same faith and devotion that my mother and father both had. Maybe I did have some sort of a mission, so I should remain open to that possibility, although it was psychics who suggested the reference to God's work instead of it coming from a religious figure.

I needed to broaden my horizons and allow myself to accept the possibility that there are people in various careers destined to do God's work. For a few moments I felt peaceful and serene, until my enthusiasm was dampened as I faced the reality of my personal responsibilities. If I had a mission for God, I simply had to wait for future events to unfold. I certainly could not ignore my responsibilities to my family.

I focused on the concept of a destiny. Supposedly, this was my destiny. I had heard those words many times before during each psychic reading. And each time I wondered what destiny really was. How did we know our destiny? Could only psychics reveal it? It was mysterious, intriguing and vaguely familiar. A slight hint of recollection permeated my memory. I could not quite grasp it, but I became increasingly comfortable with the idea.

INSIGHTS

❧ A spontaneous psychic moment can be a frightening experience, if you have no understanding of the talent. You can encounter a spirit or see something upsetting about the future, which can frighten you until you adjust to the paranormal experience. When you fully develop the extra sense, you will no longer be frightened by these routine paranormal experiences.

❧ According to palm readers, there are unusual markings on the palms of some people's hands. If you have a mystic cross in the palm of your hand, it could indicate you have strong psychic potential.

❧ Psychologists who have researched psychics know that they can predict the future. They just do not understand the mechanism or how a psychic receives the information and applies it to another person. The only people who understand the process are those who experience psychic ability.

❧ Everyone's purpose in life is to discover their own unique self and personal path in life. Through self-awareness, psychic guidance, inner-knowledge and observation you can achieve your purpose.

❧ Psychics have a unique perspective on life that most do not embrace. When you do not have the ability to receive information directly from your guides, psychics can offer information that is valuable in your living life with meaning and purpose.

❧ A psychic's prediction cannot be confirmed at the time of a prediction unless the information is telepathically received.

Telepathic information pertains to the present or past and is usually detailed and impressive. A precognitive prediction is received as a symbol or in bits and pieces of information which are clues to the future. You cannot determine the accuracy of a precognitive prediction until it occurs in some future time period.

THE GREATER MISSION

My research moved along at a faster pace than I had planned. I read everything on the subject, and talked incessantly to anyone that would listen about the paranormal concepts I had learned. There were awkward moments, however, when I discussed prophecy or philosophically debated the meaning of destiny. Most people listened politely even though they didn't understand the concepts or believe in them. On the other hand, I encountered a few reactions that bothered me.

Several of our friends couldn't comprehend my interest in psychics. Whenever we were together, they often broadcast their opinions. Their reactions ranged from a shrug of the shoulders to the cracking of jokes about psychics, or even me. One of our friends, Leon, repeatedly mocked me for even thinking I could learn any secrets at all. These comments upset me, but I tried not to let others know my hurt feelings. People often criticize what they fear or do not understand, so for that reason I usually dismissed the negative comments. However, one encounter really upset me.

We were invited to a barbecue at Leon's house. When we entered his house, he cut right into me with his critical remarks.

"Are you still going to psychics?" he asked.

"Yes, I am," I said. Trying to change the subject I commented, "Oh. By the way, congratulations, I heard you won a Golf tournament."

But the comment didn't change his mindset. When I saw the sneer on his face, I braced myself for his next comment.

Mockingly he said, "Do you mean you still haven't found the truth about psychics?"

"No, I am still researching," I defended.

"Well, haven't you heard? The truth is already known! Psychics are nothing more than modern day snake oil sales people."

"How can you say that!" I shouted. "Besides, you have never been to a psychic."

"I don't need to go to a psychic to know that. It's common sense. No one can predict the future."

"Do you always have an opinion on something you know nothing about?" I challenged.

"Hey, don't you know there are people in mental institutions who think they can see the future? You better be careful you don't lose your mind researching all that paranormal junk," Leon warned, laughing boisterously.

I had heard enough. I stormed out of Leon's house visibly upset. My husband ran after me, but that didn't help my mood.

"Hey, where are you going?" he asked.

"Home," I answered. "I am not staying in anyone's presence who attacks me with such critical comments."

These were the typical comments I had to endure every time we were with our friends or others who didn't believe in psychics. During those moments, I sometimes felt like an outcast.

My family's reaction was a bit better. No one mocked me. Instead, they referred to my interest as just something I was interested in at the moment. One or two family members considered my behavior an aberration of gullibility, which they tolerated, but did not understand. Others claimed going to psychics or believing in prophecy didn't coincide with the tenets of our religion, therefore, it had to be against our religion. I was grateful my immediate family didn't chastise me for my beliefs like some of our friends did.

Even though most of my family and friends didn't believe in psychics or prophecy, there were still a few who were bold enough to express the opposite view. However, they couldn't tell me why they believed. Nor could they provide me with the details to prove the accuracy of psychic predictions. These reactions made me more curious to want to know why there were so many perceptions about prophecy and which view was correct, if any.

Determining whether psychic predictions were true or not proved to be more difficult than I originally thought. There were no guidelines to follow to help me proceed. Fear of the unknown gripped a majority of the people I met in my search, which made my goal even harder. No one around me shared my view or my desire to unravel these mysteries. Despite the jokes and odd comments, I listened to my own inner feeling. Just thinking of the probability that there were secrets to discover motivated me enough not to be deterred by the opinions of others more skeptical.

After several weeks into my research, I uncovered a bit of information that intrigued me. Historical data indicated that interest in the unknown was not a new concept, but a mystery explored by people since ancient times. Could this information lead me to a window into the secrets I sought?

These mystical pursuits were called various names in different cultures, but almost all exploration in prophecy was based on a spiritual path. These spiritual paths were named according to their function. In native cultures the most common terms for people with paranormal powers included Medium, Channel, Shaman, Witch Doctor and Medicine Man. Other cultures conferred titles such as Fortune-teller, Oracle, Seer, Soothsayer or Visionary. People with extra-ordinary power who were members of various religions were also recorded in history. Priests, gurus, prophets, saints, mystics and holy ones were sought after for guidance as religious figures who had knowledge and wisdom that could help direct a seeker's life.

Knowing prophecy was an ancient mystical pursuit comforted me. At least I was not the only one to pursue this path. Countless others have consulted wise or psychic people for the answers to the riddle of their lives. There were passages in the Bible that could be interpreted as examples of prophecy. Even great historical people, such as Joan of Arc and Abraham Lincoln, believed in the unknown. They consulted psychics or listened to an inner mystical voice for guidance.

Joan of Arc was only seventeen years old when she led an army into battle in France in 1449, because of a mystical experience and her strong conviction it was truth. She heard voices that she claimed were the voices of St. Michael, St. Catherine, and St. Margaret, which Joan believed were sent to her by God. These voices told her it was her divine mission to free her country from the English and instructed her to go to the King of France and help him reconquer his Kingdom.

These same voices told her to cut her hair, dress in a man's uniform and go to battle for her country. After overcoming much opposition, Joan was given a small army to lead. She won many battles to ultimately help defeat the English. When I thought of her accomplishments, I could only imagine the enormous courage it took for her to follow her beliefs, despite the ridicule. This historical anecdote impressed me. How could I not continue my research?

There were reports that Abraham Lincoln not only believed in psychics, but followed their advice during his presidential years. A trance medium named Nettie Colburn was advised by her spirit guides to contact President Lincoln. After the initial contact, interaction between the two lasted a few years. During these sessions, there were always witnesses present to hear her contact her spirit guides.

Nettie, reportedly, told Lincoln not to put off acting on the Emancipation Proclamation. She also advised him through her guides to go to the front lines at Fredricksburg. Lincoln did just that with remarkable success during the Civil War. This, again, was another anecdote that fascinated me. Both of these historical figures had the courage to trust in paranormal information. Imagine where we would be today, if they had not!

These two famous people were not the only ones who had mystical experiences recorded in history. There are passages in the Bible that could be interpreted as paranormal experiences. The Reverend G. Maurice Elliott wrote a book entitled, *The Bible As Psychic History*, which was published by Rider and Company in London in 1959. The author intended to call attention to the common denominators between the Bible and psychic phenomena that he believed are apparent in the Scriptures.

The Reverend pointed out some of the evidence he believed

the Scriptures revealed: Angels visited Lot; Moses saw an angel; Aaron and Miriam saw the pillar of a cloud and were spoken to by the Lord; John the Baptist heard a voice from heaven; and Simeon received a revelation. These are just a few of the many examples he cited.

After reading his book, more than ever, I believed the secrets of life could be found through the powers of a psychic. If a Reverend could see the correlation between psychic phenomena and the mystical experiences in the Bible, then there had to be an answer to life within prophecy not yet discovered. All cultures recorded a fascination in a mystical path. I needed to complete this prophecy puzzle, even if it was just for my own peace of mind.

Exploring the paranormal is a little different from most people's pursuits, but that was not going to stop me. If people before me dared to be different by seeking the meaning of life through mystical pursuits, then I wanted to be an adventurer as well. The possibility of unraveling the mystery of prophecy excited me. So I delved into the exploration wholeheartedly and ignored those who viewed me as odd for experiencing psychic phenomenon. If prophecy was true and psychics did predict the future, then I needed to prepare for this psychic gift.

Everyday, I observed people living life without even a thought about their future. To some, the day-to-day struggle was more than enough to handle. How could people want to study the meaning of life if life itself was overwhelming for them? I wondered, however, if the circumstances of life could be changed, so we each could create a better life for ourselves.

I observed and analyzed my life for clues that would help me determine if any of my decisions affected my life in a positive or adverse way. It was easy to see how some of my decisions and actions influenced my life, especially as I looked into the past. It was difficult, however, to see the consequences of my actions at the actual moment of my decision or action. Only when I reflected on the past did I clearly see the fruits of my labor, or the mishaps of my steps. I wondered just how many poorly thought-out decisions created the turmoil in our lives which we sometimes blame on others, including God.

This observation intrigued me to wonder about destiny again. However, this time I realized we are more responsible for our lives than I previously thought. Could there be a hidden purpose for a psychic's ability other than to just predict the future? Perhaps psychics offer guidance to prevent the circumstances of life from steering us in a direction too far off course from our destined path. Could a psychic offer information that could help us change our destiny? If this was true, then there was real value in a psychic's ability to predict the future.

Through a personal contact, I had the opportunity to talk to a psychiatrist. He could answer my questions from a scientific viewpoint as well as from the perspective of his clinical experiences. He could be valuable in proving psychic ability. Laboratory demonstrations of psychic ability did not include peoples' experiences, which had to be a key for understanding prophecy. Therefore, this chance meeting at a social event afforded me the opportunity to probe his thoughts on psychic ability. Since we were in a social setting, I tried to be unobtrusive and discreet.

My heart raced when I approached the psychiatrist. Sherry, my brother's friend introduced me to Dr. Peters.

Very nonchalantly, I asked, "Have you ever had a psychic reading?"

"No, but I have studied their abilities in research projects," he replied.

"Do you believe psychic ability is real?" I asked.

His answer, delivered calmly, stunned me so much I was temporarily speechless. "Psychic power is greater than nuclear power. When we know our full, untapped mind potential, we will also understand the power of prediction."

Too shocked to speak, I just gulped. Psychic ability, according to Dr. Peters was not only real, but also, in his opinion, a great power.

I questioned his belief. "Why is psychic ability greater than nuclear power?"

"It is not for me to tell you, but rather something you need to discover for yourself," was his cryptic reply.

I was a little disappointed with his answer, but I still tried to grasp the meaning of his words. Not only did he pique my curiosity, but he also challenged me to discover the answer to his riddle.

Many thoughts flooded my mind. I wondered why he considered psychic ability to be so powerful. Did he mean psychic power could destroy a person's life? Were psychic powers, then, something to fear rather than develop? Could psychic powers, if used negatively, create an unknown force that could bring about the same destruction as nuclear power, but in some other way? Conversely, could the power be used to heal? Did he mean psychic power had to be handled as carefully as nuclear energy? I probed for possible answers to this puzzle.

As a psychiatrist, Dr. Peters treated various mental maladies, including mental illness, so did his professional experiences cause him to make that statement? Could he have seen some link between mental illness and psychic powers? Perhaps he saw people in mental institutions who were unusually psychic and couldn't distinguish the difference between a psychic vision and reality.

Could mental illness cause a person to have psychic ability or vice versa? These were questions I could not answer but wished I could. More research was needed to answer those questions.

Now, I had to determine why psychic ability was greater than nuclear energy. I agreed with the concept of the mind being a great power. Experts often explain how the real potential of our mind is yet untapped. If we develop our mind to its fullest potential, could we have a mental power equal to the power of nuclear energy?

My thoughts shifted to my childhood. Many times, I noticed how projecting positive thoughts often attracted the positive result. Whenever I allowed fear to creep in and dominate my thoughts, problems always resulted. It was obvious to me that the mind plays a major role in producing powerful results, but why do some people's minds receive it and others do not?

The mind is the only part of us that can't be dissected and studied. We know it is there, but we can't physically see its mechanisms. Not knowing how it functions prevents us from developing our full potential. Without this knowledge we can't create a better life or develop our psychic ability.

Even though the mind cannot be seen, we know there are two parts of the mind: a conscious and subconscious. We are aware of the conscious, because we process our thoughts there. On the other hand, the subconscious stores all the information from our past, present and future. It is like a giant computer. The subconscious, however, is mysterious because we do not know how it functions or how to access the information stored there. Psychic information, therefore, must be filtered through the subconscious part of the mind for it to reach the conscious mind. Somehow, a key to this power has to be in the mind. If we learn how it functions, could we then learn how to develop psychic ability? Could this be why some people have the ability and others do not? Could learning how to use our minds open the door to this ability?

According to Anna, psychic information is received in images, symbols, thoughts and feelings, which must be interpreted. But how could this information be powerful? For psychic information to be a power it must have energy. But how could the energy in psychic power compare to the energy in nuclear power? What could the power be in psychic ability that is even greater than nuclear energy? Could this power be the ability of a prediction to create change or is there an unknown force directing the information? Somehow, the force in a psychic's power has to be linked to God's energy to be as powerful as Dr. Peters believed.

When I searched for the answer, my thoughts again focused on childhood memories. I recalled a religious experience at the Saint Anne de Beaupre Shrine in Quebec, Canada, when I was in my early teens. On a pilgrimage to the Saint Anne Shrine I befriended a blind woman named Martha. She sat near me on the bus trip to Quebec. She had hoped her prayers would be answered so she could experience her own miracle at the shrine. Martha explained the history of the shrine and the many miracles that had happened there over the years. She explained how there had always been medical miracles at the shrine, especially during Saint Anne's feast day mass. This conversation influenced me. I now shared her enthusiasm and secretly hoped she would receive her miracle. I couldn't wait to arrive at the shrine, especially when I thought miracles could happen there.

When I arrived at the shrine, I couldn't believe the magnitude of people praying to be cured. The scene moved me. There were people in wheelchairs, stretchers and on other life-support medical equipment being wheeled into church. It saddened me to see them, until I focused on their strength and faith, instead of their illness. I had no idea what to expect, but I hoped to witness a miracle.

My thoughts shifted to Martha and her faith in God. All I could imagine was my blind acquaintance being able to see, as I anticipated the feast day mass scheduled for later that day. Just seeing all the crutches left by afflicted people who were miraculously cured at the shrine sent a shiver through my body.

When the mass began, more than two thousand people crowded into this huge cathedral. I waited intensely for a sign, but nothing happened. Then I heard sounds that sent goose bumps up and down my spine.

"I can see!" "I can walk!" "I can hear!" screamed faceless voices from the crowd.

Tears streamed down my face. I tried to see what had happened, but I sat too far in the back of the church to see the actual people healed. I had to wait until the mass ended to walk to the front of the church where these voices were coming from. When the mass ended, I headed toward the church altar. There I saw Martha in the front pew with tears streaming down her face. I knew something special had happened to her.

When I walked towards her, she looked at me. I gasped. Could she now see? She had not previously sensed me from this great a distance. My heart pounded as I approached her. We embraced before she said a word. Her tears now became deep sobs of emotion. She couldn't stop them, so I knew something had taken place.

Her voice then sounded the words I had hoped to hear.

"I can see images! I am no longer blind!"

This experience influenced my life profoundly. Not only

did I witness miracles at the shrine, but I learned there was an enormous power in faith and prayer. I left Canada forever changed.

Recalling this memory provoked new thoughts. Could religious miracles be connected to psychic ability? Is there some common thread between a medical miracle induced by prayer and a prediction self-fulfilled? Could the range of emotional intensity be the power in psychic ability as well as in a religious miracle? Energy had to be the force. Perhaps Dr. Peters equated the two because psychics have some powerful form of energy. There was just too much to ponder.

Sometimes I wished I had never been curious enough to seek that first psychic reading. And at other times I wished I had visited even more psychics. The emotional roller coaster I was on had a nagging drawback: I could not get off of it until I learned the truth. How do you discover the explicit truth in a non-science? It was like trying to scientifically prove that water is wet, or that sounds make music. The bottom line to both was to just have faith and continue to look for answers in the unknown. This path had to lead to at least some secrets about life.

Continuing with my quest included consulting with more psychics and researching my future through their guidance. The many consultations I explored never ceased to amaze, and simultaneously bore me. Psychics repeated the themes regarding my future. Some offered me new insights to consider. However, each psychic's style of presentation was different. The unique and rather down-to-earth style used by one particular psychic to forecast my future was also the most memorable.

I registered again at the Menlo Park Mall's bi-annual psychic fair. This time I consulted with Lori, a Tarot card reader with a little more extra flair than most of the other psychics. From a distance, I observed Lori's colorful outfit, which was distinctly different from how the other psychics dressed. Lori wore a purple and green turban that almost covered her hair. Her ears were adorned with large dangling earrings. Every finger on her right and left hand wore a ring and both of her wrists clanged with gold bangle bracelets.

When I stared curiously in her direction, my eye caught a glimpse of a rather odd-looking item on her table. The figure on her table glimmered as the sun beamed through the ceiling windowpanes and dispersed sparkles of light in all directions. I looked closer to see a glass-like figurine which no other psychic I previously consulted had ever displayed. I couldn't wait for my turn just so I could question her about the ornament she used in conjunction with the Tarot cards.

I sat across the table from Lori and immediately asked, "What is the figurine used for in the reading?"

She excitedly replied, "That's an image of an Egyptian goddess carved from quartz crystal. The crystal enhances psychic ability by increasing the energy vibrations around me and around you. The Egyptian goddess is an inanimate replica of my guide."

I gestured with a nod and a barely audible "Oh" to indicate I understood. As Lori spread the deck of cards on the table, she moved her head from side to side. I interpreted her head movement as a "No" and then gasped, thinking she saw something bad in my future. Her words describing my future still haunt my memory.

Lori predicted, "Hmm! Hmm! I sure like the way God is taking care of you! You have one man about to be put out of the barn and there is another one waiting in the wings to take his place!"

I just stared at her without uttering a word.

She continued, "I'm sorry to be so blunt but do you get my message? You will be divorced, but do not worry honey; you will have another one as soon as you let go of your present husband. And do not feel badly. You have some important business to do with this new man. And, oh my! You will ride in a fancy car driven by a chauffeur dude. You will also be prominently known for your psychic work. Just make sure you come to visit me someday in that fancy car."

Startled by her bluntness, I thanked her for the reading as my dazed mind tried to grasp the full meaning of her words. Yet another psychic predicted I would be divorced in order to do work with another man. By now, I started to realize there was some sort of destiny this other man and I were supposed to follow. This time, the prediction did not panic me. Maybe I was just becoming conditioned to my future.

Lori's humor and style of delivery captured my attention. How could I ever forget her words? Her words were so different from the thoughts in my mind that I did not question whether Lori read my thoughts or not. There was no way she could have read my thoughts with her unusual verbal style. I logged the repeated prediction in my memory. The words just "go with the flow" helped me to stay calm. These words became a comforting phrase which allowed me to let go of the prediction instead of dwelling on the need to know why.

This new knowledge changed my mindset and allowed me to believe there had to be some preplanned destiny in life. More than ever I needed to understand prophecy. If psychic ability was to be my part of a much greater plan designed by God, then I had better be willing to meet the challenge. To deny that a psychic's purpose is to guide a person to his or her destiny would be foolish.

The historical and Biblical accounts of mystics further justified my personal research and added credence to my belief in the power of a psychic. This new acceptance stimulated my mind. I glowed, as I made plans to proceed with my personal research endeavor, which included befriending a psychic. A friendship with a psychic, perhaps, would provide insights into prophecy which I could not gain through psychic consultations. I decided to follow through on Anna's invitation to meet her socially. So I telephoned her and made plans for lunch.

I met Anna at a local restaurant for our lunch date. Anna was such a positive person and I felt so comfortable in her presence. She also appealed to my religious upbringing by comparing psychic talent to a spiritual calling. She was the first psychic to connect my future psychic talent to God's work. As always, I knew her answers to my questions would facilitate my progress.

During lunch, we discussed my future again on a much deeper level than at the time of the psychic consultation. Anna tried to explain to me the strength and power of the mind.

According to Anna, our mind projects energy that creates either positive or negative circumstances in life. This mind energy also has healing properties. Supposedly, my eventual purpose was to speak in front of large groups to affect and influence people in a positive way for the good of humanity. I didn't know what that meant, but at least I could relate to the part of my speaking in front of people. I majored in public speaking in college, so that part of the prediction made some sense.

Anna explained, "I know it's hard for you to understand this now, but eventually you will know what I told you is truth. The world is destined to change for the good. There are many incarnated now who are on a mission for God. And there are many more who will awaken to their part of the greater mission. In time you will receive more guidance and others will instruct you."

I listened to her instruction without a comment before she began speaking again.

"Opening up your psychic ability and exercising the strength of your mind is your cog in the wheel of a greater mission."

"Is that all I have to do to fulfill my mission?"

"No, your psychic ability is only the beginning. God will then know you are ready. More information will be revealed to you and to others who are a part of this mission. People will begin to recognize there is a greater purpose for their existence and have a great need to discover that purpose. A nagging sense will push them along towards greater spirituality and awareness. You will then see more people who are kinder, as well as more angry and uncaring people. When that happens, you will know the plan for the greater mission has begun."

At first, this information was intense and difficult to grasp. This greater mission sounded both mysterious and important.

I tried to calm myself by asking Anna a question: "How will I know when I am doing what God wants me to do?"

"When your psychic gifts are opened up, ask God and then pay attention," Anna replied.

"How do I open my psychic ability?" I questioned.

"There is guidance all around. You just have to pay attention to the thoughts that pop into your mind during quiet moments. Learn to meditate for answers. Be still and know God."

I lamented, "But I don't know how to meditate."

Anna explained the process in simple terms. "Find a comfortable chair and put your feet flat on the floor. Close your eyes and breathe rhythmically. As you inhale and exhale, clear your mind of thoughts. Relax and focus on one thought as you go deeper and deeper into an altered state of consciousness. You can silently repeat the phrase 'I am one with God', as you listen for a thought or wait for an image. When you meditate, you quiet your mind so a spirit guide can communicate with you. In order to receive guidance you have to slow the chatter of the everyday voices by meditating. The altered state of consciousness in the meditative state makes you receptive to any inaudible voice that may whisper a thought or nudge an image from the subconscious."

Meditation sounded similar to prayer, so I wondered if there was a difference. Therefore, I asked Anna to explain it.

"In a prayer you ask or tell God your needs. In meditation you listen. Meditation adds another step to prayer. Instead of waiting for the prayer to be fulfilled, you expect an immediate answer, hopefully, to guide you from making wrong choices," she replied.

According to organized religion, attending church and praying to God is the path to spiritual knowledge and fulfillment. Therefore, I wondered who these spirit guides were that Anna mentioned.

"Why do we meditate to guides and not directly to God?"

"In order to understand the guide structure you need to view the world in terms of energy," Anna explained.

I listened intently as she continued her explanation.

"Everything in the physical world has an energy field and it consists of a certain frequency of vibrating energy. In order to stay in the physical, a human being must operate within a certain level of vibration. Frequencies are received within the normal range of hearing and sight through our senses. There are sound and light frequencies beyond our physical hearing and sight, yet we don't consciously know they are there."

"Do psychics perceive beyond this normal range of hearing and sight?" I questioned.

"Yes, we do perceive beyond the normal range of frequency and vibrations. But it takes a great deal of spiritual growth to contact the guide structure."

"Why can't we just meditate to God for guidance or personal answers? If we wanted to gain more spirituality and guidance, why wouldn't we go directly to the source for the guidance?"

Anna offered a passage from the Bible as an explanation. "The Bible states: No man can look upon the face of God and live. This does not mean that God would harm us or not want to see us. We need to understand this passage in terms of energy. Our physical vibration as a human being operates at a lower level of energy than the spiritual spheres. Our physical life actually shelters us from the higher frequencies of energy in order to protect us. Can you imagine what it would be like if you opened your front door to that amount of energy? If you were not shielded, you could be physically burned. It would be just liking receiving too much radiation from a medical x-ray."

"Are you telling me there is a guide structure in order to protect our physical being from receiving too much energy before we are properly prepared?" I asked Anna.

"Yes. A guide structure is set up to filter the energy down to the physical so no one is harmed by the energy. Physical distance does not separate us from this energy. It is our lack of understanding of ourselves and the spiritual laws that keep us from knowing the other side."

"Does that mean we can get more in touch with God's energy if we become more in touch with our inner self?"

"Yes."

"Is psychic ability, then, a gift of power?" I questioned.

"No. Psychic ability is not a gift of power. When you develop your psychic ability, you actually work towards increasing the quality of your psychic energy, not the strength or power of the energy."

"Can psychic ability be developed or do I just have to wait until God gives it to me?" I asked.

"God has already given this gift to everyone. It is the link to the other side. You have to raise your consciousness before you can develop it," revealed Anna.

"Higher consciousness? What do you mean?"

"A person has a higher consciousness when he or she can see the world from more than a physical perspective. It is an awareness that there is more in life than just the physical world. All psychic development is really spiritual growth. The first step is to understand yourself. Look inward and discover the uniqueness there. I know that a lot of this is new to you, but in time you will accept everything," Anna concluded.

I was awed by Anna's explanation although I didn't completely understand it. For years I thought we couldn't reach God because we were not worthy to make direct contact. I thought we had to prove to God our worth before we could hope for the blessing of direct communication. Now I began to understand it all had to do with the vibrations of our energy field. Communion with God had nothing to do with whether I was a good or bad person. It all had to do with freeing the physical to vibrate at a higher level and raising our consciousness through knowledge and inner awareness.

I had no proof psychic ability existed, but I trusted Anna's sincerity because of her words and understanding of the other side. I was also grateful for Anna's mentoring, which began to help me understand more about life.

I thought again of the psychiatrist and his comment on psychic ability. I now believe the psychiatrist knew more than I had previously thought. If psychic ability was somehow connected to God, then the psychic connection to this higher realm could be more powerful than nuclear energy. I searched my memory for clues to link prophecy to God. However, I could not equate the two, at least, not yet.

According to my upbringing, the clergy of each religion are emissaries of God. To know God, you attend a church, a synagogue, temple, mosque or other place of worship. Anna's sincerity and her concept of God, however, tugged at my heart. I could not dismiss our conversation as just another psychic predicting the future. In order to understand prophecy I needed to trust my feelings. This all began to make some sense.

I was at peace in knowing I was not just a person, but a spiritual soul. For the first time, I began to understand God protected us through a guide structure. So there is no way God could be responsible for all of the bad things that happened to us. We have some responsibility for the circumstances of our life, even if we don't consciously accept it. It became obvious one of our responsibilities is listening for guidance. If we do not set aside a few minutes a day to listen or reflect on the day, we can't expect our life to be free of problems. From this point I made a conscious effort to slow down and listen, even if I complained I had no time.

A short time after my commitment to this goal, I discovered a routine that enhanced the practice of listening without much effort. Everyday when I showered, I stayed a few minutes longer reflecting on my life and listening for answers. This routine became an important key in my development. I did not know all the answers but I now had a glimpse into a window of truth.

Insights

❧ From the beginning of recorded time, all cultures have pursued guidance through psychic and mystical powers. These mysteries are recorded in history, as well as in the Holy Bible. In exploring mystical powers, one can discover the deeper questions about life, as well as the answers to those questions.

❧ The positive and negative circumstances in life are created by the focus of your thoughts. The intensity and emotional charge of your thoughts are projected into the universe, which then acts like a magnet attracting your fate. When you project intense positive thoughts, you attract a positive result. If fear dominates and controls your life, you attract situations in your life which result in problems.

❧ You need to view the world in terms of energy in order to understand the psychic process.

❧ Psychic power can be greater than nuclear power because of the energy and the source of a psychic's power. This source is linked to God. Religious miracles, the subconscious mind, and the source of a psychic's power are all connected. When you become more aware of this connection, you will generate a more meaningful and fulfilling life.

❧ Psychic ability is not a gift of power. When you develop the talent, you work at increasing the quality of your psychic energy and not the power of the energy. Increasing the level of higher consciousness also increases the quality of your psychic energy.

❧ Physical distance does not separate you from God or the guide structure. Not understanding your inherent talent is the deterrent that blocks you from knowing God or the other side. When this ability is opened, you will be receptive to receiving guidance for a better life.

❧ Contacting God has nothing to do with whether you are good or bad in terms of your religion. It all has to do with your ability to free the physical in order to vibrate at a higher level of consciousness. Through inner awareness, increased knowledge and your own inherent psychic talent, you can make the connection.

❧ God is not responsible for all of the bad things that happen to you. Your emotional decisions create some of what the hand of fate deals you.

Making the Psychic Connection

L ife began to change for me shortly after I started this journey. At the time, most people didn't believe in the paranormal. In fact, there were some who thought those who did believe were strange. This worried me because I could not go back to my old way of thinking, once I claimed this philosophy as my own. I needed, however, to make a decision. Should I claim the paranormal as part of my belief system? Or should I continue to believe in the traditional philosophy my parents followed? Would I play it safe or take a risk?

I sorted through my many conflicting thoughts, debating which avenue I should follow. I thought about others who had explored unproven theories and how they, too, had to make a decision on their findings at some point in their explorations. One way or another, I had to make a decision.

There could be consequences, however, if I openly believed in the unseen world. I knew I had grown emotionally and spiritually, but could I grow beyond the beliefs of my husband and family if they didn't share in this same personal growth?

Even though I resisted making the decision, it felt as if a force nudged me to believe in the paranormal. No matter how I tried to put aside my thoughts, they resurfaced. When I began to openly discuss my views and not worry about what others thought of me, I knew I had finally adopted the new, riskier, belief system.

To fully embrace this new spiritual awareness, I had to ignore the stringent boundaries of my religion. This was hard at first to do, but eventually I was able to temporarily step aside from the rules to further explore my new belief system. Thoughts of how God might reach me now raced through my mind. What if God was trying to guide me to my purpose for being through psychic ability?

Even though the other-worldly guidance didn't come to me in the context of my religion, it couldn't be less valid. After all, religious leaders have disagreed for centuries and still do on which religion is the correct path to God. Attending a church, synagogue, temple or mosque doesn't guarantee a person following a particular religion will become a spiritual person. Therefore, why should I be close-minded to the concept that a psychic path could lead me to know more of God, too?

When I studied the history of religion, I learned of religious zealots and leaders who tried to force others into believing their respective religion was the one correct doctrine to follow. Throughout history these same people bitterly fought to convert non-followers by declaring war or engaging in some other form of physical combat. How could there have been so much bloodshed in God's name? My stomach wrenched when I thought of the many wars fought over religion. Knowing this controversy had existed for centuries made it easier for me to believe that God's guidance could be revealed through a psychic.

If I fully embraced this philosophy, then I also must heed Anna's advice and develop my own ability. If psychic talent was to allow me to be an instrument of God's work, then I had to proceed in that direction. Perhaps it makes no difference which path we follow to know God, just as long as we arrive at the same place: that of more spiritual awareness and greater trust in God.

The first step for developing my psychic ability involved meditation. However, I had to learn how to relax first before I could master it. When I meditated, I could not, at first, let go of the religious prayers committed to my memory. I had to discipline myself to just listen, which was hard for me to do.

When I meditated, I inhaled deeply enough for my diaphragm to expand and contract each time. And I listened to the Pacabel Canon, which facilitated my meditative state more than any other music or technique. When I reached a deep enough level of relaxation, I quieted the chatter in my mind by focusing mentally on the mantra, "Be still and know God." Repeating this particular phrase helped me to focus on the center of my inner mind while I waited for some form of guidance.

An image of the universe appeared to me first. It seemed as if I observed it from a distance. I couldn't stay focused on the image for long because I felt like I had just stepped into a three dimensional movie of the universe. A cool, invigorating feeling filled me. Within seconds, a sensation of movement propelled me forward, until I was travelling in that universe at a considerable rate of speed. Almost immediately this moving sensation caused an odd time and space distortion. I no longer felt physical boundaries or sensed linear time. When I stopped meditating, I remained motionless for a while trying to analyze the experience. The intensity of the ordeal surprised me, but at the same time it was addictive. Nevertheless, the experience hooked me into wanting more.

For the first few months after that intense encounter, I meditated without noting any more unusual experiences. Then, while in a deeper state of consciousness, I had another overwhelming experience. A different image appeared in my mind, which mesmerized me. I saw lights that looked like stars pulsating at various speeds move closer to me.

When I followed the display of lights, my eyes shifted, which allowed me to see deeper towards the back of my head. I enjoyed the peaceful sense that was now pervasive. I stayed in this state for as long as I could, hoping to experience more. Even though it was hard to stay focused, I persisted through sheer will. And I was thrilled and grateful for the small breakthrough.

Every night, the meditation period produced an altered state of consciousness, but I didn't always see images. I forced myself not to be discouraged, even though I questioned and analyzed why it didn't happen consistently. Did I do something different when images emerged than when they didn't? I couldn't determine that answer yet.

It took two additional months of meditating before another breakthrough in the process came. Images were projected onto an imaginary blank screen in my mind. These images emerged and then quickly vanished. During one meditation episode, a man and then a mountain range appeared. Other simple images appeared which included colorful geometric shapes or fluffy, white clouds.

Most of the time I just watched these images in my dream-like state dance across the blank screen just behind the center of my forehead. I couldn't interpret what I was seeing. Yet when images other than the usual universe image flashed in my mind, I knew something different had finally occurred.

So I contacted Anna for more advice. She invited me to visit her again, only this time she suggested her house as our meeting place. I knocked on her door and waited for Anna's response. The door opened and Anna's grandson invited me into her house, but he left when Anna finally came to the door. After a warm greeting, she invited me into her kitchen for a cup a tea and suggested that I tell her how I meditated and what thus far had happened before advising me.

When I explained my experiences to Anna, her facial expression changed.

"I am so pleased. You are beginning to open the door to your psychic ability. Keep doing the meditations exactly as you have been. More will come and eventually you will be able to interpret them."

"How long will that take?"

"It is a process, so it is difficult to predict," Anna replied.

Excited that the psychic process had begun in me I could hardly wait to try for more experiences, but I had a few questions to ask Anna first.

"Sometimes I don't see that blank screen right away," I said. "When I close my eyes, there are repetitive thoughts and instant replays of the day's worries. These thoughts pulsate across the screen, which interfere with the level of relaxation. So I try to make the screen blank, but then a headache develops. Is that normal?"

Anna replied, "Some people experience headaches when they try too hard. It is important not to force the mind to go blank because it defeats the purpose. The idea of meditation is to relax so you are receptive to guidance. It is not necessary to concentrate on anything in particular, but rather to just allow the mind to meander freely. Eventually, the mind's activity will slow and become tranquil. Then more images will appear."

Anna further explained, "If the mind is allowed to wander, it will eventually tire of the aimlessly scattered thoughts. When it has had enough, the mind will begin to seek direction. If you do not provide direction, the mind seeks a focus beyond the physical and into the psychic level of the mind."

"Anna, this sounds like hypnosis. In one method of hypnosis, the hypnotist tells ambiguous stories and gives indirect suggestions in order to confuse the mind of the subject. To stop this confusion the hypnotized person will accept the first suggestion given. This technique re-programs the subject's mind for the desired behavior or goal, which the mind then creates. However, in meditation there is no set direction so the mind shifts from reality to find something to focus on. During the search for a focus, the mind forces information from the psychic level of the mind to surface, so it finally has the focus it needs. Does that sound right to you?"

"Yes," assured Anna. "You are beginning to understand the process."

Anna left the room to answer her phone, which gave me an opportunity to reflect on our conversation. I analyzed the analogy I made between meditation and hypnosis. When I reflected on the two modalities, I thought of another observation that helped me to understand the mind and how to use it.

The mind has basic drives and needs just like the physical body does to properly function. One need the mind has is to have a focus at all times. This is an inner mechanism, which influences the behavior of the mind, as well as how we think. How and what we focus on determines whether the conscious or subconscious part of the mind is more dominant at any given time. When our subconscious is more dominant, we then have access to the level of the mind that holds true power. If we can tap into that level, we can access healing energy and psychic guidance. When there is no set focus the subconscious becomes more active trying to find a focus, thus making the subconscious more dominant. By manipulating the focus of our thoughts while we are in a state of relaxation we can open the door to the psychic level. These observations and inner thoughts excited me. I couldn't wait to explore my theory. Could this be one of the secrets for tapping into our mind power and developing psychic ability?

Anna's voice jolted me from my inner thoughts when she returned. She immediately began instructing me on a visual exercise that she wanted me to do.

"Try this focus in your next meditation. I want you to use your imagination to visualize an imaginary scene," she said.

As I listened to her instructions, I simply answered, "Yes, I will."

"Imagine you are observing activity on the other side of a window, but you are not looking for anything in particular. There is a difference between the physical window and the window in your mind. One window is imagined and is the doorway to the secrets inside your mind, and the other is a tangible window. Once you visualize this scenario you then need to trick your senses into believing there is a real door to open. As you imagine opening the door, more images will appear, which will lead you to have even more experiences. This is an important step in learning how to switch yourself off from the physical senses to experience the part of your mind that contains psychic information."

"Okay, I will try this technique, tonight."

With my acknowledgement, Anna continued her instructions.

"Remember, you are not alone in the process. Your guide

on the other side is also trying to help you."

"Is the other side what religious teachings refer to as heaven?" I asked.

"Religious teachings refer to it as heaven, but psychics call it the spiritual dimension. It is the soul's home before or after it incarnates in the physical."

"Does our guide respond to us at all times?" I asked.

"We have to first make contact and then listen for the guidance. Once we have established an avenue of communication there will be times you ask for guidance and other times it will just be given to you."

"How do we listen?" I asked.

"You slow down your busy schedule, so you can pay attention to the inward and outward signs of guidance," she answered.

"But what are those signs?" I quizzed.

"Inward signs, of course, are your dreams, feelings, inner visions and the senses which you experience, but you don't recognize or interpret as guidance. Outward signs are the coincidental moments or events which happen in life that you dismiss without stopping to wonder what they mean."

"Like a song that always plays when you ask for guidance or are in a particular place?"

"Yes. Guidance will come in patterns, especially if you don't recognize the insights right away. These patterns all have some meaning. Pay attention to the patterns in your life and you will receive the message your guide is trying to communicate to you."

Eager to reach my guides quickly, I asked Anna one more question. "What do I need to do or to overcome to reach my guide?"

"Patience is the most important trait to cultivate. It is the key to successful meditation and the one trait that will unlock the doorway to your psychic ability," reminded Anna.

Anna then offered the following analogy to help ease my concerns on how my guide would reach me.

"Imagine your guide standing on the top of the Empire State building in New York City. Your guardian is watching the crowds of people on the street below. All those people are trying to navigate their way through the other hoards of people on the street. Your guide tries to find you amongst the crowd by beaming a spotlight on you. However, instead of standing still, you are rushing around, dodging people as he or she tries to keep the spotlight on you long enough to get your attention. It is easier for your guide to make the connection if you would just stay put for five or ten minutes."

"The spotlight a guide uses to reach you is coincidence or some inner feeling. If you notice this light, you then start to look for it. Your guide now knows he or she has captured your attention, so the guide tries even harder for more of your attention. Eventually, the connection is made and there is a flash flood of information that pours into your life when you need guidance. Imagining this scenario will help you to understand the patience and perseverance it takes to make the psychic connection."

"Anna, the process is now becoming even clearer to me. I will try to prolong my meditation and be more patient."

"As I told you before, it is important to be silent," Anna reminded me. "Be still and know God, because you are already one with God."

I didn't claim to fully understand everything Anna said but I listened intently to her wisdom. I knew that without trust I wouldn't succeed. It didn't matter if I had a mundane activity to perform or a session in meditation. Without trust, faith and confidence, I couldn't succeed at anything. Although satisfied with her answers, I couldn't resist the temptation to ask one last question.

"How will I know that I have reached the psychic realm and have made contact with a guide?"

"Be patient. Get there first and then I'll explain more to you," Anna replied.

Anna and I ended our conversation. And I was grateful to have her guidance once more in this process. Each step of the psychic process sparked more questions for me. However, there were longer periods of time between my mentoring sessions with Anna, since the process in me had begun. The gap between our visits offered me an opportunity to analyze and to further understand on my own each step of the process.

For several weeks, I patiently waited to change channels during the meditative state from the physical to the mental level. I began to see more images in my mind's eye after periods of silence. First, I would try to let go of the rambling thoughts, scattered voices and other distractions. By consciously trying not to hold onto to the chatter I eventually reached a deeper level. Once in that level there was a distinct shift in consciousness. When complete silence enveloped me and there were no more distractions, I knew I was there.

In that level of consciousness flowing images of light and dark whizzed by on my mental screen. Sometimes, I saw images of varying colors emerge, seemingly dancing as the colors formed quick images. These images faded before new ones appeared. I didn't know what they meant, but I enjoyed watching them. And I began to meditate more frequently.

After a month or two, I thought it necessary to know how to reach the next level. I sought Anna's expertise again. This time

I visited her late at night. As always, her answers exhibited a calm, gentle wisdom, which made it easy for me to listen to and follow them. When she explained the next step, I became a sponge trying to absorb all her knowledge.

"To reach an advanced level you must make a more deliberate effort to reach the higher spiritual levels. You are no longer operating just as a physical being so you must begin to think of yourself in spiritual terms. In the spiritual dimensions as well as in the physical dimension, the universal law of like attracting like is applied. You will attract a higher, more spiritually developed guide or guardian if you raise your vibration to the same spiritually developed soul level."

"Do I do that by continuing to meditate?" I questioned.

"No. Now you must do more than meditate," Anna replied.

More curious than ever, I asked Anna. "How, then, can I raise my vibration?"

"You must cultivate positive personality traits such as self-love, compassion, understanding, peace, tranquility and contentment while you continue to gain both inner and outer knowledge. There are also other traits that can reverse the process by lowering your vibrations. You must guard against negative emotions such as fear, anger, hatred, pessimism, jealousy and addictions. This is the best advice I can give you to stay on the right course."

"What is the difference between a guide and one at a higher level?"

"A higher guide doesn't just protect you. It can instruct and guide you, so that you fulfill your purpose on earth. That usually involves growth and only a higher level guide knows the full spectrum of growth needed to advance your soul."

"What happens if we fulfill our purpose?" I asked.

"Your life then turns in a direction that is easier for you to follow, more fulfilling and with less problems. At that point you are able to enjoy your free will without continuously learning lessons."

"How do we grow emotionally?" I asked.

"Sometimes, we are given challenges to overcome, which assist us in our emotional growth. When we master the challenge, we gain emotional strength and increased spirituality."

I said, "Is that why bad things happen to good people? Those bad things are like hurdles in a track and field competition. Instead of allowing the hurdles to block our road, we have to find a way to jump over them so we can then leave them behind and gain the speed to go forward and live life, again?"

"That's a good explanation!"

"How will I know if I have attracted a more spiritually-developed guide?"

"The energy around you will feel lighter. And you will also feel a warm embrace around you from this energy," Anna replied.

Armed with these new tools of suggestion, I continued in my development. I read many books on psychology to gain inner knowledge and to promote the positive traits within my personality. I evaluated my negative traits and then tried to change them into positive emotions, such as self-love and spontaneity. Self-love became the most difficult to master.

When we travel the road of life, we become psychologically bruised in one way or another. Emotional scars can develop from these bruises, when we accept them into our subconscious mind. They then become our critical inner voices, which are heard over and over in our mind. Eventually, we believe we are exactly what these critical voices tell us, which either thwarts or destroys our self-esteem.

76

Consequently we never develop self-love as a result of these nagging judgmental perceptions. The lack of self-love in turn creates insecurity, poor self-confidence and a lack of trust in our feelings. All these emotions become one big vicious cycle, until we can find a way to get off the emotional merry-go-round. Until then, these negative emotions interfere with our emotional growth and our psychic development.

It didn't take me long to realize such traits were not conducive to developing psychic ability or for developing positive life experiences. Whenever I received an intuitive feeling, I often dismissed it before I acted upon it. When I later discovered the feeling was correct, it set off those critical voices and put me back on the merry-go-round.

In order to develop spiritually and ultimately make the connection to an advanced guide I needed to learn how to love myself. To help put these ideas into perspective, I imagined and compared myself to a rose bud. When the petals of the rose start to bloom, its core is then exposed to reveal the real essence of the flower. Without the core, no flower would bloom.

At the core of our being is an enormous capacity for us to love others as well as ourselves. When we arrive at that core, we are then free to bloom to our full potential, which includes our natural psychic gifts.

I struggled long and hard with the issue of self-love. I had to master it for my spiritual growth, yet it was such an up-hill battle for me. So I explored my thoughts on the reasons why so many of us struggle with self-love.

All of us begin life as lovable babies, but we are programmed along the way by our parents, teachers, siblings and peers to have either self-love or self-hate. Through our happy or painful experiences we develop varying degrees of these two emotions. If we hear praise, we then have the opportunity to develop self-love. If we hear excessive criticism, even unintentionally, we live in an environment that fosters self-hatred. By analyzing the people around me for the cause of their lack of self-love, I could then analyze those reasons and compare them to my own. This method of self-help eventually helped me to win the battle.

Reading self-help psychology books taught me that we internalize even the smallest negative comment, and program it into our sub-conscious mind. It then becomes part of our self-image. In essence our self-esteem is the result of the sum total of all our experiences in life, as well as all of the comments we have ever heard about ourselves. No wonder it is so difficult to feel self-love. Imagine how many critical voices we've heard from our parents, peers, siblings, and authority figures which we still believe describe us.

I was able, however, to control my emotions and change my thoughts whenever I thought of God in a personal rather than a religious context. In my moments of self-doubt, I thought of the following concept: If we are made in God's image, and if we love ourselves, we are then giving God the highest compliment we possibly can. When we love ourselves, we also love God. These thoughts eventually prevented me from self-sabotage and ultimately I inched my way towards greater self-love.

But first I wrote down every critical comment I had ever heard about myself from my parents, siblings, peers, authority figures and myself. It took me a week to remember all of them. Each night I chose one category and wrote those critical comments in a list. Then I gathered the lists, tore the papers into tiny pieces, threw them in the toilet and flushed them away. Those comments were the garbage I needed to rid myself from believing. From that point on my self-love and confidence began to increase every day.

One night after I had become more confident and had more self-love, I meditated for a longer period of time than usual. After several deep breaths I entered a deeper state than I had been previously able to achieve. I noticed a numb sensation around the bridge of my nose. A feeling of letting go and flying deep into the dark hallway of my inner mind took over my body. I saw several formations of geometric patterns that repetitively moved forward and then receded. Eventually, the motion of these patterns turned into a horizontal movement. Then these geometric formations moved rapidly in all directions. For a moment I felt dizzy, but I continued to watch the darting energy. Without knowing how to stop the swirling images I continued to move my eyes quickly to keep pace with the energy. Little by little I followed the patterns of light, while the energy drew me deeper into the experience.

Despite the nauseous feeling that came from looking at the swirling energy, I stayed focused on the light, hoping it would lead somewhere. After several seconds the patterns of energy dissolved into a cloud-like formation. Then a face emerged in the center of that cloud. It was an image of a man with dark hair, dark eyes and a black beard, dressed in a beige safari-type suit. He wore a large brimmed hat and carried a book with symbols and written words etched on the book cover. I stared at it for a few seconds waiting for insight, but he simply focused his glance at me without moving.

I couldn't wait any longer for his identity. So I telepathically asked why he was showing me an image of himself. He responded by telling me he was my guide. I heard him whisper a name but I couldn't hear it. I asked if he had a message or purpose for appearing to me. I watched his head nod in an affirmative motion. With my eyes still closed, I prepared to see or hear a message. Just as I saw his lips move to respond to my request, I opened my eyes. I closed them again immediately after opening them, but the image was no longer there.

This experience upset me, because I had allowed fear to disrupt my progress. Anna had warned me about fear, but I still reacted, even though I thought I wouldn't if I had an experience. Fear stopped my spiritual development this time, but I vowed I would never let it do so again.

I let go of the disappointment and continued meditating. At least, I had progressed in my psychic development. Even though I hadn't allowed the image to speak, I still acknowledged my progress in noting the guide's image. Pleased with this partial success I diligently continued meditating. I now knew I had a guide. Even though I couldn't see him, I knew he guided me. How could I not be pleased with my progress? The secrets of life began to reveal themselves.

INSIGHTS

❧ Whatever path you choose to know God is holy, as long as you arrive at the same place: developing a trust in God, spiritual growth, and unconditional love for God, yourself and others.

❧ To tap into the psychic part of the mind you must first learn how to relax and then deepen that state of relaxation by meditating.

❧ If you don't believe you can develop your psychic ability, you won't. Doubt and lack of confidence are the major blocks to success. Nothing in life can be achieved without belief, trust and confidence, including your own connection to the other side.

❧ You attract a spiritual guide, circumstance or person to you, according to whatever level of inner awareness and higher consciousness you are currently operating on in the physical dimension. Emotional growth is the key element in how we attract or how long we must endure a circumstance in our life.

❧ Lack of self-esteem shows-up in our thoughts, actions, emotions, decisions and prejudices. Ultimately they become emotional addictions to us. These emotional addictions limit our ability to recognize God's guidance in everyday life. Therefore, we must become aware of these emotional addictions and eliminate them to develop psychic powers.

❧ Problems are obstacles for us to learn to overcome, which is part of our education here.

❧
WHERE THE
DREAM BEGINS

Without warning, the process reached a new level. I witnessed vivid colors dissolve and then form into circles, squares, triangles and ovals. These same geometric shapes merged into a kaleidoscope of complex patterns. Speckled within the larger picture were intricate patterns that mimicked a mosaic painting. These were the brightly colored images that now appeared in my meditations.

A steady flow of these images dominated most of my sessions. This breakthrough in my development pleased me, but now I had to learn how to interpret the feelings that accompanied each meditation. However, I had no control over the experiences or the process, which frustrated me. There were no guidelines to follow or set formula to learn, which is contrary to other learning experiences. In fact, the process reminded me of a carnival ball-throwing game; either you hit the target or you miss it. On the other hand, the psychic door to revelation could swing wide open at any point during the process. And I had no way of knowing if or how that might occur.

Within a short period of time I noticed a particular behavior that aided my psychic development. But first I had to achieve a considerable degree of relaxation to get there. When my eyes were closed and I looked behind the center of my forehead and focused there for a period of time, images would appear in slow motion. If I stayed focused without creating tension in my eyes or forehead, the images then appeared closer and more distinguishable. For this to happen I had to look deep toward the back of my head and at the same time observe what was before me with my peripheral vision, even though my eyes were closed.

Whenever I followed this routine I fell deeper and deeper into the center of my mind. These mental exercises stretched my inner sight and expanded my senses. If I remained focused on the depth of that imaginary hallway in my inner mind, my consciousness would shift. A feeling of being in two places at once usually preceded the shift. After this move in consciousness, images would flood my mind. This happened only after I let go of the focus on my surroundings and made my inner mind my focal point.

Despite this progress I had more questions than answers. Did my mind, somehow, produce the images? Or did a guide bring the images to me? Is the ability a natural function of the mind that psychologists haven't yet proven? Or is it some form of communication with the other side that only psychics experience? Could these images be scenes from the future?

Like movies playing in fast-forward mode, the images moved quickly through my mind. My eyes tried to follow them but the images vanished before I could interpret them. When I imagined a blank movie screen in my mind and focused on the center of it, instead of the quickly flashing images, the images appeared slower and more distinct. They then moved horizontally several times, until one emerged more prominently in the mix.

Next, I had to slow the image so I could describe it. To bring it closer to me I framed the image with my mind. I squinted several times even though my eyes were closed; at the same time I looked deeper into the dark space. The imaginary space on the blank screen became smaller, larger, and then smaller again. This technique was similar to the aperture of a camera. Each time I made the image smaller and then larger by squinting, the focus of the image became stronger. If I repeated the technique, and at the same time imagined the image moving as if it were a video tape slowly rewinding, I could keep the image in view longer. Then I could distinguish the image enough to describe it. Could this be the procedure to extract the images from the mix that heralded the future?

I could hardly contain my excitement, because I knew I had discovered another bit of the prophecy puzzle. However, I couldn't tell anyone but Anna, so I had to wait until I talked to her again. That night I called her.

"How do you receive the psychic information?" I asked.

"My impressions just happen. It is hard for me to describe the process to you," answered Anna.

"Do you know anyone who could describe the technique?"

"No. Most psychics don't know how they receive the information. It just happens to them."

"How can psychics know if they are receiving accurate information or not if they don't know how the information is received?"

Anna explained, "It's all by trial and error. At first you don't know if you are correct but you give the information anyway.

You experiment first in order to understand how to interpret the information. Once you make a mistake or two, you learn how to tweak your interpretation, so it becomes accurate. After a while you learn how to discern the precognitive information from the past and the present. But only after you have learned from your mistakes."

"Wow. Doesn't that mean psychics could give out wrong information?"

"Sometimes," Anna replied, "but the ability to discern the process usually happens quickly for most psychics."

"Are there any universal interpretations of the images?"

"No, psychics need to develop their own method of interpretation. They have to learn how to interpret the images both literally and symbolically."

"Do you mean if two psychics receive the same image, they could interpret the information differently?"

"Yes. There aren't any set rules. How a psychic interprets the information depends on the life experiences and personality of that psychic."

"Does that mean if a psychic views life pessimistically he or she could interpret the image negatively and predict it to mean something bad?"

"Yes, that's right. You've analyzed and discerned part of the process, which is good. You should feel proud because your mind is powerful, and is now an asset to your mission. Even though I have been a professional psychic for more than forty years, I still can't describe the process."

I didn't know how to answer her. I could only thank her. At that point in time, I didn't think my mind was powerful, so I had no idea what she meant by that comment.

Over the course of several months, Anna and I formed a

strong friendship. Many nights, I visited Anna after my husband and children went to sleep. During our late night visits, we chatted like old friends and at other times Anna gave me instruction on psychic ability. However, there was one visit I'll never forget because the hair on my arms stood up and goose bumps tickled my spine.

We sat in her kitchen deep in conversation, when I suddenly screamed. "Oh my gosh! What was that?"

"What do you mean?"

"There was someone in the room. I felt two hands push my back. I think someone tried to push me off the chair."

"Oh, that's just Mike," Anna said matter-of-factly.

"Who is Mike?" I asked. "I didn't see anyone in the room."

"He is my deceased husband. He had a back problem. He is usually here and he just wanted to let you know that," Anna replied.

"Do you mean a ghost lives with you?"

"Yes. It's no big deal. It's just my husband. He must like you because he has never let anyone know he's here, except me."

I sensed that Anna was trying to ease my fear with that comment.

"Then you believe in ghosts?" I asked inquisitively.

"Of course I believe. Where do you think we go after we die? We don't stop existing. We just shed our physical body because we don't need it to exist in the spiritual planes. Once we have seen God and understand how to navigate the spiritual dimension, we can then visit the physical world again. Only we are then referred to as ghosts or spirits by anyone sensitive enough to know we are present."

After recalling the frightening ghost stories I'd heard, I had to ask her another question. "Can a ghost hurt you?"

"No. Hollywood portrays ghosts as evil or malicious in movies, but that isn't true."

"What about the ghost of a murderer? Can't that ghost hurt you?" I was sure she would answer yes.

"A murderer can still have some of the same personality traits in the spirit world as it had in the physical. However, the spirit doesn't have enough energy or strength to harm anyone in the physical world. Even if it tried, the ghost couldn't hurt you."

I wanted to be home before my children woke up, so we ended our conversation before it got too late. When I looked at the clock, it was midnight. I thought it was amusing for us to end it at that time. I pointed this out to Anna.

While I was in the car, I couldn't stop looking in the back seat. My experience with the ghost spooked me so much I couldn't get rid of the eerie feeling I had during my drive home. Furthermore, I couldn't understand how Anna could calmly accept that a ghost lived in her house. Even though she claimed ghosts couldn't harm you, I didn't want to ever encounter another one! I drove home hoping there were no ghosts living at my house!

When I arrived, the house was completely dark. I wished my husband wasn't asleep, because I felt vulnerable. Entering my house in the dark made me think of ghost encounters I'd heard about. My heart pounded in fear when I walked up the flight of stairs into my house. Fortunately, I made it to bed without encountering a ghost, but not without my mind conjuring up a few imaginary ones.

Over the course of several months, Anna and I continued to grow closer as friends. I felt lucky to have a spiritual guide from the higher realms as well as one on the earth. Anna's encouragement motivated me to meditate often and for longer periods of time to develop the ability.

I had no new images or experiences until my daughter and I attended a dance competition in a nearby state a few months later. The weekend away provided a bit of relaxation for me. There were no household duties to distract my attention, which was a welcomed respite from my routine chores. I had no plans for the night other than my usual meditation.

I closed my eyes, played soft music and inhaled deeply. In my mind's eye I could see shades of yellow and orange emerge and then form a pattern. This pattern formed a huge sphere of warm colors that danced in various directions. As I looked deeper into the image, I began to feel the warmth of the colors. After a few seconds I no longer saw the image. Instead, I saw streams of the warm, bright glow of yellow light enlarge beyond the visual area in my mind. A second later the warm light enveloped me. I still sensed the boundaries of my physical body, but I could see the vision of energy with my eyes tightly shut and feel the radiating energy around me. I didn't open my eyes. I simply allowed the experience to continue, while I waited for insight.

This omnipresent feeling was that of a gentle, loving energy. Could I have experienced self-love in some unusual way? Or could this feeling of love be from a source on the other side? I realized this energy could only compare to a fraction of what God's love must feel like. Nonetheless, the energy soothed me. So I stayed as long as I could in this altered-state of consciousness. When I awakened from the experience, a strong feeling of calm and inner peace filled me. Could this have been the experience Anna described on how to recognize whether a higher guide is present or not?

I didn't receive an answer. Even so, I couldn't stop questioning whether or not the experience was a sign from God.

Concerned my personal views were drastically changing, I had asked God to give me a sign. I wanted God to answer whether or not my budding psychic awareness was indeed part of the plan God had for me. After a minute or two a sense of fear welled up inside me when I began to believe more in what had been prophesied. It was not a fear of the unknown, but rather a fear of change. Whether I wanted it to or not, I knew my life would be different once the door to my psychic ability was fully opened. I just didn't know if life would be better or worse as a result.

The other side had another opportunity to contact me the next night. The same feelings of warmth enveloped me, and the images reappeared. According to Anna, anything repeated had significant meaning. Therefore, this experience had to be another breakthrough in the psychic process.

This yellow-orange light created overwhelming feelings of love and peace within me. How could it not be a sign from God? The vivid colors and feelings gave me an inner serenity. No longer did my developing psychic ability seem just a prediction. Since this experience, the pieces to the prophecy puzzle began to fit together. Everything predicted seemed possible to me now.

As I progressed further along in the process, the quality of my dreams were enhanced. They changed from unremarkable reveries to ones with detailed scenes, rich in vivid colors and now lucid. The lucid dreams made me feel as if I watched the dream as an observer instead of a participant. These dreams had more value psychically than the usual ones. In lucid dreams I was consciously aware I was dreaming during the actual dream, so I could analyze the meaning of the dream before I was awake. Whenever that happened, I became my own psychic because these dreams were precognitive and easily interpreted. These lucid dreams didn't occur all the time, but when they did they were always powerful.

I logged bits and pieces of dream recollections in a notebook, so I could assign meaning to the dream symbols. At times, dream patterns emerged, but I didn't know how to interpret them. Then I had a dream I knew was different from my previous reveries.

The images in this dream appeared in a predictable structured order rather than as a random collage of images, so I knew they had meaning. The dream showed me an image of a plane crashing into an ocean. Images of deep-sea divers searching for the plane's missing black box appeared next in the dream. I could see the divers disappear into the white crests of the waves as they searched for the flight recorder. Then I heard a voice mention flight recorder and the word sabotage. With those words I opened my eyes and bolted upright. I no longer saw the dream images, but the memories still lingered.

When I realized the dream had to be a scene in the future, my stomach churned with fear. Somewhere in the world a plane would crash. I didn't know how to react to my interpretation. Could I have seen the future? Or could my dream have been generated by fear or a previous activity?

I telephoned Anna to tell her my dream and then asked, "What happened to me? Did I have a dream that foretold the future?"

"Some dreams are precognitive glimpses of the future. You will have to wait awhile before your dream can be discerned as precognitive. Dream symbols have no set meaning. So you have to analyze your dreams to know their meaning."

"Do you think this dream was precognitive?" I asked.

"The only way to know for sure is to wait and see if the dream comes true or not."

We ended our conversation with Anna reminding me to be patient. "All great things in life take time."

Two weeks later the media flashed a story on the morning television news. The headlines screamed, AIRPLANE PLUNGES INTO OCEAN: BLACK BOX IS MISSING.

I called Anna to discuss the news and how it related to my dream.

"Since my dream showed me these details, could I have done anything to prevent the accident?" I asked Anna.

"No. Psychic visions and dreams of global situations don't provide enough details for us to accurately predict the situation. Therefore, potential disasters are the most difficult to prevent because of the lack of detail. It is even harder to predict if the destinies of a large number of people are involved," explained Anna.

"Do you mean fatalities in disasters are people who have reached their appointed time of death?"

"No. Accidents happen, but they have nothing to do with destiny. Our guides provide warnings to prevent accidental death. However, sometimes we aren't listening or we can't understand the signs they try to communicate to us."

"Do you mean guidance comes through in a dream, a vision or coincidence?"

"Yes. There are people who change their plans at the last minute, but don't know why they do other than to cite a strange feeling. In some cases they avoid a disaster by heeding that feeling. Sometimes there are blocks put in our path, such as a traffic delay, oversleeping or an alarm clock misfunctioning. These blocks, which are really signs of guidance, can help us avoid a problem, including accidental death when we pay attention to them."

"Then I shouldn't be upset when I am delayed in traffic, because the delay could be my guide's way of protecting me?"

"That's correct! Coincidences and our frustrations have meaning in our lives."

"Is there ever a time when an accidental death is destiny?"

"Most are accidents. However, there are some that could be destiny. Some people may have chosen to die a certain way for a greater purpose because they chose that destiny when they were still in spirit, even though they don't remember it. Have you ever noticed the out-pouring of love after a disaster like 9-11 or the sudden death of a child? People become spiritual and treat each other better at those times. In essence, death served a greater purpose by trying to teach us what we are supposed to be striving for in this life. In other cases, a person's appointed time of death was on hand and he or she just happened to be present at the time of the disaster. And of course, there are times death is an accident."

"Is there a way to tell the difference?"

"Unfortunately, no. When it is an accident, God often tries to turn the incident into something that is for our greater good. That way the person who accidentally died can be credited with a higher purpose and revered in spirit for the contribution that soul has made to humanity."

"That's amazing. Then I guess we are here to become better persons?"

"Yes, that's true."

"How should I deal with future dreams? If I dream of an accident or another plane crash, should I think it is precognitive?" I asked.

"In time you will recognize a dream that is precognitive and when you do, it doesn't mean you will be able to prevent what you see. Take one step at a time."

"Do most people have precognitive dreams or just those who have psychic ability?"

"All have the potential, but sensitive, creative people are more prone to psychic influence."

I heard my husband enter the house, so I thanked Anna and said good-bye. We had plans for dinner and I wasn't even dressed yet.

The memory of those people who perished in the plane crash nagged at me. Could those passengers have done anything to change their fate? If the passengers had an intuitive sense of the disaster, perhaps they could have changed planes or cancelled that particular flight. What if some of those passengers, before they boarded the plane, had a sense of doom, but they just didn't listen to their inner voice? I now saw value in prophecy. You can change your life for the better if you listen for guidance and interpret it correctly. This insight excited me. Perhaps God wanted me to tell people about this guidance or to eventually teach them how to listen. Maybe this was the purpose of the mission God intended for me and the reason I had to develop the ability. How could I not proceed?

Two months later, another precognitive dream came to me. This time, however, the dream involved me. According to my dream, I lost control of my car and hit another vehicle on a rain-slicked road. In the lucid dream, no one was injured.

I telephoned Anna again to ask for her opinion. "Did this dream mean my future included a car accident or did it have a symbolic meaning?"

"The dream warned you about an accident, so be careful driving. Dreams of accidents are usually some kind of warning. The dream could be symbolic or it could be literal. There is no way to tell that yet."

For months, I drove my vehicle cautiously without an incident. I thought I had changed my fate with the extra caution. At least I thought so until a rainy autumn day six months later.

I drove my van down a side street during a torrential rainstorm. I approached a driveway on the street that was hidden from my view, when a car suddenly pulled in front of me. I slammed on my brakes to avoid the accident, but my van skidded on the rain-soaked leaves that covered the road. I lost control of my vehicle when I tried to steer my van away from the car to avoid the accident. Without any control of the van I now headed straight towards three or four big oak trees. There was no way to avoid a collision. I had to either steer the van into the trees or into the car.

I needed to make the decision quickly. At that instant my dream came flooding back into my memory. My van hit the car in my dream, and there was no damage to either vehicle. Within a second I made the decision to follow what had happened in the dream; so I steered the van into the car rather than into the trees.

The jolt from the collision came quickly. To my surprise, there was minimal damage to both cars. The damage to the car was on the same side and almost in the exact place as the car in my dream. I glanced at the tall, sturdy oak trees after the accident and paused for a moment. If I had steered the van into the trees instead of the car, I more than likely would have suffered injuries.

Instinctively, I reacted to the dream guidance, even though I hadn't recognized it as such. I quietly thanked God and the spiritual guide who saved me from injury.

For the first time, I thought I understood why life didn't always go as well as we wanted it to unfold. We needed to ask for guidance and watch for it. If we didn't expect guidance, then we also wouldn't recognize it when our guides tried to reach us.

Unfortunately, we have been told that everything important in life can only be seen, heard or felt. We have been conditioned by science, education, religion, society and our family to navigate life through our physical senses only. Yet, we receive guidance mostly through our sixth sense. If we don't believe in a sixth sense, then how can we recognize guidance?

Before my journey into the unknown, I could only imagine what a great philosophical thinker or famous inventor experienced the moment their apparent discovery was conceived. I thought of Plato, Edison and Einstein with deep awe and appreciation for their talents. I could not compare my insights to their achievements, but I now understood what they must have felt at the moment of their inspiration.

I reflected for a moment on that first psychic reading and how it had changed my life: What seems at first glance to be negative may not be when you look back at the experience with hindsight. I didn't debate my thoughts anymore whether I should or should not explore the depths of the psychic world. Happy to be on the trail of uncovering a mystery elusive for centuries, I felt confident and serene. All the secrets of this phenomenon now seemed within my reach.

Since dreams were now a regular source of guidance for me, I made a point to remember them. After a short time, it was easy to discern the precognitive dreams from those that had no meaning. The important dreams were vivid and seemed real. They created a strong sensory response in me that could easily be mistaken for a nightmare. All of them, however, etched a deep impression in my mind.

I had one dream that I regretted I couldn't interpret until it was too late. It was another dream of a car accident, but this time it involved my children. In the dream my son had a car accident, but it was in the driveway of our house. The car was heavily damaged and the passenger was injured, but I couldn't see the passenger. Then my neighbor and her son walked toward me in the dream and told me about the accident. I awakened from the dream a bit puzzled. If the dream was precognitive, then why did the scene of the accident happen in my driveway?

When my son left to pick up my daughter from school the next day, I wanted to warn him about my dream. However, I decided to wait until I had interpreted the part about the driveway. When I arrived home from an appointment, my son's car wasn't there. He was already more than a half-hour late. I opened my car door, and then noticed my neighbor and her son walking towards my driveway. My heart pounded as I remembered my dream.

"Your son and daughter were in a car accident in front of the school. Jimmy wasn't injured, but Teri Ann was. However, it isn't serious," Trish informed me.

I raced to the scene and saw my daughter being placed in an ambulance. It was at that moment I realized the driveway meant 'near home' and not literally in the driveway. If I had interpreted the information correctly, I could have prevented the accident. The accident resulted in a concussion and serious debilitating headaches for my daughter. Everytime she suffered from one of those severe headaches, I remembered the dream and how I couldn't interpret it.

It became clear to me that we often receive the correct guidance, but can't always interpret it correctly. I realized I should have interpreted the scene in that dream symbolically, instead of literally.

There was one dream, however, that didn't fit into the categories I had discovered. This one put me in touch with the other side. It started mundanely, but moved in a different direction quickly. The dream centered on several of my relatives. I watched each relative show me preparations for an upcoming celebration. I couldn't identify the relatives, because I didn't see their faces at first. As the dream progressed, I realized I was communicating with deceased members of my family. I walked amongst them, but they ignored me. They were only concerned with their preparations for a party and completing them on time. I saw my grandmother, my Uncle Frank, my Aunt Faye and her husband Harold.

While they chose their duties, I just watched and listened. My aunt planned the menu. My Uncle Frank planned the official greeting. My Uncle Harold hurried about planning the list for the invitations to the party and how he would announce it to the others. And my grandmother chose to meet the new soul arriving into the spirit dimension. Her duty was to lead that person to God and then to the celebration. I tried to communicate telepathically to let them know I was there with them, but I still couldn't attract their attention.

Then my grandmother turned around, and gasped when she saw me. At first I was upset by her reaction. I thought she would be happy to see me. Instead, the startled look on her face frightened me. Why is my grandmother angry with me? She had always been such a loving person. Then I heard my grandmother telepathically speak.

"You can't stay long. You don't belong here. It isn't your time. Get going! It's dangerous for you to be here long," warned my grandmother.

I moved away from my grandmother just long enough to see my Uncle Harold excitedly clap his hands in glee. Shocked and confused, I tried to determine where I was or why I was there.

Then my uncle announced, "Oh Boy! Another one is

coming to join us! There's going to be a party just like old times."

When I heard that announcement, I woke up with a jolt and sweat trickling down my face. I felt I had just been thrown by some force. My heart thumped in fear. I knew this had to be more than a dream. It felt as if I had just been with all my dead relatives, instead of just seeing them in a dream. Immediately, I realized the meaning of the dream and the plans for the celebration; someone in my family would soon join them in the spirit world.

For a few weeks I couldn't tell anyone my dream, not even Anna. The dream had frightened me. I was too afraid Anna would validate this dream. If this were a precognitive dream, then it could mean I actually traveled to the spirit world and communicated with the dead. It also meant an end to a relative's life. I just didn't know who was going to die. Both thoughts disturbed me.

Within a month of my dream, my Uncle Tommy learned he had a serious illness. Six months later he died. However, I knew he was going to the other side to celebrate his new birth date into the spiritual realm with my deceased relatives.

This knowledge comforted me, but I couldn't help but be upset. I was upset not only because I missed him, but because I had also received that information in a dream six months earlier. When I told Anna about the dream, she tried to comfort me.

"In time you will adjust to your psychic ability, as well as have more experiences dealing with the other side. Remember, seeing sad moments is just as much a part of psychic ability as seeing the good moments."

"Do I have to always see death?" I asked.

"No. You won't always see death. It is blocked from us most of the time. It is good that you had that dream, because you gained insight into the spirit world."

"Does that mean I will have more dreams of death?"

"No. It just means you will see the other side so you can help others not to fear it. Remember, death is a part of life."

I left Anna's house dazed and repeating those words, as if I was trying to convince myself. I mumbled the words softly trying to remember why the phrase seemed to be a part of some distant memory I couldn't quite grasp. Over and over again, I said those words, trying to understand their importance to me. I knew I had heard them before, but I didn't remember when or where. All I could think of was the phrase: Death is a part of life.

INSIGHTS

୬ If you do not receive guidance on your own or you do not understand the guidance that reaches you through meaningful coincidences, dreams or introspection, then you can find the guidance through a psychic. Psychics can point out the next steps in life that you must act upon. If you are on or off your path, guidance can reach you through prophecy. You might also be directed to another path to avoid disaster.

୬ If you do not expect guidance, then you will not recognize it if guidance is trying to reach you. Coincidences and signs can allude you without your ever recognizing or understanding these signs as guidance.

୬ Circumstances in life that seem negative can have a different meaning, when you look back at the experience. After a lapse in time, a serious problem can be seen as a blessing in disguise. Problems are simply obstacles placed in your life to allow you to learn how to emotionally respond and intellectually respond as part of your education as a human being.

୬ Your dreams are messages from your sub-conscious mind. Studying your dreams can give you psychic insight into your life.

My Secret Life

I had the luxury and freedom to explore the paranormal without the time constraints of a full-time, nine-to-five job. My husband and I were self-employed in a seasonal business. As a stay-at-home mom, my business duties started when everyone retired for the night. The business accounting and billing continued often into the wee hours of the night so the records were ready for the next day's business. When my husband left for the office, I was a full time stay-at-home mom, again.

The psychic encounters and paranormal research consumed my leisure time during the day. When my husband came home in the evening, I tended to other activities and not the paranormal. This lifestyle afforded me the opportunity to live a secret life. Anna and I were the only ones who discussed my supposed mission. How could I tell these predictions to anyone but Anna? Most people viewed psychics as odd and unbelievable. No one at that time thought of a psychic as an emissary for God. Of course, I still didn't have proof the predictions were true. But I had begun to believe in the ability because I knew something paranormal had started to happen to me. However, I still didn't understand the prediction regarding a mission. Nevertheless, I persistently pursued this path hoping to discover the truth.

Living with this secret pulled me in two directions. I had intended to tell my husband about my developing psychic powers, but he didn't believe in them. Therefore, in the daytime I explored the unknown, and in the evening I was, again, a traditional wife and mother. I didn't dare reveal what I had learned about psychic powers to anyone, so I kept my spiritual activities a secret.

My family considered me an open book and not the keeper of secrets. Consequently, no one suspected my beliefs were in a state of flux and that I was on the path to developing psychic powers. Many times I wanted to share this with others but feared their reaction to my beliefs. So for now I had to keep my quest a secret.

There had to be some truth to what had been told to me by psychics. Otherwise, I wouldn't have been able to discern the process. I just didn't know if everything predicted was true. Even though I knew I had a long way to go before my ability was fully developed, I was, however, pleased with my progress. I, at least, had some paranormal experiences to indicate some proof in the predictions.

Summertime meant a break from the more concentrated exploration in the world of psychics than the other months of the year. My husband stayed close to home during the summer months, so I didn't have as much freedom as I did in the winter months. Anna, also, had a lot of visitors in the summer, so she was not as available to me as in the other months of the year. However, I didn't mind this time off, as the more leisurely lifestyle in the summer offered relief from the more arduous moments of my exploration. This provided a time for me to reflect on everything I had already uncovered about prophecy and the other mysteries of life.

Live entertainment at the Garden State Arts Center, an outdoor stage arena in New Jersey, was a popular entertainment venue in the summer. We attended the concerts at the Art Center in the summer and then hibernated in the winter, rarely enjoying any entertainment together. Over the years we had seen a number of popular stars in concert at the center, but Bob Hope touched my heart the most.

When my son was eight and my daughter was four, they both attended the Bob Hope concert with us. I carried a bouquet of red roses to the concert for my children to present to Bob Hope. During a pause in the concert my daughter carried the roses and my son led her toward the stage. Bob invited both of them on stage. He lifted my daughter into his arms and kissed her on the cheek. Then he shook my son's hand and made him the butt of his jokes, while he still held my daughter in his arms. Quick-witted Bob made my son part of his show and the audience roared. Of course, both children were thrilled and none of us ever forgot that moment. These Art center concerts were always memorable events. I did not, however, expect my first outward sign of psychic ability to occur on one of these summertime jaunts.

On that occasion, my husband and I sat in the center section of the outdoor arena about thirty-five rows from the stage. While waiting for Wayne Newton's performance, I noticed a blank movie screen set-up on the stage. I assumed his performance for the evening also included some movie clips. Wayne stepped onto the stage to thunderous applause and he belted out a couple of songs before he spoke to the audience about his life and family. I expected his stage technicians to project images on the movie screen once he addressed the audience. However, halfway through Wayne's performance the white screen still remained blank. This distracted me from his performance. I tried to be patient, so I lost my thoughts in the melody of his voice.

After several songs I saw an image fill the entire screen. The profile of an old woman with deeply etched lines on her face appeared on the screen. When I looked closer, it was an image of a Native American Indian woman. Wayne Newton's ethnic heritage was part American Indian, so I assumed the image of the woman belonged to a member of Wayne's family. Satisfied the screen was no longer blank I confidently waited for Wayne to identify this woman and reveal a story about her.

Wayne sang several more songs without making a comment regarding the Indian woman's identity. As I fidgeted in my seat, I couldn't focus on his songs. The woman's image on the screen begged to be identified but he just continued singing, oblivious to the image behind him.

I couldn't wait any longer. I leaned toward my husband and whispered, "Do you see the Indian woman on the movie screen?"

"What woman?" he replied.

Pointing, I said, "Right there! There is an Indian woman's picture on the movie screen on the stage next to Wayne. Can't you see it?"

Puzzled, my husband asked, "What are you talking about? There isn't any image of a woman. There is only a blank, white screen."

When I realized Kevin didn't see an image on the screen, but I did, I didn't say another word. When I looked back at the screen, the image had disappeared. I slouched in my seat, trying to look inconspicuous because I felt so embarrassed. I couldn't believe what had just happened. Why did I see the image and my husband not see it? It was so vivid and detailed. Could I have had a psychic experience? Could this be what happens when a psychic predicts the future?

Once I realized I had experienced a psychic moment, I then became excited. This could be the psychic breakthrough I had hoped to reach. If the vision indicated the door to the psychic level of my mind had opened, then I could expect more of the psychic gift to follow. I tried to remember all the details so I could tell Anna. I was so thrilled something significant had happened.

The image of the woman seemed more like a brilliant photograph than an image. The woman's face had deeply etched lines around her eyes, mouth, forehead and cheeks. I estimated her to be at least eighty years old, because of the wrinkles in her skin. In fact, I had never seen a face so wrinkled. However, I thought of those lines as marks representing the years of enlightenment she gained from her life experiences.

The image lasted for more than thirty minutes, which seemed a long time for a vision. I could see the woman's profile, her long braids and every detailed line on her face. Those lines proclaimed great wisdom. Yet, there was no image on the screen except for the one created by my imagination. It didn't make sense that the image could be so sharp and detailed, yet not be seen by anyone but me. Could these illusions be a part of everyday life for psychics? If they were, then being psychic took courage. Could you imagine what would happen if a person experienced a psychic moment, but didn't know he or she had psychic tendencies?

I stopped reflecting on the vision to focus on my husband. Secretly, I hoped my husband wouldn't question me about it. I wasn't prepared to address the issue with him. Fear of his reaction consumed me. What was he going to think of me if these visions happened on a regular basis? How would I fit into society with a psychic gift? Wouldn't that make me odd or unconventional in most people's eyes? I also wondered if the psychic ability could be shut off once the ability fully opened. I quieted my fears with thoughts of Anna. I needed to talk to her again. For now, though, I had to think of some excuse for my odd behavior to dissuade him from questioning me.

The ride home from the concert, at first, seemed uneventful. I chattered incessantly about Wayne's superb performance. However, that discussion didn't last long because he changed the direction of the conversation.

"Hey, tell me. What happened to you tonight? That sure was funny when you thought you saw an Indian woman," he teased.

"Kevin, that isn't funny. You're mocking me again."

"Oh, come on. Don't you think it's a little strange for you to see an Indian on a blank screen?"

"Not if it were part of my psychic ability."

"You aren't psychic! It's just your over-active imagination."

"Not yet, but I am trying to develop it."

"That's ridiculous! You aren't psychic nor can you develop it."

I refused to say anymore, so the remainder of the ride home was quiet.

I called Anna the next morning to make plans to meet with her. We met for lunch at a restaurant down the street from her house. I had a lot of questions about the previous night's experience, so I was grateful for this opportunity to be with her.

"Anna, do you think that mirage represented a part of my psychic ability?" I questioned.

"Yes," Anna answered. "You will have these visions as you open more of the window into the psychic realm. Just don't be frightened. This is a normal part of the process."

"Do you experience your psychic ability in the same way?"

"Yes, but I no longer project my thoughts outward. Now I see images inside my mind, which are also sharp. When you see them inwardly instead of projected outwardly, you will access the information quickly."

"Will this type of extra-sensory perception end at some point in the process?"

"No. You will have more of these images. As you develop the ability further, the illusions switch to inner visions. You also need to know that in the beginning you might see negative visions rather than positive. Once the power is fully developed, the negative images will diminish."

"What do you mean by negative images?"

"You could have visions of airplane crashes, murders and other types of death."

Startled by her comment I screamed. "What! Why develop psychic ability if you have to see destruction and death?"

"Don't be frightened. It's a temporary part of the development process. You're strong. Remember, you have a mission to complete. You weren't born to just live out your life. Once your ability is fully functioning, God will give you other instructions."

I didn't want to hear either one of those comments, so I tried to change the subject. Thoughts of death flooded my mind. I began to question whether I wanted to continue the process.

Trying to forget my fear of the powers, I asked Anna another question: "Do you suppose that the woman on the screen is my guide or a member of Wayne Newton's family?"

"It is your guide. She probably projected the image to

attract your attention. Are you still meditating?"

"Not as often as I had been."

"That's why she appeared. Her presence was intended to remind you to keep connected as well as coax you to complete your lessons, so you can get to where you are supposed to be. The other side is watching you closely so you won't fail at your mission. You will probably be told again if you don't focus on your purpose. That guide is a temporary one. American Indian guides are often around people who first begin to open the ability. A new guide will then be assigned to you when you have progressed further."

Knowing I was watched so closely by the other side annoyed me. I never liked being told what to do and now I had unseen guides dictating orders to me. However, I didn't dare tell Anna my feelings. I dismissed them until I could reflect on this. Frankly, I was quite surprised by my strong reaction, which made me realize these old issues were emotional buttons I needed to address before I progressed on this path. I fired more questions at Anna, so I could hide my emotions before she asked why I had become so quiet.

"When you first experienced your psychic gifts, did you feel you were different than other people?" I probed.

"Psychics operate at a much higher level of perception than most people. Consequently, people who are not perceptive look at us strangely but our insights and perceptions seem normal to us. Those who don't perceive at this level are fearful because they don't understand. And it is human nature to criticize what we fear or don't understand. Don't take the criticism personally. We are all on our own path and in time those who don't understand will have the opportunity to do so."

"Have you always been happy being psychic?"

"Sometimes my sensitivity overwhelms me and I cry at inappropriate times. However, I have never regretted being psychic. Looking at the world with this wisdom helps me feel a deep inner peace that I probably wouldn't have had otherwise."

"Do we have any control of the circumstances in our lives?"

"Yes," Anna responded. "We are here to learn how to exercise our free will. Sometimes, we make decisions and use our free will recklessly. When we use it recklessly, problems and challenges occur, which we then must meet as destiny."

I was glad to hear we have free will. It made me feel better about being so closely watched by the other side. I continued asking questions because I wanted to learn as much as I could on psychic powers in this one encounter.

Anna continued her teaching. "Some people want psychics to make decisions for them. Psychics point out the next steps in a person's life, but we can't magically bring to fruition what we see psychically. We see what is supposed to happen, but you can exercise your free will either to avoid it or take action to attract it to you. For example, if I predict a relationship for a person, it doesn't happen automatically. He or she can't just sit home waiting for a soulmate to knock on the door. A person must take some action to reach his or her destiny."

"Is that what happened at the concert last night?" I asked.

"Yes, but it didn't happen without effort. You worked at quieting your mind by meditating, and you explored your inner self by reading and acquiring knowledge. With emotional growth and increased self-love, you were able to finally shift your reality into a different realm. Most people never quiet themselves long enough for their guide to reach them. Then these same people wonder why they have so many problems."

I addressed Anna with another question, hoping she would not think I was too inquisitive. "Now that my ability has begun to open, can I ever shut it down?"

"You need to control it, not shut it down. If you block psychic ability after it has developed, you could suffer headaches."

"Why would that happen?" I asked.

"Psychic ability involves a good deal of energy. Psychic information comes into our conscious awareness through the mind. When you open the window into the psychic realm, you open yourself to an additional burst of energy that flows into you. This energy has to either be used, directed or released. To release it a psychic must acknowledge the information and express it. If there is a long dormant period when psychic information is ignored, the energy builds in the person to create pressure in the head and a dull headache."

She then reminded me, "This is your destiny. You have incarnated now for a specific reason."

This time I didn't respond. I just listened quietly. In the back of my mind I heard this slightly rebellious voice softly chant the words, no one can tell me what to do. When I thought of the other side watching me to make sure I meditated and listened, I balked at the idea of a mission. I accepted the psychic ability, but I didn't yet believe this part of the predictions.

"Someday, you will be in front of large groups of people speaking God's words of love and using your psychic ability. You will be in the media, but not for the sake of fame. Instead, it will be the beginning of your work as God's instrument," continued Anna. "So just let the events unfold and someday you will understand."

We ended our mentoring session and I left the restaurant. Conflicting thoughts bottled in my mind. It was hard for me to understand how developing my psychic gifts could lead me to be an instrument of God's greater plan. It almost seemed silly and trite to think of psychic work in the context of God's work. Again, my religious beliefs had influenced me. I admitted to myself that ministers, priests, rabbis, clerics and other religious people had missions for God, not psychics. How could a psychic be an instrument of God's work?

I didn't verbalize that thought to Anna because I didn't want to hurt her feelings. It was difficult to accept this part of her interpretation of my future. How could I talk to anyone about my "mission"? In the context of religion I would have to be a nun, priest, minister, rabbi or cleric to have a mission. I decided to put the prediction aside because I didn't want to wrestle with it anymore.

Only a few people around me ever talked about psychics, so this topic couldn't be discussed with many. When I talked to psychics, most couldn't offer explanations for their psychic ability or how or why they had the talent. Textbooks offered academic knowledge, but parapsychologists couldn't offer concrete information to prove or disprove psychic talent. Anna seemed to be the only one who had the expertise to understand and explain this ability. I trusted Anna, so I accepted her advice to just let the events unfold until I had an inside look into my own psychic awareness.

I searched my childhood memories for examples of my imagination as a child or some other experiences that could indicate a propensity for psychic ability. I recalled several episodes of trying to tell my mother about a being who radiated light and talked to me during my dreams. My mom usually labeled the vision a figment of my imagination and dismissed it. So I stopped telling her these experiences. Although I remembered the episodes, I couldn't recall the specific details.

I searched for clues in my past of people who could have influenced my development in a psychic direction. As far as I could tell, I had had a normal childhood. I had loving parents and an extended family of grandparents, aunts, uncles, and cousins to interact with on weekends and summers. I was the youngest of three children. I had an older sister who sometimes complained I talked in my sleep because we shared the same bedroom. On occasion she would listen to my nighttime chatter and then tell me the next day what I had said during my sleep. Despite our five-year difference in age, we enjoyed playing together and interacted well. As siblings, we had a close bond and still do. In fact, my sister had an interest in Astrology. She studied it for years, but gave it up because the accuracy of it was too scary for her.

I also had an older brother who lovingly teased me into doing things for him. I often walked our family's hunting dogs in the fields behind our house to maintain the dogs' sense of smell keen. It was my brother's job to exercise the dogs and prepare Duchess and Fortuneteller for hunting, but my brother learned early how easy it was to bribe me into doing it for him. I didn't mind, because I liked being alone in the fields or in the woods near my grandmother's house. It provided me an opportunity to think, plan and analyze life. Sometimes, I received answers to my questions during those times in the field. When I got older, my brother and I spent hours analyzing people and the world around us. We both liked to delve deep into the meaning of things. Perhaps that's why I jumped into this quest. Analyzing how or why something works was familiar to me.

We were a close-knit family with many fond memories of big gatherings with my aunts, uncles, and cousins that were always fun. My happiest family get-together was always on Easter.

All the cousins from young to old gathered to participate in a huge Easter egg hunt. I looked forward to the family event at my grandmother's every year.

My mom was a perfectionist and my dad was easy-going, so their style of relating, though opposite, made a perfect match. They were devoted to each other and their kids. Despite their personality differences, their affection and deep love for each other set an example for me. As a result, I grew up to be sensitive and caring of others and believing all people were equally loved by God. Neither parent had much education because of their having to pitch-in and help their respective families with chores and farm duties in the late 1920s. However, they valued education so keenly that when they married, they vowed to send their children to college. And that's exactly what they did. My mom worked when it was unusual for a mother to and my father worked two jobs to send their three children to college. Remembering their determination and commitment to a goal made me determined to succeed in my goals. And today, at 88 and 93, they are still an influence in my life.

My thoughts turned to fishing and how I refused to let my father and brother go fishing without me. Revisiting my stubbornness and determination to succeed in this goal made me chuckle. When I was seven, I threatened to hide in the trunk of the car if my father didn't take me fishing on the opening day of trout season. It worked, and I went fishing with them every year on the opening day of the fishing season until I married. For nearly fifteen years I stood next to my father and fished off the banks of the various fresh water fishing holes throughout New Jersey. The best part of the experience was enjoying the beauty of nature and hearing the sounds of the fishing lines splashing in the water. The roar of the swift-running water in a babbling brook always mesmerized me and put me in deep thought. Recalling this made me realize these fishing adventures taught me how to relax, which probably facilitated my ability to meditate now.

There were times I danced for hours in front of the large mirror in my parents' bedroom. I loved creating tap dance and jazz routines to express my creativity when I was a teenager. However, I recalled how the movement in my dance routines often sparked imagery that I thought was just a part of my imagination. This memory made me remember thoughts which I dismissed as normal but that I now realize were images of the future.

The previous memory triggered other recollections when I danced as a teenager. I saw myself as a writer after the age of forty-five; I also remembered telling myself I would marry someone with a common first name, but an unusual last name. I couldn't confirm the vision now about being an author, because I wasn't even forty, yet. However, the memory of the name I related to because my husband had a short first name and he had a numeral listed after his last name. This memory intrigued me. I wondered if my dancing at that time was a form of meditating. That made sense as to why I received those images then.

As I recalled another incident in my childhood, I chuckled when I remembered some studious efforts. At twelve, I often hid in a closet reading my brother's college textbooks on Psychology and German. I had an overwhelming hunger for knowledge that is still with me today.

Nothing surfaced in my mind to indicate any childhood experience that could be described as paranormal, until I recalled how I almost died when I was four years old. I had repeated episodes of breathing difficulties from the croup, a common childhood respiratory condition. This one episode frightened my parents.

When I was four years old, I woke up in the middle of the night gasping for air. The wheeze in my throat didn't stop. Instead it intensified, which created long gaps between breaths. My parents woke-up from their sleep in a panic when I approached their bed, not able to breathe. My mom cuddled me in her arms and shouted for my father to get some honey. I found it more difficult to breathe with each gasp and wheeze. I heard my mother shout to my father to hurry because I was turning blue. Tearfully, I heard her pray to God for help as she waited for my father to bring the honey. She pleaded for God to make me better. My mother's voice faded to a barely audible mumble in the background when I became dizzy. In the eerie silence, I then heard a voice speak within me.

The voice assured me, "You will be okay. Just listen to me."

This voice then gave me more instructions: "Do not take deep breaths. Slowly breathe through your nose and do not fear. Your fearfulness is causing you to stop breathing."

I followed the instructions and tried to calm myself. I consciously heard my mother's voice again praying while my father got a teaspoon of honey ready to soothe my cough. Then I heard the voice tell me she was my guardian, there to protect me and keep me safe.

I swallowed the honey and the croup attack stopped. I felt an incredible calm envelop me. Then I heard my mother thank God as she held me in her arms crying in relief. The next morning my mother made a call to the doctor.

The doctor told her, "The next time your daughter has a respiratory problem and there are blue tones in her skin color, take her immediately to the hospital. She could have died from asphyxiation last night."

I never questioned the voice or ever told my parents about

it. I simply accepted it and forgot it until now. Remembering that incident made me think of an experience shortly after my croup attack. During surgery for a tonsillectomy, the face mask that administered ether for my surgery covered my mouth and nose. Within seconds I was no longer conscious. I could see myself on the operating room table and the doctors frantically working on me. Then I became aware of a dark tunnel with a light at the end of it. I kept falling into that tunnel trying to reach the light, but I couldn't. Over and over I tried to get through the tunnel and near the light. Then I awakened while still on the operating table and heard the doctors say there was a problem. Then they moved around me quickly and put me out again. I didn't awaken again until I was in recovery. However, I was the last child to recover from the surgery. All of the other children who had tonsillectomies were already discharged from the hospital. They told my parents they had a little problem with me because I reacted to the ether and might have an allergy to it. My mother didn't think anything of it because the doctors told her I was all right. For years I repetitively re-lived the experience by having a dream of falling into a black tunnel and trying to reach the light at the other end. Recalling this incident flooded my mind with more questions. Could I have almost died again? Could I have received some guidance during those experiences that I wasn't supposed to know until now? Could I already have had psychic ability and not have known it? Perhaps, there was something to the predictions after all.

I telephoned Anna to tell her the details of my recollections. Pleased to hear about my experiences, she identified the voice for me.

"The inner voice you heard was a spiritual guide assigned to guide and to protect you in this life and in the next dimension,"

Anna informed.

"Why do we still have a guide when we cross over into the next dimension?" I questioned.

"The operative currency in the next dimension is not the monetary system we use in the physical. It is more important to gain knowledge and understanding in the physical than to simply accumulate material possessions. These memories and stored wisdom become the currencies we use to navigate the spiritual planes. In order to advance in the spiritual planes you must have wisdom. There are many levels to the other side just as there are educational levels here in the physical. We continue our growth in order to reach a higher level of existence above the reincarnation cycle. Guides are there for us until we reach their level and no longer need to incarnate in the physical. Our knowledge and wisdom continue on the other side."

"How could I have been in communication with a guide when I was only four years old, but not be in communication with one now?" I questioned again.

Anna replied, "Somewhere in childhood you may have been punished or ridiculed for showing a tendency towards psychic ability. Formal schooling doesn't allow for this kind of expression. For the first decade or so we are conditioned to follow what others say. Our natural psychic tendencies are submerged deep into the sub-conscious where we don't have memory of them. Without knowledge there is no spiritual advancement to reach the level of communication necessary with a guide."

"We are actually more advanced spiritually as children than we are as adults, unless we consciously develop in that area?" I asked.

"Yes. That's right. Children are born with inherent spiritual knowledge and psychic ability. The trauma of the birth process erases most of those memories. Through our imagination, bits and pieces of those memories surface. However, society and our educational institution condition us to stop using our imagination. So we function most of the time without these original spiritual insights."

I probed for more information, "Does that mean we are already psychic?"

"Yes. Developing psychic ability is an awakening process rather than a new process. In Greek, the word psychic comes from the word psyche. Psyche actually means soul or spirit. Therefore, psychic ability is not limited to a few gifted people. Every person born into this world has the potential, because it is a means to advance the soul. However, like any talent, there are varying degrees of the ability. And just like other creative talents, some people may develop and use the talent as a profession and some may use it as a tool for personal satisfaction."

I was grateful for Anna's understanding and knowledge, but I also had to recognize that my mind just couldn't absorb any more new information. I reached this point now. Fortunately, Anna recognized my fatigue, so we ended our conversation. Just before I said good-bye I asked one more question: "What would you suggest I do now to continue developing?"

"Continue meditating, but be aware of the bits and pieces of information that flash through your mind. Pretend you are already psychic and then pay attention to everything you feel. Most of all, don't let fear inhibit your process. And call me if anything more happens."

Those last words triggered reflection on my part. Fear is a big block to our psychic development. Anna repeatedly referred to that emotion as a deterrent. Could there be anything to fear or is it just our own fear that impedes progress?

Thoughts of hypnosis entered my mind. I recalled my experience in college with hypnosis and wondered if it could enhance the process. Hypnosis helped me control pain. During those sessions I entered deep levels of hypnosis and used imagery to relieve the pain I had. I now wondered if these same deep hypnotic states of consciousness could facilitate the psychic process. I decided to seek out a hypnotist for a few sessions in order to research its effects on my development. But I had to keep this a secret, too.

The following week I made an appointment with a hypnotist. I explained the purpose of the appointment to him and he agreed it could help in my development.

He directed me to another section of his office. I sat in a comfortable recliner chair and listened to his instructions. His voice was soothing and melodious, as well as soft in tone. He told me to close my eyes and just relax as I listened to his words.

"With each beat of your heart, you let go of all the tension in your body and you allow all of your muscles to relax."

The muscles in my body became limp and loose and I allowed my body to sink further and further into the cushions of the chair. Then I began to hear more of his suggestions.

"You are tuning into your psychic mind through meditation, and other altered states. Eventually, you will receive psychic information when you are conscious and in a normal state. When you see images, you are now able to slow them down, so you see them more clearly and can describe them. Little by little you become more sensitive to your surroundings and the people around you. And you now use your senses to absorb psychic impressions that you accurately interpret. You now apply the psychic information to your life and you begin to recognize the guidance around."

121

Soon I could only faintly hear his words as I drifted in and out of consciousness. Then I could feel myself physically and mentally let go. I was somewhere between consciously hearing his words and drifting into an altered state. Deeper and deeper I allowed myself to roam into the dark mental screen behind my eyes. Then I was able to see pictures rapidly move across the blank screen. I began to see something different. The images slowed enough for me to describe them.

After about twenty-five minutes the hypnotist counted me out of hypnosis and back to being awake. I remained quiet for a moment adjusting to my awakened consciousness before I engaged in conversation.

He asked me, "How do you feel?"

"I feel fine and I am very relaxed." I then added, "When my eyes were closed and I was deep, I could see moving pictures flash in front of my eyes, but my eyes were closed."

He didn't respond to my comment. He just instructed me to return next week and gave me a copy of the audiotape of the hypnosis session. I left his office but the experience nagged at me. I remembered seeing these images before this experience. I couldn't remember when, so I just let it go.

The next morning I telephoned my mother. While on the telephone, my mind drifted as I stared out the window. As I listened to her, I recognized the hypnosis experience in my current daydream. As I talked on the telephone, moving images flashed in front of my eyes. I realized this was the familiar experience I was trying to remember after I awakened from the hypnotic state.

I connected the two experiences and was delighted with the insight. The images in hypnosis were the same as what I saw while awake. These were now outward images like the first image I had of the Indian woman. I became increasingly aware of these mental pictures. Each time the pictures occurred I worked at trying to slow them down. Eventually, I was able to slow the pictures enough for me to recognize them clearly. I didn't know at the time these images were part of clairvoyance.

When I made the connection, I knew I had also entered another level. I was on my way to being closer to opening this door within the psychic realm and I had no doubt it was within my reach. Soon my psychic ability would no longer be a secret.

INSIGHTS

❧ An image or illusion of an image projected by the mind is considered to be a visual hallucination, according to Psychology. Psychologists term the experience a hallucination, but they can not prove how or why the hallucination occurs. The same experience from a different perspective is considered a psychic moment. There are many different perspectives in life, which suggest that not everything you hear, see, learn or believe in life is the absolute truth. Based on the differing opinions of what is fact or truth, all of your personal experiences have merit.

❧ Psychics operate at a higher level of perception than most people do. Consequently, people who are not quite at the same level of perception do not understand and are quick to label psychics or paranormal experiences as strange. Developing your psychic ability takes courage and self-confidence to stay the course.

❧ Psychic ability is a natural gift that is suppressed by society and the educational system. Neither allows for the expression of the imagination. A diversion from the prescribed course material or a day dreaming episode is often criticized as unacceptable behavior. This attitude inhibits the imagination and the creative expression in children, which then blocks their inherent psychic talent from being expressed, until they seek instruction and a reawakening of the ability.

❧ Problems are not always pre-destined, but are often caused by the reckless use of free will or by negative emotions that can cloud perception as you make a decision. Your decision can then set off a whole chain of events that you must meet as your destiny. You can have some degree of control in your destiny if you do not allow emotions to dominate your decisions.

&❧ You may wonder why you have so many problems but you never look for the reason in your past decisions. You may never quiet yourself enough to receive spiritual guidance, yet then blame God or some other source for your problems. In order to change your life you must take some responsibility for the circumstances in your life. Listening for guidance or paying attention to the subtle coincidences in life will help direct you to a better life. In other words, you must take some action in order to be led to your destiny.

&❧ The stored wisdom and memories gained in the physical are the operative currency in the next dimension. When you reach the spiritual planes, you use the wisdom and memories you achieved in your physical life to navigate the spiritual world. The next dimension is a mental world, so you live in that world through your memories and communicate telepathically with others in that dimension, as well as in your former plane. Spirits who contact the physical world communicate through telepathy. This communication reaches the physical world through thoughts that enter your mind or through feelings your body experiences.

&❧ Several guides are assigned to oversee your journey on the earth, as well as when you cross to the other side. There is a connecting network of guides helping us at all times. By embarking on a path of higher consciousness to re-awaken your psychic talent you can consciously connect with your guides.

Opening the Door
to the Psychic Realm

The frequent episodes of vivid images, spontaneous visions and precognitive dreams convinced me I was on my way to understanding the psychic world. Each new experience moved me one step closer. The process, however, required dedication to achieve these deep altered states of consciousness. Impatience often dampened my enthusiasm and fear interrupted the process. Nevertheless, my will to unravel the secrets of this realm outweighed the obstacles and steadily pushed me forward.

Undeveloped inherent psychic ability, I suspected, affects our lives in ways of which we are not yet aware. Could using this natural talent solve problems? Could psychic ability help us develop a closer connection to God? Could psychic powers have more of a purpose than just foreseeing the future?

I reflected a moment on psychic ability. If there was an underlying purpose to prophecy not yet discovered, then psychic ability could be a way to know God. This premise, I speculated, was an important insight. Could this be the secret God wanted

127

me to discover?

I pondered on what I might experience when the final breakthrough into my psychic ability occurred. According to Anna, psychic development involved the understanding of certain principles that couldn't be rushed. She explained that psychic ability progresses the same way as we learn in a traditional school. You can't advance to a higher grade until you master the educational level of the current school grade. The psychic process had an order of progression to it, too. To develop this ability you must learn how to relax, be receptive to impressions, interpret the information, and then learn how to turn the gift on and turn it off at will.

Once I gained knowledge of the process, I speculated on the difference between an ordinary person and someone who was psychic. If psychics predicted the future, then there had to be a plan to life, proving destiny isn't just a composition of random experience. There had to be heretofore unknown rules that guide us to what we call destiny. Psychics, I imagined, comprehend the rules to the game of life more than most. And I suspected these unstated laws operated according to God's will, but without our awareness. These laws or rules were some of the secrets I sought.

For now I concerned myself with my budding psychic talent. I wanted to succeed, so I needed to understand more about the ability. Could I handle seeing something traumatic? Would I be able to read a person's mind once the ability developed? Could the development be stopped once it began? Unfortunately, the answers to these questions couldn't be determined until I progressed further.

For now, I directed my desire to learn in another direction. I reflected on how much I had changed since I began this journey. Before I explored the paranormal I had become a shadow in the background of other peoples lives. I had no personal identity, because I allowed my opinions to be carbon copies of others' beliefs. I was a mother and a wife but I forgot who I was as a person. My journey in the paranormal, however, helped me to rediscover the truth of who I was. It also changed my belief system just as the first psychic had predicted.

Studying the paranormal taught me we are so much more than physical bodies. We have a unique spiritual self, which is part of a much greater plan. And we have an obligation to discover this uniqueness and develop our soul's full capability to love, so our piece of the plan can fit into the bigger puzzle. When a large number of people complete this task, then the nearly finished puzzle will usher change into the world for the good of humankind. Knowing this made me more determined than ever to do my part.

Could God have given us a tool to navigate life more easily, but we haven't made the connection necessary to make use of it? In horror, I thought of the people who were persecuted for centuries for possessing these misunderstood abilities. Women were labeled witches and were publicly stoned and hanged in the United States. In other countries women were publicly burned at the stake when they were accused of possessing psychic powers. Estimates indicate there were more than several hundred thousand so-called witches put to death during the period from 1484 until 1722. Could this history of psychic persecution still affect society today?

Psychics are no longer executed, but the prevailing attitude of fear, skepticism and criticism toward psychics hinted there is still a form of persecution present today. Could I have reacted skeptically and mistrustingly toward psychics because I unknowingly allowed history to affect my beliefs and attitudes? Even though I couldn't prove it, I knew my answer was affirmative.

I thought of the passages in the Bible that could be interpreted as episodes of psychic phenomena. When these Biblical events were recorded in the Bible, the word psychic didn't exist. During the course of history, the meaning of words has changed and new words have replaced old ones. Could the seers and prophets mentioned in the Bible be what we now call psychic?

I thought of Jesus and how he exhibited qualities that could be considered psychic talents in today's world. Only His abilities were greater than the powers possessed by psychics today. Perhaps Jesus exhibited a more advanced psychic ability not yet discovered or gifted to anyone. I reflected on Moses, Abraham, Isaac, Buddha, Allah, Mohammed, Hare Krishna and others worshiped in various religions. They all possessed great mystical powers that could be interpreted as psychic powers in today's world. Could psychic ability be the common thread in all religions? If so, then religious differences could ultimately be resolved, so people of all faiths could worship without fear of persecution.

I telephoned Anna to discuss these new insights. Anna was attentive as she listened to me babble the news to her. I talked non-stop, forgetting that Anna probably knew and understood these insights already.

She said, "I think you have discovered a bit of truth not recognized by most people. Keep searching for answers and you will uncover a lot more."

"How long do you think it will be until I have another experience?" I asked.

"Your breakthrough into the other side can't be timed. It is not just one spontaneous experience. The ability must be cultivated, maintained and controlled. And you must remember it is a process."

"Is there any way to speed up the process?"

"Self-confidence and self-love fostered the development of psychic ability. Focus on the revelations in your inner self for greater awareness and ability," Anna responded.

I retired for the night but couldn't sleep. When I shut the light off in the room, I noticed a new phenomenon. In the pitch black of the night there were specks of light floating in the room and illuminating the otherwise dark room.

I closed and then opened my eyes several times, but they didn't dissipate. Instead, these bits of light, which were suspended in mid-air, filled the entire room for more than ten minutes.

The only procedure I observed that was different from the other nights centered on the bedroom door. This was the first time I had ever closed the bedroom door when I went to sleep. With the door and the window drapes closed there was no outside light source to filter these specks of light from my view, so I assumed that's why I saw them. I relaxed, closed my eyes, and had a good night's sleep. When I awakened the next morning, I called Anna hoping she would have an explanation.

"Anna, do you have any idea what happened to me last night?"

"You experienced the energy remnants of your own aura. Your heightened emotional state contributed to the formation of those bits of lights."

"What do you mean by energy remnants?" I questioned.

"There is an electrical and magnetic field around all living things. We call this electromagnetic field a person's aura."

"But why did I see these sparks of light in the air rather than as an aura around my body?" I questioned.

Anna explained, "Our aura consists of energy, which continuously flows around our bodies. Electrical charges of the aura break off to form sparks of electromagnetic energy. Our aura sheds the expended energy just like our skin sheds dead cells."

"What more do you know about the aura?"

"The aura extends six inches or more beyond the physical body. There are various colors in a person's aura, which are clues to the person's emotional and physical state. A trained observer can detect the first signs of illness or healing by observing the colors and texture of the aura."

"That's incredible! What are these signs?"

"The auras of healthy persons flow continuously around them and there is a smooth rather than porous texture to the auras. When there are breaks in the aura or dark, murky, grey or black colors, then illness is usually present. Illness manifests first in the aura before it manifests in the physical body."

"Can I train myself to see an aura?"

"Yes, but you need to defocus your eyes and at the same time look at the energy field around the person. However, it is probably easier to feel a person's aura then to see it."

"How do I do that?"

"Pretend you are stroking a person's aura. Put both of your hands about two or three inches over the person's head. Then allow your hands to move alongside the person's body toward the feet, keeping your hands about two or three inches away from the body. You will have either a hot or cold feeling all around the body. If you feel warmth and then cold or absence of feeling or vice versa, then you have felt a break in the aura. The break indicates there is illness in that part of the body."

"Do you think I could do it?"

"Yes. Practice eventually will make you sensitive to the subtle differences."

Anna suggested it was time for me to experience a past life regression. Past life recall, according to Anna, could help me further my self-awareness. It could change my perception of and further develop my ability.

Before ending our conversation I questioned Anna about reincarnation. "Have we all had a past life?"

"Yes. We have had many lives but we don't remember them, unless we delve deep into the subconscious mind. The theory of reincarnation suggests that we never die. We simply pass to another state of existence until we are ready to incarnate in the physical again."

"Why do we have to reincarnate?"

"Are you totally without fear, ego, greed, jealousy, hatred, prejudice and impatience? Do you love all things equally? Are you kind, compassionate, empathetic and loving at all times? Can you embrace a person of a different race, ethnic group or sexual orientation without thinking they are different from you? And do you love yourself enough not to have feelings of self-doubt, inadequacy, insecurity, fear and guilt?"

"Of course not, I can't answer yes to all those questions."

"We reincarnate to perfect our soul because we can't learn all of those lessons in one life," explained Anna.

"Can knowing about a past life help me in this life?"

"You could recognize patterns of behavior or circumstances that have stopped you from accomplishing your goals in this incarnation. Or you could recognize a fear from a previous life that is holding you back in this life. A past life memory could spur you on to greater achievements. And it could trigger the development of your psychic ability or bring it to another level."

"Will we ever stop fearing death?" I asked her.

"Certainly. When people recall past life memories, they usually recognize that there is no death."

"Will I remember a past life?"

"Through visualization techniques and hypnosis most people can trigger the memory of their past lives. Hypnosis is a heightened state of concentration during a deep relaxed state. You are not asleep or unconscious during hypnosis, so you will remember everything," explained Anna.

"Should I do anything to prepare for the regression?"

"You could practice entering a trance state, so it will be easier for you to do so in the regression."

"Okay, I will play my hypnosis tape and meditate more often this week."

We ended our conversation by setting a date for the regression. The idea of having lived before intrigued me. I imagined several scenarios set in different countries, hoping one of them was my past life. One thought consumed my waking hours: Could I have had a famous life or lived in an exotic country? I couldn't wait for the scheduled appointment to discover more about my life journey.

Immediately, I started preparations for the regression. I researched the philosophy of reincarnation and again meditated on a regular basis. In the morning I meditated and at night I entered altered states of consciousness using self-hypnosis, which put me deeper into a trance state each time. The intense periods of concentration during meditation and self-hypnosis developed the psychic part of my mind faster than I had expected. And I wasn't prepared for it.

One morning, while sitting at the kitchen table, a few days before my scheduled past life regression, I heard some unusual sounds. When I listened more intently, I heard a series of sizzling and crackling sounds all around me. The sounds became louder and seemed closer. It felt like electrical currents buzzed around me. At the same time my senses expanded beyond my normal energy field and my body tingled all over. These unfamiliar sensations weren't painful, but they weren't pleasant, either. A light-headed feeling interfered with my concentration, but I remained calm enough to allow the experience to continue. This electrical buzz lasted nearly ten minutes, but nothing more happened until I tried to stand up.

When I stood, a terrible feeling of fear gripped my body. My face became hot and flushed. Within seconds a sick feeling churned in my stomach. I gagged, but I grabbed my throat with my hands to stop the sensation. Emotions welled inside me like a water pipe about to burst. I closed my eyes but saw only undistinguishable images flood the blank space within my mind. A sense of doom overcame me and a dark foreboding filled my mind. I knew the thoughts and images warned me of something, but I had no idea what.

I paced the floor hoping to either release these feelings or to understand them. As I paced, I pleaded for an answer. I sensed death on a grand scale.

My first thoughts centered on my family, hoping it didn't involve them. However, the intensity of my feelings didn't change, so I knew these feelings didn't pertain to any of my loved ones. Anna had taught me how to focus on a person to receive psychic impressions and then how to interpret that information. If after focusing on a person you still felt the same feeling of anxiety, then the information didn't pertain to that person. I managed to quiet my thoughts about my family, but I still had to contend with those feelings while not understanding their meaning.

That night, I meditated but couldn't relax enough to enter an altered-state of consciousness. I tossed and turned in bed, still anxious and sensing doom. After an hour I lost my patience, so I sat upright. This time I had a queasy, trembling feeling that made me nauseous. I paced the floor again, trying to rid myself of these feelings. I knew this couldn't be a health issue because there were no other symptoms. So the anxious feelings had to be psychic information I couldn't yet interpret. Could my body and emotions act like a barometer each time I received a psychic feeling or impression? If so, then I didn't want the ability.

Two hours later, I received my answer. The news hit the airwaves: PLANE CRASHED IN LOCKERBIE, SCOTLAND. ALL ABOARD DIED. Now I knew why I had sensed so much death. When I acknowledged I had sensed this disaster before it happened, my anxious feelings disappeared. The psychic door had opened.

This was the moment I had been working toward, but I wasn't excited. Those feelings disrupted my life beyond anything I could have imagined. Up until now I enjoyed the journey and looked forward to the ability, but not anymore. Now, I didn't want to be psychic. Receiving psychic information was too much like listening to a television with a broken antenna broadcasting only irritating static. When you've had enough, you shut it off.

I needed to tell Anna but I knew she would be upset about my reservations. I telephoned her and described my experience.

"You tapped into an expanded energy field and received insight into a global situation. That's wonderful! It also means you opened the door! But why do you sound so sad? You should be thrilled,"

"Anna, I felt so emotional when I received the information. Is this how I will receive psychic impressions?" I asked.

"Sometimes you will receive it that way and other times you won't. You will become accustomed to the feelings, so they won't affect you as much as in your first experience."

"The feelings overwhelmed me. I am not sure psychic

ability is for me," I confessed.

"You sensed a huge disaster. That's why your feelings were so intense. Besides, it's too late for that now. You have already opened the ability."

"Do you mean I can't shut it?"

"The ability can be controlled, but once it's developed you can't stop it. Besides, you can't say no to God."

"But those feelings were painful and frightening," I lamented.

"That was a temporary condition. When your psychic ability functions on a daily basis, you won't feel it so intensely in the physical. And you will have more control over it. Developing psychic ability is like learning to talk. Once you learn how, you never stop talking. You can control the amount and the flow of information, but you can't eliminate the communication between you and your guides."

"Then how do I learn how to control it?" I asked.

"You must think of the ability as an errant child who needs discipline. You train your guides to only give you the information when you ask for it, unless there is some danger lurking around you. Eventually, you will master the technique. But now you need to brace yourself for more psychic impressions."

"What more could happen to me?" I fearfully questioned.

"If the door is only slightly opened, then you might only tap into disastrous scenes of the future or have nightmares. If the door is fully opened, then you will see more positive scenes of the future. The negative then will be veiled from you, unless the situation can be changed by some action."

"How do we fully open it?"

"Fortunately, you will only have to endure one or two days of not knowing whether it is opened up or not. The past life regression will help to round out the ability and push you through the door if you aren't already there. Just be patient. And remember, the pain will only last for a few days. I know you can handle it."

Meekly, I said to Anna before we ended our telephone conversation, "I just hope you are right."

Upon reflection, I recognized a bit of irony in the situation. I could almost touch the secrets I had desired to know for so long, but now I wasn't sure I wanted them. The secrets to psychic powers beckoned me, but fear held me captive.

INSIGHTS

❧ Psychic ability provides communication linking you to God, of which you may not yet consciously be aware. Without higher consciousness or inherent ability you are missing an important means by which you can enrich your life.

❧ The process of acquiring psychic ability is similar to the educational structure of school. In order for you to advance to the next grade you must first learn the basic principles, gain knowledge, analyze and interpret the observations. Once you have mastered these lessons, you can then advance to the next step.

❧ If you live in the shadow of another, you will forget your own soul's importance within the greater scheme of life. Therefore, you will never fulfill your life's purpose in this lifetime. Every soul is unique and you have the responsibility to develop your soul to its fullest potential. If you allow others to control and manipulate you, your soul will not be free enough to develop emotionally and spiritually to fulfill its purpose.

❧ Mistrust in yourself and lack of self-consideration can force your personal boundaries to collapse. When you have no boundaries, you can be dominated or coerced into being what another person wants you to be, rather than discovering the uniqueness of your soul and purpose. You will be vulnerable to other people who will direct your life, instead of you mastering your own destiny.

❧ Today, textbooks and science offer little proof that psychic ability is real. The only avenue available for you to know whether prophecy is true or not is to personally experience the ability.

❧ Psychic ability is the common thread within all religions that could ultimately dissolve religious differences and bring all people back to God. The word psychic or paranormal didn't exist during biblical times. Some of the mystical experiences in the Bible were not described as a psychic event because of the language used during that time. Today, if you examine those events you will see how they could be defined as psychic experiences, according to the language of the twenty-first century.

❧ Your psychic ability can be developed more quickly if you increase your self-love and self-confidence. When you are confident and exhibit self-love, you are able to decipher guidance from the conflicting thoughts that emerge in your mind. Self-doubt, fear, inferior ego or the pre-conditioned voices of society all deter you from recognizing your true guidance.

❧ There is an electromagnetic field around all living things. This field is called an aura. Some studies indicate that a person's degree of health can show up in the aura as a break in the flow of energy or by emanating a specific color. Once you are aware of this phenomenon, you can train yourself to see or feel auras.

❧ You have had many past lives, but you can't usually remember them. Bits and pieces of these past lives can surface in your memories as fears, talents, likes and dislikes. Through introspection and past life study, you can discover your past lives.

To the Other Side
and Back

Impressions entered my mind like the click of a mouse moves the cursor on a computer screen. My mind's focus, whether I wanted it to or not, shifted to a constant state of psychic reception. Hour by hour, with each new experience my life changed. However, I still had no control, which meant the ability was only partially developed.

According to Anna, the lack of control made me more vulnerable to sensing death and having nightmares. Negative events pulsate stronger energy into the universe than positive ones. Therefore, until I had more control, it was easier to receive those negative impressions.

The awkwardness and lack of control of my budding psychic ability presented some unexpected revelations. A few days after the ability had developed, Marla and Paul, our friends for many years, joined us for dinner at a local restaurant. Soon after we sat down for dinner an impression of Paul flashed in front of me. I tried to block the flow of information without letting anyone know my psychic state of mind. A vision, however, repeatedly flashed, until I couldn't ignore it any more. I saw a vision of Paul with another woman. When I realized it meant he was cheating on his wife, I gasped so loudly that everyone thought I was choking. I couldn't look Paul in the face without seeing the vision. I gasped again, but then quickly pretended to hiccup to avoid questions about my odd behavior. For the remainder of the night I pretended to be attentive to the conversation, even though I was caught up struggling to ignore the vision. This experience made me realize secrets were no longer secrets, because I could now see beyond the words and circumstances in front of me.

When we went home that night, my husband fell asleep as soon as he flopped on the bed. I, however, couldn't sleep or stop myself from thinking about my experience. Marla was a friend, so I wondered if I should tell her about my vision. Would I be more of a friend not to tell her or more of a friend if I warned her about her husband's affair? Either decision created a moral dilemma and put me in an uncomfortable situation. I struggled long and hard over this situation, but decided to spare her the anguish.

It had been less than twenty-four hours since I penetrated the psychic level in my mind; but I had already decided I didn't like having the ability. The lack of control made me feel so emotionally vulnerable whenever I had a psychic experience. So I retired for the night annoyed with my supposed destiny.

A nightmare a few nights later disturbed me so much I wanted to call Anna in the middle of the night, but I waited until first thing in the morning. In a dream I saw myself in a coffin. Everyone in the dream thought I had died of asphyxiation. However, I was actually alive, but no one knew it. When the coffin was carried to the cemetery plot, I banged furiously on the inside of the coffin and yelled loudly, but no one heard my muffled cries for help. Just before the coffin was lowered into the ground Anna heard a sound in the coffin.

She yelled, "Stop! She is not dead. Open the coffin." When I heard those words, I woke up from the dream, sweating profusely. My heart raced and I was panicked until I realized it had been a dream and wasn't my reality.

With a sigh I headed for the kitchen for a bottle of water. On the way back to the bedroom I heard voices whispering. I thought my children had left a television on downstairs, but it wasn't on when I checked. I went from room to room trying to determine the origin of the voices until I discovered the voices sounded loudest in the hallway. I positioned myself against the hallway wall to better hear and observe the paranormal activity. When I stood erect, the voices were loud. When I slightly bent away from the wall, the voices became audible whispers. The next time I heard the whispers, I recognized their source. They were spirit voices and I heard them all around me.

These voices made predictions, but I could only hear the words in the last part of each sentence. These words were repeated over and over but I couldn't hear the prediction: This was going to happen and that was going to happen. When I heard several voices repeat those words and I still couldn't determine the prediction, I became angry. I decided that no one from the other side had the right to invade my life in this manner. So I shouted for them to stop immediately.

It was difficult enough to hear the voices, but even worse to be teased about knowing the future without being told it. I had had enough of these psychic experiences and I wanted the quiet life I had enjoyed before my exploration.

I again addressed the audible whispers even though I had no idea who had spoken to me. "If I hear you one more time, I will not do this work!"

The barely audible conversation immediately stopped and I never heard them again.

I telephoned Anna early the next morning to tell her what had occurred. This time, however, I enjoyed a peaceful, serene mood. I was confident the other side had listened to my commanding request, so I felt I had gained some of my control back.

"What did my dream mean? Did it mean I was going to be in a situation where I could die?" I asked.

"No, of course not. The dream represented your fears and the lack of control you feel. Precognitive dreams are expressed symbolically and not literally."

"That's a relief to know, but why did I hear spirits?"

"Your spirit guides wanted to attract your attention, so you wouldn't abandon your mission or stay so fearful. You probably heard them talking about you. Didn't you ask for a sign to confirm your destiny?"

"Yes, I did. But didn't my guides realize hearing them would frighten me into abandoning the mission?"

"Of course your guides were aware of that risk. However, they also knew how to motivate you. Pushing you to such a limit forced you to act. As a result, you didn't let fear stop your progress or emotionally cripple you. I think they accomplished their goal. Don't you agree?"

I laughed, "Yes, when you explain it in those terms, they did succeed. I don't feel threatened anymore."

"Good. Then let's do the regression tomorrow. You will understand more after you remember some of your past lives."

We ended the conversation and confirmed the appointment time. I imagined all sorts of possible scenarios for my past lives, but I also hoped the regression would fully open the ability, so I'd have more control. Once I had that, then I could concentrate on developing the application and interpretation skills.

The next day I embarked on my past life odyssey much earlier than the scheduled appointment time. Even though I was early, Anna invited me to join her for a cup of tea. Afterwards, she escorted me into her office and asked me to lie on the couch. I made myself comfortable and tried to quell my enthusiasm so I could relax. She explained some visualization and hypnosis techniques she would use, and instructed me to say whatever I sensed, felt, thought or saw during the regression. Anna also told me not to dismiss anything as my imagination. According to Anna, it was more important to express the information then attribute it to my imagination and negate an important part of a past life memory.

After the initial preparations Anna then instructed me to close my eyes and visualize my body growing beyond the boundaries of my feet. At first, this was difficult to do until I managed to gain control of my imagination. Then she instructed me to imagine my head growing beyond its physical parameters. The sensations from the visualizations immediately expanded my sense of self. And I felt larger than my five feet, three-inch height. This expanded sense of self reached a few inches beyond my physical self. I couldn't see the increase in my electromagnetic field, but I knew I had just penetrated the boundaries of my aura.

Anna instructed, "Tighten each group of muscles in your body, hold the tightness for a few seconds and then let go of the tightness in each muscle group. This technique will relax your body."

She continued to guide me into a deeper state of relaxation. I let go of my everyday thoughts to experience what seemed like time slowing down. I could hear the clock in the background ticking ever so slowly, but Anna's voice seemed distant. I recognized the sensations as the same feelings I have had in previous hypnosis sessions, so I knew my awareness would soon shift to another level and into a deeper altered state.

Time seemed to pass even more slowly. I could feel my consciousness slip and alter when I reached the next level of consciousness. A fleeting glimpse into a window beyond the physical world moved rapidly past me. I slowed it down the second time it appeared until it hung enticingly in front of me. Round and round the image swirled until my mind was in tempo with the image.

The conscious level of my mind altered again and this time my consciousness reached an even deeper level. I could hear Anna's voice faintly in the background, but I focused on the sensation of moving quickly down a dark tunnel. Within a few seconds in that state I felt something happen to my body. A sensation traveled up from my feet toward my head. A minute later there was a strange absence of feeling in my lower limbs. I felt a tug at my body but I ignored the feeling.

I heard Anna's voice direct me. "Imagine you are flying above buildings searching for a familiar place from a time period before your present life".

Anna's voice sounded distant but I followed her directions. I waited for an image to appear. I noticed images forming that were vaguely familiar to me. The images appeared and at first, I thought I was asleep and in a deep dream state until I heard Anna direct me again.

The sound of Anna's voice jolted me back from my deep dream-like state to a more conscious awareness as she posed a question to me: "Do you see any images?"

I mumbled a slightly audible, "Yes."

"Good. Now allow yourself to focus on the image, but at the same time also try to slow the speed of the images. Carefully scrutinize those images. Choose one which has some meaning to your present life and stop there."

Bits and pieces of images darted back and forth but I focused my attention on one. I then told Anna, "I can see a huge stone building with wide steps and a large, ornate front door."

"Open the door to the building and tell me what you see or sense," she directed.

I imagined the door to the building had a doorknob. I then mentally opened it and walked into an enormous hallway. This great hallway had walls on both sides decorated with framed portraits. I tried to audibly explain the images but I couldn't speak in more than a whisper.

"Remember you can speak loudly during the trance. Speaking won't affect the hypnotic trance," Anna reassured.

"Look down at your feet and describe the kind of shoes you are wearing if you are not barefoot."

I glanced in the direction she suggested. At first, there was no image. Then an image popped into my mind. I gazed at the image for a few seconds before I slowly described it to her.

"The shoes are a shiny brown with tied laces to match. There is another pair of shoes next to the first pair. Both pairs look like men's shoes but one pair is smaller than the other," I replied.

"Do you see any images besides the shoes? And can you sense who is wearing the men's shoes?" she asked.

"I am wearing the smaller pair of shoes and my father is wearing the other pair. We are in a school building. I just received an award for excellence in academic achievement. My mother has just approached me. I can see these odd-shaped, laced shoes peeking out from underneath her long skirt."

"Is it a high school or college?" asked Anna.

"I think I just graduated from high school. I have to say

good-bye to my parents because I am leaving for medical school. My parents are pleased and proud when a few of my teachers congratulate me and wish me luck."

"Look into the eyes of your mother and father. Do you recognize either one as someone you know in this life?"

"I don't recognize my mother as anyone I know today. However, my father is my husband in this life. He is also a medical doctor in that life. He is upset that I have chosen medical research for my career instead of practicing medicine like he does."

"Can you sense any information on why you chose medical research as a career?"

"I was an only child who preferred reading and studying to socializing with others. I didn't like dealing with people, so I chose research rather than to practice medicine like my father. He is disappointed in me, but he won't verbalize his anger and disappointment. He has stoically tried to accept my decision, but secretly he can't forgive me."

"What I want you to do is advance time in that life by projecting yourself fifteen years into the future. I am going to count from one to five. When I reach the number five, you will be in that same life, but 15 years later. When you are there, describe the images or tell me what you sense."

I drifted in and out of consciousness each time Anna spoke to me. The hypnotic experience seemed easier whenever I saw the mental images. There was a change in the speed of the fleeting images. An image immediately appeared after the other image disappeared. The pace of the images slowed, so I no longer had to strain to see them. I reached an inner threshold of consciousness, which thrust me into a level deep enough to reach my memories.

I experienced the memories now as if they happened at that moment. I checked my physical body for signs that I still had contact with the physical world. Within my body I noticed an absence of energy. Again, I assumed this lack of feeling was a normal part of the trance.

I heard the number five and was transported forward in time. I saw myself in a laboratory researching the effects of a vaccine for preventing children's crippling diseases. I wanted to find a cure before the number of cases multiplied, since there was an epidemic at the time.

Anna again instructed me to go forward in time. When she counted to five, this time I saw myself as a grown man in my sixties and engaged in medical research at the Sorbonne University in France. My name was Gabriel and I was married, but my wife was no longer with me. She died during childbirth. After my wife and child died I focused only on my research work. Research papers and the books I had written were stacked neatly on the office bookshelves.

Anna no longer directed me because the images were distinct and moved in slow motion. I described everything I saw in my previous life including the pressure I felt to complete my book. From a distance I watched Gabriel writing relentlessly to complete the project.

I heard Anna scribbling notes relentlessly. For most of the time, however, I focused more on the images than the sounds of the room. And I was so deep that I felt I lived the story at that moment instead of recounting it.

I described what I saw in a trance-like state, unaware of Anna. My voice sounded anxious when I explained I needed to complete a research project within a certain time frame. I saw myself write continuously to complete it on time. It was a few days before my sixty-fifth birthday when I saw I had just finished a book based on my latest research project. It included detailed case studies of paralysis in children and the research on its prevention.

When I saw the book completed, I announced, "I can go home now. My work is completed."

I saw myself as Gabriel in the late 1800's lay on a couch in the living room. The fabric and color of the couch attracted my attention until I sensed a change in my body. Again, I couldn't feel energy in my body. I struggled to understand the feeling, but images flashed so rapidly I couldn't concentrate on that. I saw Gabriel go to sleep, but when I watched him I saw something unusual a few seconds later.

I saw an etheric replica of my prone body leave my form. I didn't know what had happened to me but I felt a tugging sensation. It felt as if something was leaving me. I couldn't stop the sensation so I just continued watching this spirit body rise above me. The image faded until I couldn't see it anymore. Now there was only total darkness around me. I felt strange and not in control, yet I didn't have fear even though I was immersed in nothing but darkness.

It felt like a very long period of time passed, but it lasted only a few minutes. Even though I saw nothing, I still felt an odd sensation. It seemed as if I moved at great speed. I had no idea what had happened to me, but I didn't care either. I allowed it to continue because I was confident I'd soon see the images again. However, I didn't expect nor was I prepared for the image that emerged in the midst of this darkness.

First I heard beautiful melodious music and then an incredible inner peace enveloped me. I didn't feel my body anymore, but I ignored that sense while I waited for something more to happen. I saw images of a face appear faintly in the darkness, but it was too far in the distance to see clearly. I struggled to see it, but I moved deeper into this tunnel of darkness instead. I could see the vision move toward me, so there was a feeling of motion. I moved toward it and it moved toward me.

When the face appeared closer, I glanced in its direction and gasped. It appeared to be Jesus. I couldn't utter a word. He had the most loving, deep blue eyes that twinkled when you looked into them. An indescribable feeling of love filled me in the presence of His image. His melodious voice mesmerized me, when He addressed me by name.

He embraced me and then said, "Gabriel, you have completed everything you agreed to accomplish in your allotted time on the earth."

I was enveloped by a feeling of love which penetrated me to the core of my being. This feeling couldn't be described or compared to any love I had ever experienced. He looked into my eyes and nodded. I knew at that time that He saw into my soul.

Then He spoke again. "I am rewarding you with time travel."

I couldn't define the term, but I soon experienced it. With that announcement I was transported at great speed into a moving pattern. The pattern resembled the mathematical symbol for infinity, but I couldn't compare the speed to anything I had ever before experienced. I continued to move rapidly in this moving pattern as if I was trying to reach a particular destination. I seemed to travel on some accelerated transport vehicle; however, I couldn't see any vehicle. I only knew I moved at an incredibly fast speed in a pattern similar to the sign of infinity.

This sensation of motion eventually stopped when I looked down in the direction of earth. In my first image, I saw horses, wagons and old-fashioned stagecoaches move on the dirt streets below. The second image flashed next to the previous image. I saw people I currently know walk on the streets. Others drove cars on paved streets and highways. The third picture linked to the other two and looked like the frames of a photographic negative. The third image showed me some unusual vehicles moving oddly on the earth but I couldn't identify them. The earth appeared to be quiet and peaceful as people moved about their business. When I added the third image to the other two, I noticed the three visions represented the past, the present and the future. Either my psychic sight had developed during this experience or God had given me a message.

The sense of speed increased around me. Even though I suspected there could be some danger associated with this enormous speed, I responded with trust. I realized, however, I was some place other than in the past life regression I started in Anna's office. I had no idea where I was or what had happened to me. My thoughts shifted to the time period before I moved at this great speed. I compared those moments to my current experience. It was obvious to me I was somewhere in time looking at the earth. Could I be on the other side but not know it? When I became aware that I viewed the earth in a future time period, the voice of God spoke to me. "Would you like to go further into the dimensions?"

Still in awe, I mentally thought 'yes' before I verbalized the answer. Within seconds, I started to move again. This time I moved laterally. I was swiftly transported to another level on the other side. Instead of just motion I had the sensation I was moving toward the stars. As before, I could only see darkness until the travelling stopped. Once the sensation of speed ended, I again saw images. And I could not believe what I saw.

I observed a white city. Everyone was dressed in white clothing. It looked just as normal as if I were watching people walk on the streets of New York City on a routine day. I observed the people happily co-operating in harmony with one another. No one suffered pain or disease. And they all radiated happiness and love.

Puzzled to see such harmony on earth, I wondered if I had peeked into the future conditions of earth. I fantasized about how wonderful life would be if this were our future.

Off in the distance, amidst the white-clothed figures, I saw the former Russian Leader, Nikita Kruschev embrace the former American President, Dwight Eisenhower. They acted as if they were best friends. I couldn't understand why I saw those images or what could have happened to bring about this change in circumstances.

When I observed their camaraderie, I realized I watched them interact in the spirit world. I wondered whether I had observed them from a distance or from some point in the spirit world? As I asked myself that question, I again experienced a tugging sensation in my body which jolted me.

Then I heard Anna's voice command me to return. Her voice authoritatively counted backwards from ten to one, but there was an anxious tone to her voice. When she instructed me, I experienced a quick descent. I raced in a downward spiral toward my body. I didn't understand what had just happened. I thought, "Why are you ending this state?" Then I heard a voice in me answer, "You have work to do on the earth, so you don't belong in the spiritual planes at this time." None of this made sense to me.

Anna counted rapidly and forcefully. When I opened my eyes, I couldn't speak.

Anna commanded me, "Don't move. I have to get something hot for you to drink. I will explain everything in a moment."

Before Anna left the room I began to shake. I couldn't stop the sudden shivers or the twitching. She ran around the room gathering blankets and piled them on top of me. She adjusted the thermostat in the room to eighty degrees. I still couldn't stop the shaking. Anna seemed alarmed but I wasn't frightened. I thought I this was normal behavior for a past life regression.

She returned to the room with hot coffee for me to drink and said, "Don't elevate your head until you stop shaking. Drink the coffee from a straw and don't move until your body feels warm."

Now concerned, I asked, "Anna, is everything alright?"

Anna mumbled, "I'll explain everything in a moment."

I wondered why Anna seemed so anxious and disturbed. Could she be disappointed with the regression? I thought it had been successful.

The uncontrollable shudders stopped as quickly as they started. And Anna regained her composure enough to explain the details of the experience. I didn't know what had just happened, so I was anxious for Anna's clarification.

"You left your body and entered the spirit world. I had to stop the regression before you crossed the line between life and death. If you had stayed longer in that condition, you could have become comatose or died."

I was too stunned to speak, so I just listened as Anna continued.

"When you said you had completed your work and you were going home, I knew what was going to happen to you. At that moment, your faced changed. Your countenance looked young and beautiful. In fact, it looked almost angelic. Your face exhibited pure beauty with an incredibly peaceful, serene, expression. I stopped writing just to watch your face, because I anticipated what you were about to experience"

"But why did I shake so much?"

"The violent shaking was your etheric body coming back into your physical one. The different temperature range between the two bodies caused the shaking. Your spirit was out of your physical body and you needed to synchronize the two when your spirit body reentered your physical body."

"Do you mean I actually visited the spirit world?" I asked, overwhelmed by her explanation.

Anna answered, "Yes. And I waited thirty years to witness it again. Many years ago, while living in Florida, I regressed a man into his past lives. In that regression he experienced the same out-of-body experience as you and described exactly what happened to you. The details were all the same including the description of God, the time travel and the white city."

Again, I was speechless. I didn't know how to react. However, I knew there had to be some explanation for my not being able to feel my body during the regression. Anna was my mentor, so how could I not believe her, but I also needed more details.

"How could my soul leave my body?" I asked.

"Your soul as Jane was the same soul in Gabriel when he lived in France centuries ago. Your physical body was the only difference between you and Gabriel. You re-experienced that life because it must be important for you to know that information. There is a continuous cycle of death and rebirth in order to fulfill our souls' lessons."

I was mystified by the experience. I had never even heard

of an out-of-body experience before the regression.

"Take time to reorient yourself to the waking state. After you feel totally cognizant, I would like to discuss the experience further. I feel blessed to have witnessed this twice."

It took me sometime to feel coherent again. Then I addressed my questions to Anna. "Why did you end the regression? Couldn't we have learned more if I stayed longer?" I asked.

"No. It was too dangerous for you. A longer period in the spirit world could have confused you and put you at risk of not being able to find a way to re-enter your body."

"Is that what happens to a person in a coma? Does a person in a coma stay trapped between the two worlds because the person is no longer aware of the body?" I questioned.

"Yes. That's correct!"

"I heard you, but I didn't want to come back. Could a person in a coma hear, but not want to return?"

"Yes, a comatose person can hear the physical world, even though the person is not consciously aware or able to respond. At the same time the comatose person tries to function in the spirit world thinking it is the physical world. This confusion could cause the person to be trapped between the two worlds for an indefinite period of time."

"Why wouldn't a person in a coma not want to become conscious again?"

"The soul spontaneously leaves the body to avoid severe pain as a way to endure the trauma, while the body tries to heal. During trauma the soul hovers near the body or it enters the spiritual dimensions. The further the soul penetrates the spiritual planes, the more there is risk for confusion. Eventually the soul must choose whether to return to the physical or remain in the spiritual plane."

"What determines whether a person stays in a coma or not?"

"If the person's body can heal enough to support a normal life, it will then return. If the soul knows its body can't sustain life, then the soul must decide if it wants to endure the pain and return to the physical body, even if it is only for a short time."

"Should we speak to a person in a coma, even if they can't respond?"

"Yes, of course. Are you feeling more aware now?" Anna asked, concerned.

"Yes, I do feel better. Does this usually happen during a past life regression?"

"No, what happened to you is extremely rare. God intended for you to have the experience in order to receive the information for some benefit or purpose not yet revealed."

"Do you mean God could have given me some knowledge I am not consciously aware of at this time?"

"Yes. When you saw the vision of the past, present and future I had a psychic impression you received knowledge about the future."

"I don't know that. However, the images moved as rapidly as you could flip the pictures in a photo album, which didn't allow much time for me to decipher them."

"It doesn't matter, because the images were probably impressed into your memory to be revealed at the appropriate time."

"The beauty, peace and love surrounding God's presence are all I remember about the experience."

"You will remember more. I suspect you gained knowledge about the future as well as about God. I think you will know more tomorrow."

"Perhaps I will."

"Did you see any other religious figures, especially from other religions?" Anna asked.

"No, I only saw Jesus and I heard the voice of God speak through him. Could that be who we all see when we reach the other side?"

"No, I suspect whatever we believe is God while we are on earth, is what we will eventually see when we reach the other side. But we will all hear the voice of God," she said.

"Then there is a difference?"

"Yes. Jesus, Moses, Abraham, Buddha, Mohammed, Hare Krishna and the other mystical figures in the various religions represent God on earth. When we reach the other side, we will see who we believed was God's representative, according to our religion. That familiar being will lead us to God, and we will then know there is only one God for all of us."

I left Anna's emotionally numb from the experience and deep in thought. I embarked on this journey to unravel the secrets to mystical powers and the answers to some of the mysteries of life. And now I knew even more than I could have ever imagined.

INSIGHTS

❧ You have an allotted time on earth to accomplish what you agreed to accomplish in your current life. If you accomplish your predestined goals in your physical incarnation, you are then rewarded in the spiritual dimension, as well as in your next physical incarnation. You are rewarded with a greater wisdom to navigate more easily the spiritual dimension and your next physical incarnation. You then bring that ability into your next life in order to have the wisdom and the guidance to create a better life in the physical world.

❧ There is great harmony in the next dimension. Almost everyone in the spiritual dimension relates to each other with love, compassion and understanding. The physical earth is destined to achieve that same harmony.

❧ If you have an out-of-body experience, you may suffer an intense physical shaking when your spiritual body reenters the physical body. This clashing of energy occurs because of the different temperature ranges between the two bodies. Sometimes, an out-of-body experience can occur during the dream state. A shaking can occur or you may wake up with a physical jolt if the out-of-body experience occurs during sleep.

❧ A person in a coma experiences a deeper than normal out-of-body state. In this deeper state, he or she is caught between the two worlds. Such a person can still hear you talk to them while in a coma, but they can also hear the sounds of the spiritual dimension beckoning them to come to the light. Moving deeper into this in-between state can cause death. There is an incredible feeling of love from the light and a feeling of love at the same time from the loved ones on earth, which creates a spiritual tug of war. Eventually, the person in the coma makes a decision with the help of the other side's guidance. This decision has nothing to do with your love, but ultimately depends on the physical condition of the body and whether the person in the coma could gain more spiritual growth by returning to consciousness or by passing on to the other side. When the person in the coma recognizes his or her body can no longer maintain an acceptable quality of physical life, he or she makes the decision to permanently leave the body.

❧ When you reach the other side, God's presence is overwhelmingly beautiful and nothing less than pure unconditional love. In the presence of God's unconditional love you are forgiven for any of the mistakes you made in your physical incarnation. As your gift to God, you forgive those who are still in the physical for any of their negative activity directed at you. You will also forgive those who hurt you. The goal of the soul in the spiritual plane is the same as the goal in the physical: soul growth.

❧ When you reach the other side, you will first see the religious figure you are most familiar with who represented God on earth, according to your religion. By seeing the figure you are most familiar with, you will successfully navigate the planes to reach God. You will then witness other religious figures, also. Even in spirit you look to the familiar for comfort and to guide you to a deeper understanding of God.

❧ There are subtle messages and meaningful coincidences in life to prod your memories or to stimulate you to reflect on those memories. By taking time for these quiet moments of reflection, you open yourself to receive guidance. Your guides can coach you to stay on your path or to take a different path. This guidance can make a difference between a happy, fulfilling life or a life with many challenges to overcome.

❧
DEATH IS NOT THE END

The regression proved to be beneficial in more ways than I had anticipated. Not only did I remember my previous life, but also the memory of it offered me an explanation for a long-time passion I couldn't understand. For no apparent reason I had an obsessive desire to research information for the sake of learning. I often browsed the local library for whatever topic commanded my attention. I never understood why I had this passion. Now, however, I had the answer. According to my regression, I had been a medical researcher in a past life, but it wasn't my destined path in this life. Knowing why I had this interest helped me to better understand myself.

When I awakened the morning after the regression, I looked in the mirror and saw my face radiated from the inner peace I now had. The past life experience inspired me to continue on this quest to discover more of what might be buried in the unknown. When I thought of the lives of the mystics recorded throughout history, I imagined their moment of enlightenment and what it must have been like. Could I possibly gain this same wisdom?

After my morning chores were finished I headed for brunch at Anna's, but not until after I reflected on my out-of-body experience. This time, however, I focused on God and not my past life memories. I recalled how I had never doubted the existence of God or the afterlife, but now thought it a blessing to have proof of those beliefs. Death held no fear because I knew it wasn't an ending. It was part of the full circle of life.

I no longer had to deny my religion in order to believe in the psychic world. Convinced religion and psychic phenomenon were both vehicles to God, I embraced both with confidence. Religion presented the principles and rules to know God, whereas the paranormal fostered a more personal approach to experience God. On the other hand, without religion I couldn't have developed the discipline necessary for me to embrace the paranormal as a way to know God, too. My belief in religion allowed me to trust the paranormal experiences I had because I trusted God. Both modalities provided a way for me to reach God, but with greater confidence and conviction than if I had only approached Him on the traditional path.

Again, my life changed as a result of the regression. Whenever I thought of God, I experienced an incredible feeling of love. And the memory of the other side seemed more beautiful than anything I had ever known. The love, peace and beauty I felt and saw on the other side were indescribable. Sometimes, I wished I were still in spirit, because I longed for those feelings again. I couldn't discuss my experience with anyone except Anna, because I feared being ridiculed or regarded as emotionally unstable. Who would believe I had encountered God?

The focus of my thoughts shifted to a fantasy. Wouldn't it

be wonderful if we could all experience God like I had? Perhaps people then would love one another and not feel hatred or prejudice. It was a dream, but I had hope. With that, the telephone rang, which abruptly ended my fantasy.

"Will you be here soon?" Anna asked.

"Yes, I am just leaving. I'll be there in fifteen minutes." I replied.

"Good, I am anxious to know more."

When I arrived at Anna's she was already at the door waiting for me. She greeted me and asked, "How do you feel?"

"I feel fine," I exclaimed. "Can we do another past life regression?"

" Oh no! I can't regress you for a long time. You were too comfortable in the spirit world. It would be dangerous for you to do it again so soon."

"Why is it so dangerous?"

"Because you had a near-death experience without any physical trauma to cause it. I suspect you are prone to out-of-body experiences, which means your soul could spontaneously leave your body at will. If you travel too far out of your body, you could die. Our soul is attached to a cord. If the cord is severed, death follows."

"How could something like that happen?"

"Sudden shock from either staying too long or going too far into the spirit dimension while out of body could sever the cord. In less serious situations your soul could come back into your body not completely aligned. This could cause mental illness."

"Could I prevent that from happening?"

"Probably not. Some people may be more prone to this behavior than others."

"Why do you suppose I had such an unusual experience?"

"We are in a period of enormous change and it is time to be awakened to our purpose and part in the greater plan. You were exposed to the other side in order to awaken your soul to its purpose. Once your soul is awakened you will then awaken others to their part of the greater plan. Understanding the paranormal and developing your psychic ability are the vehicles you need to fulfill that purpose."

"How did I achieve this level?"

"In our incarnations on the earth we learn spiritual, emotional, intellectual and physical lessons. When our lessons are complete, we then stay in the higher planes of existence. On that level we can choose to become a master, a guide for another person, or choose to reincarnate for a mission. If we volunteer for a mission, we then incarnate to serve God for the good of humanity."

"When a person seeks to know the meaning of life or to understand the unknown, could that be the start of the awakening process in them?"

"Yes. It is the start and also the path that leads the seeker to his or her purpose."

"Is there a way to serve humanity before the greater plan unfolds?"

"You need to pay attention to the synchronicities and the patterns in your life. Those are the ways in which the other side guides us."

"Why don't we have conscious knowledge of our purpose when we are born?"

"The physical plane is too dense for us to continue active communication with the other side. So we are subject to free will and often make decisions without any guidance. These emotional decisions create our challenges or cause consequences, which in turn wreak havoc in our lives."

"If we connect with the other side and receive guidance, does our life then have less turmoil?"

"Yes."

"Why is it so difficult for us to receive that guidance?"

"Telepathy, which is the universal means of communication between all souls, is easily blocked, so we don't communicate with the other side. Because our communication capabilities are limited, we are assigned guides that act like coaches. These guides try to keep us on our path by sending subtle messages and meaningful coincidences to prod our memory or to stimulate us to set time aside for quiet reflection. During those moments of reflection or meditation, we are more open to receive the thoughts our guide sends us. This information is in the mix of all thoughts, so it has to be recognized as guidance and then interpreted. We aren't automatically aware of our purpose here. Nor do we understand all of our experiences. We have to uncover our reason for being here."

"Did I have the out-of-body experience to help me recognize I had a mission?"

"Yes. The experience triggered the memory of your purpose, which is what you needed to know to push you in the right direction. Evidently, you denied your thoughts in the past, and ignored coincidences, so the other side had to create a memorable experience that you couldn't deny. You can't teach others until you believe and understand."

I smiled at her comment, but accepted it because I had just asked God for a sign a few days before I had the regression.

"Now that you have more understanding I want you to go back into your memories to determine more of what you experienced while you were on the other side. I am sure you received more knowledge than you are aware, so I want to stimulate those memories. Lie down and just relax. I will hypnotize you into a light trance, so you will remember the knowledge you gained during the regression."

I quieted myself and closed my eyes. Anna counted me into a light altered state of consciousness and directed me to remember the regression experience before she questioned me.

"When you traveled to the spirit world, did you sense a vehicle or did you travel without one?"

"I remember moving very fast on some sort of transport vehicle. It wasn't a vehicle like a car, but some other vehicle I don't think we have access to in the physical."

"Hmm! That's interesting. Did you see the spirits of your deceased loved ones?"

"I saw the faces of a lot of spirits, but I couldn't tell if they were deceased relatives or not. Most of the spirits were engaged in activity. In fact it looked similar to the activities on the earth, but everyone moved much slower and more deliberately. The spirits also seemed to ignore me."

"Perhaps you didn't see deceased family members, because it wasn't your time to cross over. Therefore, no deceased member of your family had to greet you or encourage you to go toward the light."

"Could that mean you don't see loved ones when you're visiting the spirit realm, unless it is your time to die?"

"Yes. I think that's true. If you had gone too far in the spirit dimension, a family member would've told you to go back, just like your grandmother did in one of your previous dreams. Passed loved ones must only be present when it is a person's time to leave this earth. Maybe that's how we know whether to travel toward the light or return to our bodies."

Anna continued, "Did you have feelings of pain or receive a sense of what it is like to die?"

"Death seemed similar to a dream state. You are aware you are dreaming, but you allow it to continue, even though you don't know how it is going to end. I knew I was someplace other than on your couch, but I allowed it to continue. I felt no pain, so I don't think death is painful."

"When you were out-of-body and viewing the earth, did you get a glimpse of the future?"

"I saw only a vision of the earth spewing light which radiated in all directions. It looked to me as if God's presence was on earth. I didn't see destruction. I saw a change in people's behavior and they all radiated love. The image of the earth was awesome. I think that's the message God wanted me to understand. Eventually, our future will be just like that image, and God's presence will be present on the earth."

"That's incredible!" Anna exclaimed. "Will it happen in our lifetime?"

"Yes. I think that's the message God tried to give to me when I had the vision."

She then asked, "Did you receive any indication whether or not a particular religion was more correct than another?"

"No, there was no favored house of worship. It doesn't matter what religion or path we follow. The only thing that matters is for us to express love for God, oneself and one another. There are differences in the world for a purpose. When we dissolve our differences and accept all people, God will know we are ready for the Christ energy and we will be able to accept that gift from God. At that time, we will learn the truth in all mysteries and the Christ energy will heal us and restore the earth to light. The Christ energy has no religious denomination connected to it.

It is a universal energy connected to the Source and an energy of love, truth, and healing. Love is the pervading energy on the other side, so I could only interpret that feeling as a message: We are loved, and we are to love ourselves and others."

"Is there a reason why God can't come before those conditions are fulfilled?"

"God's energy vibrates at a much faster and higher rate of vibration. Our physical bodies can't handle that intensity until we have raised our energy vibrations. Love produces the higher vibration, so loving ourselves, as well as others, is a key condition. When we experience the Christ energy, we will be given the power to manifest. Therefore, our thoughts and actions can only be expressed with unconditional love or it could cause the opposite."

"What if the condition of the earth deteriorates into wars or even the possibility of a nuclear war instead of us working towards peace and the brotherhood of all? Would God still come to the earth? And would God punish us for our behavior?" Anna asked.

"I can't imagine God punishing us, because I experienced God's energy as infinitely loving. However, I do believe God would do something to stop our destruction if we continue on that path. We all have a piece to the greater puzzle. When the puzzle pieces come together, the course of history will be altered for the good of humanity."

"What a wonderful thought! If there is only one God, why are there so many religions?"

I hesitated a second while I recalled a vision, and then I interpreted it. "Religion allows for people in various cultures to express their individuality. We all have a unique soul and a specific purpose to uncover and to fulfill in our lifetime. It is this singular expression that allows each religion to contribute to God's plan. The doctrine of each religion has a piece to the puzzle. Religion safeguards the puzzle from being revealed, until God's greater plan can manifest on the earth. The right time is crucial for the success of the greater plan, because we will know all of God's secrets at that time. And we have to be ready for the truth, which could be different than our current beliefs."

"Do you think the symbol of infinity had any meaning or message behind it?" questioned Anna.

"The sign of infinity indicates life continues beyond the loss of the physical body. And I believe God tried to remind me that there is no death. We live in one form or another for eternity."

There was a lull in our conversation, so I used the time to open my eyes and sit in an upright position. Anna refilled our cups with coffee, as I reflected on the answers to all the questions. To my surprise, there was a shift in my consciousness. Words began to dance in my mind.

I blurted out to Anna what had just transpired. She grabbed a piece of paper and handed it to me. "Your guide is trying to come through. Just start writing and the words will eventually flow."

When I received an image, I then scribbled the word down on the paper. When my consciousness shifted back to a less intense state, I knew I had a complete message. I looked at the paper and read what I had written.

Death is not the end; it is just the beginning.
It is a step in a new dimension to evolve in new work.
You graduate from the earth plane to another school of learning.
And when you finish your schooling on the other side,
you return to the physical dimension again to begin all your new lessons.

"Anna, it's as if someone forced me to write the words. I saw the words inside my head before I wrote them down. Have you ever experienced this?"

"No, I don't receive information that way, but we are all unique instruments in this work so guidance can come in many ways. The information you received is a channeled message from your higher self. You used a form of automatic writing to express this. Channeled information is usually informative and inspirational, which is meant for personal growth or as a message for the general population rather than an insight into an individual's tomorrow."

"Could I have spoken the words instead of writing them?"

"Yes. There are people who channel information by speaking instead of writing the words."

"What does the term higher self mean?" I questioned.

"All psychic information is received from a higher realm. This realm could include your own higher level of perception, or guides from the spirit world. Our higher self is not bound by the restrictions of a person's current personality. There is a greater awareness of life in a person than just knowledge of the physical world. This greater awareness allows a person the freedom to explore the deeper memories of the sub-conscious mind, which is the storehouse for all knowledge learned from previous lives as well as from the current life."

"Anna, did the other side push me to develop my psychic ability when I channeled that definition of death?"

"Yes. The channeling experience was supposed to motivate you and to help you to trust in your ability. It will also be the way you will first use that psychic ability. You will channel messages from the other side to teach and guide others, because you can enter into a deep trance very easily. This trance state will help you develop more of your clairvoyant ability. After a while you will guide others and predict their futures."

There was a moment of silence between us. It was late and I knew I needed to be home before my children came home from school. When I left her house, Anna and I hugged and thanked each other for the enlightening information we received that day. It had become evident to me that channeling was another step in my development.

Anna made one more comment before I left her house. "Do you realize what has just happened? You have begun to teach me! We have reversed roles. The out-of-body experience gave you more knowledge and increased your ability. God wanted you to have these insights as part of the preparation for your role in the plan."

I humbly acknowledged Anna's comment and marveled how God communicated with us through insights, coincidences and paranormal experiences.

The next morning, I reflected on my experience with Anna, and analyzed everything again. Then other memories began to come into my awareness. I searched for clues that would indicate how or why this path had become my destiny. A glimpse of early childhood flashed in my mind. I saw myself around the age of six. Then an image of a funeral popped into my thoughts. It confused me, because the image was so vivid it made me feel as if I was right there. At the same time, it was as if I was transported back in time, rather than just remembering it.

I saw myself as a little girl sitting in the third row of pews close to the center aisle of my church. The church was very small, and my attention was focused on the funeral. Within a few minutes of this image I saw my grandfather, father, mother, uncles and aunts walking slowly behind a coffin being wheeled towards the altar. My paternal grandmother had died. This was my first funeral so I observed everything intensely. The ritual and events were strange to me, but it was the crying that puzzled me the most.

Perplexed by my relative's sobs I tried to understand their tears. Just as quickly as I asked the question I received an answer. My relatives viewed death as an end to life. However, I knew my grandmother was with God and I would see her again. I recalled thinking about how it isn't painful to die because we return to the earth plane after our experience in the next dimension. I thought about how we should know this, but then an inner voice reminded me that people here don't know that anymore. Somehow, that knowledge is erased at birth. This memory stunned me. How could I have had so much wisdom at six, but not have that same wisdom now?

I tried to remember more, just so I could understand my unusual reaction at such a young age to death. Then I remembered a wish I made the day of the funeral. I wished for God to help me find a way to teach people it wasn't sad to die, because we were all coming back. And we would see each other again. The memory of that wish stopped my thoughts. What seemed like a little girl's plea at the time could have more meaning than I had suspected.

Could that experience have been a glimpse of my future? Could it have been a guide revealing my mission for the first time? Or could I have created my destiny with that wish?

I couldn't answer those questions. However, I now realized I couldn't avoid this path in my life, because it had to be my destiny. Whether it was pre-planned before I was born in the physical or whether I created my destiny with that wish, didn't matter anymore.

If my path exploring the unknown was pre-destined, then I must have chosen to re-incarnate for a specific purpose. If I created this path because of a wish, then I must have asked God to find a way for me to teach people this message. Either way the psychics' predictions and my supposed mission finally made sense to me.

The image of my grandmother's funeral made me hungry for more memories to prove my path in the paranormal was God's intended purpose. I searched my memory again, but drew a blank. However, a few weeks later the image of a nun at a holy shrine popped into my thoughts. When I realized this was another clue to the destiny riddle, I gasped.

There were tens of thousands of people on a pilgrimage at the Saint Anne shrine located in the Quebec province of Canada. On the second day at the shrine, my mother and I wandered away from the church down a narrow dirt road searching for a place to eat lunch. When we finished our meal, we exited the little restaurant and headed towards a souvenir store. Before we reached our destination, a nun dressed in full habit stopped us. She gathered a group of people around me and then handed me a newspaper article she asked me to read to the small crowd.

According to the article, her name was Sister Anne Marie from Chicago. When she was sixteen, her long hair became tangled in a machine at work. Her entire scalp and one ear were ripped off of her head from the accident. There wasn't any hope for her to live. However, Saint Anne appeared to her and told her she would survive the accident and would be miraculously healed. When she saw Saint Anne in the vision, the agonizing pain gripping her was immediately released. Her doctors diagnosed her condition as grave and hopeless. Yet, she miraculously recovered. According to the article, the incident was placed on a list of miracles for the Catholic Church to investigate. When I completed reading the article, the group looked at the nun in awe and acknowledged her miracle. Meeting and hearing her story had influenced all of them.

The next day while walking on the church grounds, my mother and I accidentally bumped into Sister Anne Marie again. She gathered another group of people and asked me to read the article. This group responded in the same manner as the other group of people.

An experience on the last day of the pilgrimage made me wonder what Sister Anne Marie meant by her last comment to me. My mother and I were on the steps of the Basilica waiting for the candlelight procession to come to an end. The French Cardinal had just ended the procession by giving the crowd a blessing. When he walked past us, we had the opportunity to kiss the Cardinal's ring before he re-entered the church. Kissing a Cardinal's ring is a custom in the Catholic Church that is considered an honor. By kissing the ring you receive a special blessing. We then turned around to head down the steps. There stood the nun smiling directly at me.

This time we instantly embraced each other. It was obvious we both felt it was no coincidence that we had continued to bump into each other, despite the tens of thousands of people at the shrine. She didn't gather a group of people this time. Instead she delivered a message.

"You will be a missionary in this life!" said Sister Anne Marie.

Apologetically I responded, "Oh no sister. I am sorry but I am getting married in two months."

"That's okay. You will be married, but still be a missionary in this life. It's God's calling for you."

Our eyes locked onto each other's and then we said good-bye.

I wondered what she could have meant by that statement. How could I be a missionary and still be married? I thought people who had taken religious vows were the only ones who could be on a mission for God. Now I knew the truth. We can have a mission for God but not know it. All of us have the potential to do God's work whether we belong to a religious order or not. The recollection of the nun's message sent shivers up and down my spine. How could I continue to ignore what psychics had told me about a mission? Even though I didn't understand how being psychic could have anything to do with being an instrument of God's work, I decided I needed to heed all of those signs. If I ignored them, I could be dismissing my purpose and God's plan for me.

Could other people dismiss guidance as a coincidence and never receive the answer or the help they seek? Could this be why so many people search for their purpose but never find it? These were more of the answers that were unraveling before me.

Insights

❧ No religion on earth has all the answers on how to reach God. Each religious doctrine provides a clue to the greater puzzle. God did not entrust one religion with all the answers. This is God's way of safeguarding the greater plan so it can manifest on the earth at the right time.

❧ Your higher self is not bound by the restrictions of your current personality. To reach your higher self you must gain a greater awareness of life by probing the deeper memories of your subconscious mind. Observation, analysis, introspection, meditation and hypnosis are all means to a greater self-awareness.

❧ Religion and the paranormal are both vehicles to God. Our path to God can include both modalities. Religion is a formal path, that teaches us the discipline needed to know God at a basic concrete level with rules to follow on how to worship and know God. We learn by example and repetition, which is the foundation to any learning before we can experiment, observe and come to our own conclusions. The practice of worship in all religions teaches us the discipline necessary to open the avenue to our own higher consciousness. Through this avenue of higher consciousness, we have the opportunity to experience God at a more personal level. This combined approach to God can help us to gain greater confidence, faith and conviction in God, as well as in life.

❧ Throughout history, psychics, mystics and seers have brought messages from the other side to generations of people. However, most of these messages were not heeded, but were met with persecution. Imagine how history would have been rewritten if societies in previous generations had acknowledged these messages.

❧ A paranormal experience is a way for God to get your attention. The psychic experience teaches you there is more to life than just the physical world. There are numerous examples of these occurrences in the Bible, accepted during ancient times as common ability. Would God have permitted these experiences on an almost daily basis during that time and not allow them to occur during modern times? Paranormal incidents demonstrate there is a God trying to guide us.

❧ Out-of-body experiences can occur naturally. However, forced situations could put you in physical danger and could jeopardize your life. When you physically leave your body, your life energy is depleted. If you remain out-of-body too long, your life energy can be damaged by this depletion. Mental illness could occur if your etheric body does not re-synchronize fully with your physical body when it re-enters.

❧ You incarnate again and again in order for you to learn your lessons. In each incarnation your soul strives for perfection. You are not expected to learn all your lessons in one lifetime, so you are continually reborn to continue your spiritual educational.

❧ You are loved and God wants you to love others. There are differences in people in the world so God can use our reaction to these differences as a teaching aid and as a barometer of our readiness for knowledge and change. God will know we are ready by our reaction to the various people. When enough people on the earth can openly accept others despite their color, race, religion, sexual preference or other differences, a messiah will be identified. We will recognize God's loving energy around this person.

❧ During the birth process, you intentionally forget your knowledge of life after death and the reincarnation process. If you had all of your memories, it would be difficult to focus on the main lesson of your spiritual and emotional growth in this lifetime.

❧ For each of you, your lives are also a test, to evaluate how well you have learned during your journeys. You will ultimately pass or fail your tests. You will grow with your calling, or fail in your lesson. No matter what the result, God will continue to unconditionally love you.

THE SECRET PURPOSE
OF OUR MEMORIES

Quiet moments became precious gifts for me to savor because it was during those moments of silence my knowledge stretched and my psychic ability deepened. My thoughts this time were held captive by a memory. In fact, it was impossible to stop thinking about Sister Anne Marie, even though the encounter with her took place more than twenty five years ago. I scrutinized the experience several times just to be certain I hadn't missed any details of the old encounter. When it first occurred, I questioned for years what the nun could have meant by her prophetic comment.

Nevertheless, the memory of it faded after a few years, and I dismissed it from my thoughts. Now, however, I had a new perspective.

Recollections of the event suggested it was more than coincidence or it wouldn't have been spotlighted in my memories. Moreover, this was the second time someone informed me I had a specific, pre-destined goal to accomplish. I believe everyone has a purpose, but only a few people have the good fortune to know it. On the other hand, I became convinced the unknown held the keys to the answers I sought in life. In fact, my self-discovery journey into the paranormal set the groundwork for me to discover my purpose and some of the secrets of life. Could it do the same for others?

When I reflected on the answer, I discovered a pattern present in our lives. A guiding force seems to nudge us along a path, even when we have no conscious knowledge of it. It doesn't matter whether this unseen force provides a religious experience or a psychic one, because both types of experiences share the same purpose. Even when we are consumed by our struggles, this unseen force continues to guide us toward our destiny hoping to awaken us to our purpose. And coincidences and odd experiences are a part of that guidance.

I agonized over the opportunities I missed, because most of the time I attributed odd experiences to my imagination. On the other hand, how could I have thought otherwise? If an experience didn't conform to my belief system, I dismissed it as meaningless or untrue. Could I have created a more harmonious life, if I had recognized sooner that coincidences and some strange experiences had meaning? The answer was obviously yes. Therefore, the boundaries imposed by my inherited belief system no longer made sense. So from this point on, I would look to non-traditional avenues rather than traditional ones for guidance, as I continued my research for additional proof to support my new belief system.

According to Psychology, we learn from example by following in someone's footsteps or by imitating what others already know. Throughout the centuries, organized religion has provided the rules for humanity to follow. These same rules provided a method for people to imitate so our faith in God survived. In addition, religion satisfied our spiritual hunger, and people used it for generation after generation to search for the meaning of life. However, I now had more than just religion to satisfy my hunger to know God. I had psychic ability to see beyond and into the unseen world for my answers. This intrigued me, as well as set me free to experience life from a whole new perspective.

What if more people embraced a belief system that accepted paranormal experiences and psychic ability as a normal part of the human experience? Could adding these beliefs inspire greater inner peace in a person's life? Or could recognizing guidance in everyday life help others feel a closer connection to God? The answer to those questions had to be yes because those benefits had already manifested for me.

My thoughts sparked images that unexpectedly popped into my mind. They alternated between an intuitive flash of information and a scene from my past. In fact, the images flashed in my mind like the pages of a book rapidly being turned, which made the images difficult to decipher. When I intentionally slowed them, bits of the images resurfaced, which allowed me to finally identify them.

The first vision I recognized surprised me. A photo image of my deceased uncle floated into my thoughts. However, the image changed quickly to a scene inside of a church with a vision of an altar prominently in view. Before I could reminisce about my uncle, the scene changed a second time just as rapidly as I could snap the lens on a camera. This time a panoramic view of a street, with me looking skyward, filled my mind. Finally, the sequence of images ended with one of me engaged in serious conversation with two classmates in my junior high school cafeteria.

I had no idea what this meant. On the other hand, there

had to be some significance to the memories or they wouldn't have been centered around a theme and remembered in such rapid sequence. Now, my task was to uncover their significance.

As soon as I regained my normal state of consciousness, I focused on remembering one childhood experience at a time. So I directed my mind to first focus on an image of my deceased uncle. My recollections of him centered on a period of time in his life when he was in a coma with an inoperable brain tumor. Nevertheless, I didn't think there was anything significant to this memory, until I recalled the command of an inner voice. This voice relentlessly kept at me to visit him and told me he would respond, despite the coma.

What surprised me the most about this memory was my response to it. Without a second thought, I listened to the inner voice and immediately acted upon it. I even nagged my mother until she agreed to take me to see him. On the other hand, I wondered why I acted so quickly then, but hesitated to believe or act with that same conviction, today. Could we be more sensitive and psychically aware as children than as adults? And could our trust and spontaneity as children give us that awareness?

Years ago, when I entered my Uncle Frank's hospital room, he exhibited no emotion that day. His eyes remained open, blankly staring into space. I kissed his forehead and addressed him by name, but he stayed perfectly still without flinching a muscle. I lovingly stroked his forehead and told him how much I loved him, but there was still no reaction. I slipped my right hand into his, hoping he would squeeze it but he didn't. For the fifth time I told him I loved him.

Then it happened. Tears rolled down his cheeks. I asked him to move his finger to let me know he understood. He responded with a faint squeeze of my thumb and his reaction melted me into tears.

His nurse informed me it was the first time he had reacted to anyone in more than a month, which gave me hope.
However, she made another comment I didn't know how to handle. She informed me that I had freed my uncle from his confused
state the moment tears formed in his eyes.

Dumfounded by the comment, I asked her to clarify her
remark. She explained that a comatose person's soul remains
trapped between the two worlds until a person from this side or
the spirit world succeeds in creating a reaction in the person. In
addition, any reaction could be strong enough to jolt a person
from the confused or trapped state of mind.

According to the nurse, the reaction could be a tear, a
movement or a moment of recognition or it could be a reaction
to spirit loved ones beckoning for the person to come join them.
Once the comatose person comes out of their confusion, he or she
can make a choice to either continue living in a paralyzed state or
decide to cross into the spirit dimension and become free.
Unfortunately, I never had a chance to fully understand her comments, because my uncle died the next day.

In retrospect, the nurse's explanation sounded vaguely
familiar to me. Then I remembered why. Anna and I had discussed the comatose state after my past life regression experience.
The regression provided information on how it felt to be in a
coma and how a soul needed to be persuaded to make a choice to
enter the spirit world or to re-enter the physical world. Could I
have helped my uncle make his transition? If so, then at least I
knew he was at peace. I accepted that conclusion, but now I wondered why I had this memory. Could the other side want me to
remember more details about death or the comatose state?
Or could it just be another sign of guidance? Neither answer was

clear, so I continued to reflect on my thoughts and memories.

Next, I searched for a time when I looked intently up into the sky as if I were observing a plane. Eventually, I recalled the incident, but was surprised to discover it wasn't a plane in the sky, instead, it was a vision.

On Easter Sunday, when I was about eleven years old, a whisper distracted me from a game of hopscotch. A faint voice told me to look up. When I directed my eyes toward the sky, I saw a huge, white cross directly over me and the surrounding area. There wasn't a cloud in the blue, sunny skies, nor were there any commercial or sky-writing planes in the sky. Therefore, I eliminated all possible physical explanations for the vision. And I just stood in the street with my eyes fixated on the cross.

Seeing the cross made me think of my maternal grandmother, and a comment she frequently made to me.

Whenever I visited my grandmother, I usually washed her feet and combed her hair to make her more comfortable, since she was confined to a wheelchair. She expressed her gratefulness with the sweetest gesture for the small amenities I offered her. She assured me God would bless me for caring and showing my love for her. So I couldn't help but wonder if the cross in the sky was a sign of God's blessing. Naturally, my first instinct was to tell my mother, but the inner voice said no. The whispered voice simply told me that she wouldn't see the cross, so I quietly accepted the vision without telling anyone.

Visible for nearly a half-hour, the cross eventually faded, but my belief that it was a sign of God's blessing didn't. I quietly accepted the other side or the possibility God had communicated with me, but I never told a soul this secret. Could God have really communicated with me? Or could this experience indicate I had psychic ability, but couldn't develop it until the right time?

Remembering this now made me quiver, but I pressed my memories for more information.

When I focused on the church scene, an image of the Blessed Mother came to mind. So I braced myself for another religious memory. I didn't, however, connect the church or Mother Mary to anything significant, because there is a statue of the Blessed Mother in every Catholic Church. On the other hand, a vision of an unusual experience nagged me. I forced myself to recall the details, but couldn't until I remembered the church hymn I often sang. This hymn, called the Ava Maria, made my spine tingle whenever I sang or heard the song. When I, again, focused on my faded memories, I remembered an unusual experience I had once during a novena mass.

While singing the hymn, I glanced toward the statue of the Blessed Mother. The shock of what I witnessed made me gasp. The eyes of the icon were moist with tears. When I looked closer, I saw tears trickle down the statue's face. I reacted by shifting my eyes away from the statue and back to the prayer book clutched in my hands. Despite my shock, I immediately forced myself to regain my composure, so I could assess what I had just witnessed. At the time some possible explanations came to mind but I dismissed the experience as nothing more than my imagination.

I glanced at the statue one more time. Nevertheless, the tears were still present, but this time I could see them better and in more detail. Now, I knew it wasn't my imagination. I wanted to tell my mother, but intuitively I knew she wouldn't see them. I continued to watch until there were no more tears. At the same time, I tried to understand the message behind the vision. However, I never told my mother or anyone else about it.

In retrospect, I remembered receiving a telepathic message at the time, and instructions not to reveal it. What message could I have been given that I no longer remember? Thoughts questioning what I heard that day repetitively circled in my mind. No matter how I tried, not one bit of the message resurfaced. The forgotten message and the tears bothered me because I wasn't sure if they were tears of joy or sadness. I wanted to know more, especially whatever was buried in my subconscious. Could developing psychic ability give me the key to unlock the memory of this message?

Again, this experience reminded me of other experiences that would be considered psychic or paranormal. Could a religious and psychic experience come from the same source, but be labeled differently according to our perception and purpose? Could being psychic help me to understand God? Could the other side want me to see the connection between religious experiences and the paranormal to entice me to reach my purpose sooner? I didn't know any of the answers, there was still much to ponder.

There was one more incident, which I hoped would put all the pieces of the puzzle together. I needed to recollect a memory from my school's cafeteria. After trying unsuccessfully to remember a conversation I had more than thirty years ago with my seventh grade classmates, I focused on other memories of junior high school hoping to stimulate the memory of the cafeteria scene significant to me. Within a few minutes of focused concentration, I remembered my discussion with friends. During our conversation, we talked about the possible causes and cures for cancer. Moreover, I recollected a comment I blurted out to my friends, which astonished me.

"Someday scientists will discover that cancer comes from the food we eat and the cure will also be discovered in the food," I commented.

When I realized I had made a statement more than thirty

years ago that researchers were just now studying and reporting, I became more intrigued with the memory. I had made the comment but didn't think of it as a prediction at the time. In fact, I stated it as if I were an authority on the matter and it was already an accepted belief. Could this mean I had psychic ability years ago, but didn't have knowledge of it? Could recalling memories be another step in the psychic process? Or could our memories be another way the other side guides us?

After I recalled the details of the last vision, I telephoned Anna to tell her what had just happened. Anna sensed my urgency so she invited me to join her that night for dinner. Before we ended our conversation I asked her a question.

"Why do you suppose I remembered those childhood experiences one after another?"

"I will meditate on it and tell you when I see you tonight. You should also meditate for the answers. Your psychic ability is developed, so you can now receive information too. It's important to meditate for answers to specific questions, so you can develop interpretive skills. Those skills will be necessary when you do readings."

"But Anna, I prefer not to do readings. Guiding a person's life is too much responsibility. Couldn't I teach about the ability, instead?"

"You can educate people about it, but you still may have to guide people by doing readings. You may not want to, but if you are supposed to use your psychic ability that way, then you will have to fulfill that destiny to achieve your purpose in this life."

"Do you mean we can't change destiny?"

"No, of course it can be changed. Look at the circumstances of your life. You were on a different path before you had your first psychic reading. That reading challenged your beliefs and set you on a quest for the truth. You made a decision and then acted upon it. You could have decided there was no truth to the prediction and not explored it further. Even though you were destined to be psychic, it didn't happen automatically. You had to exercise your free will by choosing whether to believe, not to believe, or to explore further. By making decisions and taking action we set our fate into motion and sometimes we divert it into another direction."

"What would have happened if I hadn't listened?"

"Your guides would have worked overtime by providing coincidences, odd experiences, memories, and dreams to attract your attention. It's our guide's duty to inform us of our purpose and keep us on our path, but we have to do our part by listening for and observing the signs of guidance."

"But what if we don't observe the signs or listen to them?"

"Blocks are then put in our path and doors are closed, which usually creates more dramatic circumstances in our lives than coincidences. However, when problems occur, we often question why and then look for the answers or some understanding of those circumstances. During that period of time, our guides work on overdrive to reach us."

"Is that why life doesn't always go smoothly? Are the rough times presented as lessons we have to learn or extreme tactics our guides use to reach us?"

"Yes. That's right. Whenever there is a problem, we need to analyze what the other side may be trying to tell us. There is a destiny, but not all of it is pre-planned. When we make decisions, even if those decisions are made subconsciously, we exercise our free will, so it doesn't happen automatically. However, whenever we make a decision, take action or have repetitive thoughts, we create karma, which becomes another part of destiny we eventually have to meet. There is a really fine line between destiny and free will. That's why it's so difficult to understand."

"What part of destiny concerns our guides the most?"

"All of it. We have lessons and goals our soul chose to complete in this lifetime, as well as the destiny we create with our thoughts, intentions and actions in this lifetime as well as in previous lifetimes. So I think it is important for you to understand those childhood memories, because that information will help you to fulfill your own destiny."

"Okay. I will meditate before tonight's dinner."

It became obvious I had grown emotionally and spiritually, because I no longer exhibited fear when I encountered a new experience. Instead, I accepted it as a part of the guidance around me. And I approached it as if it were a lesson, challenge, or opportunity to learn something new. Furthermore, I could see there is a plan to life, which we call destiny. Some of our destiny is preplanned and some of it we create with our own thoughts, intentions and actions even if we weren't aware of it. In addition, I learned we have the potential to be chosen for a mission for the good of humankind. We just have to show God we are ready for it.

The daylight hours faded into night, but I managed to spend a little time in meditation before I left for dinner at Anna's. When I arrived, Anna once again greeted me before I rang the doorbell. She seemed just as excited to see me as I was to see her. I followed Anna into the kitchen, but before I pulled up a chair she began to excitedly question me.

"Did you receive any insights during your meditation?" asked Anna.

"I repetitively heard the word "guidance" and the phrase,

"now is the time." However, I couldn't decipher what it's time for me to know. Did you receive answers when you meditated?"

"The other side wanted to show that you have always been guided, even when you were not aware of it. They were confident you would believe this and continue in your psychic development, once you saw the extensiveness of the guidance. Because religion has always been important to you, your guides counted on the religious memories to create an impact on you."

"They indeed captured my attention, however I paid more attention to the religious ones. Looking back at those particular memories made me wonder if God was trying to reach me for a particular purpose."

"And that's exactly what your guides hoped to accomplish. You were harder to reach than most. Even with your strong faith in God, you still had to have proof for everything. Your skeptical nature indicates just how difficult it is for God to communicate with us or for us to recognize guidance in our lives."

"I know I am analytical, which is sometimes a detriment, but at least I see the truth now. Do you know if there is a purpose for our memories?" I asked.

"Memories prod us to reflect on our life and to look for insights or for clues to the lessons and goals we are supposed to accomplish in this lifetime. Some of the insights support our emotional development, which can then push us toward our purpose. Other flashes of memories point out pertinent information we might have overlooked, but needed to act on. Over a period of time we then notice that coincidences and unusual experiences have meaning, which in turn, helps us to recognize guidance on a regular basis."

"Do memories enhance the psychic development process?"

"Absolutely! Recollections of memories not only show the

192

depth of emotional growth in our lives, but they resurface from the part of the subconscious mind that also holds our psychic talent. Exercising the part of the mind that holds our memories also frees the mind to release bits and pieces of psychic information."

"Is that another reason for my vivid memories?"

"Yes. Memories help deepen psychic ability and increase interpretive skills," Anna replied.

"I also noticed that analyzing the meaning of memories seemed to be a catalyst for more images and impressions. It made me recognize another pattern in our lives that I haven't verbalized."

"What's the other pattern?"

"Have you ever questioned God or sometimes blamed God for your problems? But when the problem is solved, you quickly forget the incident."

"Yes, I've experienced that a number of times, but haven't we all?"

"After the problem is resolved, we seemed to then understand the reason we had the problem. In retrospect, we learn the purpose and how it was there only as a challenge for us to conquer."

"Yes, exactly! I don't even regard problems as problems anymore. They are just challenges. Our task is to find a way to overcome the challenge, so we learn the lesson the problem represents. It's our choice on how long the difficulty remains in our life, which is how we use our free will. God then knows we are ready to uncover our purpose and meet the challenges of our mission, when our perception embraces this philosophy."

"Do you think there is some knowledge stored in my mind that I don't know consciously?"

"Yes. How many people have religious experiences that are

193

also mystical? Only a small percentage have such experiences, so I believe you were given knowledge you aren't yet supposed to remember. Furthermore, other people who have had experiences centered around the Blessed Mother have often received messages. If you meditate on it, I think you will receive the answer."

"Anna, can you hypnotize me or put me into an altered state to help me remember the information?"

"I could, but I don't think the other side wants you to remember that yet. When it is important for you to know, your guides will alert you. What were your thoughts immediately following those experiences?"

"Both incidents made me feel that God had communicated with me. In addition, I had this gut feeling there was something I needed to reveal or announce, but couldn't at the time."

"Can you now see that at some level you knew you had a mission long before I told you?" Anna asked.

"Yes, but why don't we have conscious knowledge of it?"

"All of us have knowledge stored in us that we need, including the purpose of our life. However, it can't surface into our conscious mind until we are ready for it. There are steps we need to take before we can know our mission."

"Do you know the steps?"

"When we become aware coincidences have meaning, the other side perceives we are ready to be awakened to our purpose. Our guides then take more aggressive action by providing more and more coincidences to convince us there is more to life than this physical world. The rate of our acceleration depends on our ability to recognize and act upon the guidance. When we can overcome the negative patterns in our lives, our successes become the stepping stones that lead us to our growth. The barometer the other side uses to measure our readiness is our emotional and spiritual growth. Furthermore, when we develop a burning desire to understand our purpose, the other side then knows it is time to guide us in that direction. The next step in our development is the cultivation of our natural psychic ability which connects us even more to our guides. We then have glimpses of psychic impressions or feelings on a regular basis, which adds to our knowledge of life."

"Does reflecting on our past and analyzing it indicate we are ready?"

"Yes. It's part of the process, and it's a way we communicate with our guides. And coincidences and psychic experiences are some of the ways our guides communicate with us," Anna answered.

Anna's profound comment ended our evening, and I went home to contemplate the next steps in my journey. All my reflections on the unusual moments and memories in my life proved to me that our memories were more than what they often first seem to be. Yet, most of the time, we see them only as memories and not as clues into the meaning of our lives. Moreover, I looked for the moments of synchronicity in my life, and I made a greater effort to recall and analyze my memories, as well as to scrutinize them for patterns. Recalling our memories is another way the other side makes us aware. With each step into the unknown I had a greater understanding of my purpose and the meaning of life. And I couldn't wait to delve even deeper.

Insights

ॐ Memories that repetitively resurface in our thoughts have meaning, so it's important to reflect on them. They could be a form of guidance or a lesson we need to learn before we can move forward in our lives.

ॐ If we reflect on the past, we will see there is a pattern that exists in all of our lives. Whether we recognize it or not, there's an unseen force that guides us toward our destiny, even when we are consumed by our struggles.

ॐ We are more psychically aware as children, because we have a greater trust in those around us and our experiences are more spontaneous. However, those traits diminish when we get older and so does our ability to act on hunches or gut feelings. In order to become sensitive as an adult to paranormal activity, we have to consciously foster those traits.

ॐ When a nagging feeling to know our purpose haunts our thoughts, it may be the other side alerting us we have a mission to do God's work. And the first step to knowing that mission is for us to pay attention to coincidences, odd experiences, dreams, memories and moments of synchronicity. These are the tools the other side uses to communicate with us.

ॐ Destiny may seem predetermined, but sometimes we must be guided to that destiny in order for us to react and exercise our free will. We set our fate into motion with our action and some-times we divert it into another direction. Destiny is like the path of a ball rolling on the ground. The ball has momentum and direction, yet it is subject to the action and motion of the forces surrounding it. At each moment in time, the ball has a direction and a destination. However, as the ball continues on its path there are forces that influence it.

❧ We attract the circumstances of our life by our thoughts, intentions, actions, soul lessons, and goals, as well as our past and present karma, which we then call destiny. However, those circumstances are controlled by our actions, which we call free will. Whether we act or not, we exercise our free will which ultimately creates the rewards or consequences of our life. If we accept fate as unchangeable and take no actions or make no decisions, we still affect destiny. Consequently, no decision or no action is a passive decision.

THE BREAKTHROUGH:
DIRECT COMMUNICATION
WITH A GUIDE

K nowing there could be a message buried in my sub-conscious mind haunted my thoughts. Question after question raced through my mind. Could the forgotten message be personal? Did it pertain to my future? Was it a mystical message communicated by a higher power? Did it reveal definitive insights into the meaning of life or life after death? Or was it a message about the future of humanity? And if so, was it hopeful or dire?

As I pondered that last thought, I wondered if the message could have been an ominous one? Just the thought of receiving a dire message made me queasy. I searched my memories for details of the incident but I remembered only feelings of joy and exhilaration. Therefore, the message couldn't have been foreboding. Besides my memories, I had only one other clue about the message. When the other side decided the time was right, I would receive it once again.

After uncovering some of the secrets of the unknown, I became complacent and a bit lax with my development and research

However, the intrigue of a mystical communication changed my attitude and piqued my interest. Determined to uncover the message, I renewed the quest as fervently as when I first began the journey.

On the other hand, there hadn't been a dramatic breakthrough in my development for more than six months. There were sporadic flashes of psychic episodes, which included telepathic communication, an occasional insight into the future, and a disembodied voice that called my name. However, I still didn't have enough control of the ability to enter the psychic mode at will. Nor could I communicate directly with my guide the way Anna could with hers.

Anna explained to me that I needed to use my psychic ability in order to control and develop it. According to her, the sporadic episodes of psychic insights didn't provide enough experience for me to learn how to master the ability. Thus, Anna challenged me to either offer psychic consultations or to teach about the ability in order to develop it further. This was a difficult decision for me, because I was comfortable with my knowledge and current level of power. So I turned to meditation for guidance and for the strength to take action.

Because I meditated on a regular basis, it was easy for me to enter deep states of altered-consciousness. Bright colors and vague images usually appeared in the initial stages of most of these meditations. However, this time I asked for a comprehensible sign to guide me in making the decision. I made myself comfortable and quickly entered the relaxation ritual. This time, however, the rapidly moving images were more vivid than usual.

A few seconds after beginning the meditation, I saw several bright colors burst onto the blank screen in my mind just like the fireworks of a pyrotechnic display. This sudden burst of red, yellow, blue, and orange riveted my attention toward an inner vision. Waves of sharply-defined images and brilliant colors pulled me into what seemed like a dark tunnel. Trying not to be fearful, I remained focused on the vision instead of the dark tunnel. Could I be at the threshold of a doorway into my mystic mind where psychic information is stored? This could be the point where direct communication with a guide is possible. That possibility titillated me.

I didn't dare move because I didn't want the experience to stop. I saw nothing but darkness inside my mind. And my senses became so keenly aware that I heard electrical sparks crackling around me. Could this unique moment in my meditation be an opportunity for me to reach a guide directly?

I searched for an image - any image to clarify my experience, but I still saw only darkness. This long period of darkness began to unnerve me, but I held on. Finally, I glimpsed something in the distance that moved toward me. I waited for it to come closer and felt proud I hadn't succumbed to my fear.

A few seconds later, I began to decipher the images. I first saw a pastel hue of the color violet, which moved toward me down a dark hallway inside my mind. Then the violet color morphed into transparent visages that looked like spirits. These faded and swirled from one side to the other before their direction abruptly changed. The visual odyssey continued, but the hues of the various shades of purple and violet still reminded me of spirit images.

When I glimpsed the images again, I received another impression. This time the spirits marched toward me like soldiers in the line of duty. Secretly, I wished their march toward me included an order from the other side. However, they dissipated into a formless shade of purple, which changed my mood from exhilaration to despair. Obviously, my interpretation of the vision wasn't correct, because I didn't make contact with a guide.

Disappointed but determined, I continued the meditation and hoped for another chance to make the connection. Therefore, I tried a different approach, hoping to coax my guides to make the connection. Perhaps they would communicate directly to me, if I talked directly to them. As I inhaled and exhaled deeply to continue the deep state of meditation, I focused on one question and repeatedly posed it to my guides: Should I offer psychic consultations or teach about the ability?

With each breath I waited for an indisputable sign that would lead me in some direction. At the same time, I scanned my body for physical signs, but there were only a few miscellaneous scenes that drifted on and off the imaginary blank screen in my mind. Images of a house I didn't recognize, the number five, and the face of a friend appeared and then dissipated. However, none of these impressed me as the guidance I had hoped for.

Aware of my own impatience and wandering thoughts, I recaptured the previous moment of focused concentration by taking a few slow, deep and deliberate breaths. In addition, the sounds of a meditation tape playing in the background focused my attention. The taped music recreated the sounds of ocean waves hitting the sand and then crashing against the stone jetties on a beach. This stimulated my imagination, so I purposefully savored the moment and continued the meditation.

During this time, my senses embraced the sounds of the ocean and my mind conjured up a sensory experience so real I forgot I was in meditation. An imaginary cool breeze gently caressed my face and moistened the air around me. With the sound of each ocean wave I let go physically and entered into the previously inaccessible levels of my mind.

I surrendered to the sensations and enjoyed the experience without interpreting it. But then, a yellow ball of light appeared amidst the shades of violet color that dominated the imaginary screen inside my head. I tried to follow the ball of light, but it moved too rapidly. Intuitively, I knew the bright yellow light was leading me in a specific direction. Excitedly, I thought this could be the answer to my questions.

When I focused on that thought, the light slowed enough for my eyes to adjust to it. Teasingly, it morphed back and forth from a small ball of light to a larger ball of light and then back again. And the intensity ranged from the soft glow of a nightlight to the blinding intensity of a spotlight. In addition, the continuously moving light looked like an animated display that mimicked my own indecisiveness. Could this be my guide's way of making a comment about my not being able to make a decision?

Once the thought popped into my mind, the pattern of light changed. Instead of rapidly moving, the light deliberately and slowly moved from the left side of the blank screen in my mind to the right side, each time pausing a few seconds. There was a deliberate change in the speed of the light, which correlated with my thoughts. By now, I had learned to recognize images, feelings and symbols as the language guides use to communicate. So the moving lights had to have meaning or the speed wouldn't have changed so dramatically. Could one of my guides be getting ready to communicate with me? The possibility made my adrenaline pump faster, and my eyes locked unflinchingly on the light.

Without warning the light changed again. It danced into a swirling pattern of light and formed a ball. A few seconds later, the circle of light morphed a second time, but this time it formed into the shape of an old-fashioned key. Instantly, I knew the key to my question was forthcoming. The next image had to be the answer. So I waited with great expectation. A feeling emerged instead of an image and it again pulled me deeper into my mind. I experienced a sensation of traveling, but I wasn't in a vehicle. Waves of light-headedness and a whirling sensation enveloped me. For a moment I thought I was losing consciousness, but then realized it was a new level in the psychic process.

Even though the sensations were vivid, I struggled to keep my eyes closed. In fact, the intensity convinced me this experience could be another opportunity for me to reach my guides. Like a rapidly descending elevator, the sensation of dizziness continued until I arrived at a deeper level of the meditation. A feeling of warmth embraced me, which reminded me of the mid-morning rays of sun when I sunbathed on a beach. Could this warmth be the embrace of one of my guides?

I waited patiently for an image to appear. Instead, I experienced only strong sensations. In fact, my senses expanded two feet beyond the boundaries of my body for about thirty seconds and then returned to their normal parameters. I felt a bit strange, but there was no pain. Instead, I experienced a numbing sensation in my nose and forehead. After a few minutes, my aura again enlarged, and it increased my awareness beyond the usual range of my senses. However, this time they didn't return back. The facial numbness increased and my inner mind automatically concentrated on my sensory awareness. I felt like a radio antenna broadcasting and receiving signals.

My senses then tuned into the world beyond. And I could hear the sounds of muffled whispers. I could hardly contain myself. I had waited for this moment for a long time. It was the defining moment between haphazardly receiving psychic information and having control of it. Now, I could receive information by consciously meditating for it or by shifting my consciousness into an altered-state. I was sure an avenue of communication had been established with my guide.

A few seconds later, the vision of a speaker's lectern flashed in my mind. But as soon as I interpreted this, another scene appeared. This time I saw an image of a psychic reader. Could this mean I had to do both? In addition, the images repeatedly flashed as if to defy interpretation.

Then an outline of a figure appeared. I couldn't determine the gender, but the face appeared briefly. I sensed a feeling of love embrace me. It had to be one of my guides, so I was euphoric.

Next, a buzzing sound and whirling sensation raced around me. And the possibility this could be the breakthrough for me to communicate directly with a guide thrilled me. Then the buzzing sound became a whisper of voices, this time more distinguishable. The whispers morphed next into an inner voice. I still felt facial numbness and light-headedness but my awareness remained focused inward. I struggled to hear the muffled voices. And then, a voice suddenly delivered me a whispered message: "We can't make all your decisions, because you have free will. We can lead you in a direction with our guidance, but ultimately you must make each decision and then take action. In order to strengthen your psychic ability and allow it to evolve, you must make the decision. When you do, you will own the responsibility and have full control of your psychic ability."

Like the flashes of sudden ideas, thoughts of advice rapidly flowed into my mind. And a force seemed to control my inner thoughts when it communicated with me. I expected to see images when my guide communicated. Instead, I heard words that weren't audible sounds to my ears.

The words seemed distant and then I realized I heard them with my mind and not my ears. It was an odd sense because

I thought I heard words but I wasn't really hearing them in the usual way. This must be what psychics refer to as hearing their guide. As I sat speechless, the palpitations in my heart sounded louder than the message. Still awed, I struggled to regain my composure before I could fully comprehend the words. I had experienced a psychic's sense of hearing in the spirit world. My guides set the rules for me and now I had to either cross the line or deny the opportunity. It was my decision to make and a sense of urgency commanded me to take action. I had hoped my guides would make the decision for me, but instead they placed it directly in my hands. My eyes opened, but my thoughts rode a mental roller coaster. And this sent my thoughts tumbling in all directions.

To stop the whirlwind of thoughts, I tried to explore a more tangible solution. I asked myself some questions to put the dilemma into perspective for me, so I could make my decision on what I thought I should do first. Was I ready to apply my psychic ability as a personal consultant and offer psychic readings to the public? Was my ability to interpret psychic impressions developed enough to accurately read others? Did I want the responsibility of guiding a person's life? Without another thought I answered no to all of those questions.

On the other hand, Anna had encouraged me to offer the consultations because she thought I had developed my ability enough to guide people. Nonetheless, I still believed I wasn't ready for the responsibility. In fact, I cringed when I thought about incorrectly interpreting an impression, especially when I knew that person counted on my guidance. So I decided the first avenue for me to pursue was to teach others what I had learned about the paranormal. Once I had more confidence, then I would offer individual consultations. Besides, teaching would allow me more comfort because it was a natural path for me. At one time, I had been a high school teacher, so I knew I would enjoy teaching about the paranormal.

Finally, I made the decision to teach first before I offered readings. And that decision ended my mental torture. Now, I focused on implementing the plan, instead of agonizing over what I should or should not do. Moreover, I had a definite focus.

Before I offered the course, however, I wanted to do research on the concept of time and how it related to the future. I thought this information would help me to understand how destiny and prophecy are related, as well as increase my ability to interpret psychic information. Again, I turned to my own thoughts for answers. This time I analyzed the concept of time and how it relates to what we label as the future.

By using a mechanical device we measure time to gain order in our everyday lives. The familiar phrase, "what time is it now," indicates we view time mostly in the present. The hands on a clock click from minute to minute in what we think of as continuous movement.

Next, I imagined an event in the future as a fixed state that moved on an imaginary conveyor belt defined as time. That image made me realize that we think time moves the future into the present and then into the past. However, can we isolate a point in time and pronounce it as the present or the future?

If I am reading a book or a magazine, the page I am currently reading would be the present. If I planned to read more, then the next page would actually be my future. The first words on a page that you read can be considered the present. As you continue to read, the previous words quickly become the past. Time seems to flow without us giving it much thought. Now, I wondered if destiny flows in the same way or do we have some control over it?

When I observe nature, I see perfect examples of how motion is a part of our lives. There is motion in the ebb and flow of the tides and in the orbit of the moon. The planets revolve around the sun. Everything is in motion, even if we don't consciously observe it. So how could time or the circumstances that determine the future be constant? When I pondered these points, I realized our past choices bring our present circumstances. Therefore, decisions about our current circumstances actually determine our future. This revelation impressed me, because I could now see how teaching these concepts could help others to know how they could effect change in their lives.

Next, I pondered the ability of psychics. Could a psychic really predict the future, if the future can be changed? After analyzing all the readings I had experienced over the years, I concluded that it was more accurate to say that psychics predicted the probability of the future, rather than the future. Therefore, free will can be exercised at any moment in our lives by our making a decision, which will then alter our future.

I searched my mind for a hypothetical example. The vision of a tall building popped into my mind, so I imagined a scenario about the future using that image. I imagined being on the top of the building and being able to see the flow of traffic beneath me. When I looked just beyond the street below me, I imagined a white car and a red truck traveling at excessive speeds and headed to the same intersection. If I had to predict the future for these two drivers, it was easy to see from my vantage point the two vehicles were destined to collide with each other. Instead, I considered a different scenario.

I visualized that seconds before reaching the intersection, the driver of the white car made a sudden decision because he was distracted by a store window display. In addition, he reduced the speed of his car and then parked it, so he could shop in the store. Because of his decision, he didn't reach the intersection at the same time as the truck driver. Therefore, he avoided the predicted vehicle crash. What happened to destiny in this hypothetical scenario?

This imaginary example showed me fate wasn't automatic or all pre-destined. Some form of guidance can alert us to danger or keep us on our path. Distracting our attention could be a way the other side guides us. We could also be guided by more dramatic signs such as: dreams, spirit encounters and coincidences. This imaginary scenario fascinated me so much I searched for an example of destiny that actually happened to illustrate this point.

An experience Anna had with a client popped into my mind. She did a psychic reading for a girl who was visiting the United States from Russia. Miriam scheduled a reading with Anna to help her decide whether to go back to Russia or stay in the United States and work for her uncle.

Anna told Miriam, "The man you are in love with will ruin your life because he will never marry you. You should stay in the United States. You have a major health problem around you that needs attention."

However, Miriam went back to her boyfriend in Russia, instead of following Anna's psychic insight. Miriam discovered she was pregnant, but her boyfriend refused to marry her. During the pregnancy, she developed a mole on her chest, which her doctor diagnosed as benign. Six months later, the mole turned into deadly skin melanoma.

When she returned to the United States for medical treatment, the doctors told her that if she had come for an appointment sooner, the mole could've been removed before it became cancerous. Unfortunately, she died two years later. Could she have avoided this fate? If she had made the decision recommended by Anna, Miriam would probably still be alive.

This showed me how one decision can affect a person's fate. Our so-called destiny had to be more of a probability rather than something that happened automatically. Therefore, psychics predict the future, but our decisions and actions ultimately create our destiny.

I was comfortable with this part of my research. Now, I wanted to explore other concepts. Anna and I had never discussed the religious viewpoint on psychic phenomena, and I was curious to know Anna's opinion. So I telephoned her. I directed our conversation toward religion.

"Do you believe psychic consultations go against our religion?"

"Absolutely not! Our Catholic religion believes in miracles and the intercession of saints. A number of years ago, alleged miracles in the Catholic Church stimulated interest in the paranormal among research scientists. In fact, a research scientist, Dr. J.B. Rhine, conducted numerous studies that compared the paranormal phenomena of Parapsychology to the mystical events in Christianity. According to his research, there were definite similarities between the two."

"What are they?"

"Psychic healers who demonstrated the mind-over-matter phenomenon were documented in Rhine's laboratory and other research centers as creating physical healing in themselves, as well as in others. This research indicated there is a correlation between miracles in the church and the psychokinetic energy demonstrated in the laboratory. Dr. Rhine also observed that telepathy was similar to prayer, and seership and revelation were comparable to clairvoyance."

"Could some mystical accounts recorded in the Holy Bible be attributed to psychic ability?"

"Yes. There are events recorded in the Holy Bible that could be considered paranormal events, even though these events have been interpreted in other ways. When the Bible was written, the word psychic or paranormal was not part of the vocabulary until modern times. Therefore, biblical events were not described as psychic events, but could be described that way today."

"But, there are people today who would never agree with that view."

"Yes. That's true. However, there are numerous examples in the Scriptures, which indicate most of the main characters in the Bible didn't live by faith alone. There were many mystical signs and wonders that bolstered their faith. There were angel visitations and accounts of Biblical characters who heard the voice of God. For example, angels visited Lot, Jacob, Moses, Joseph and Mary, and there are the accounts of Elijah being touched by an angel and receiving a message. In fact, even Jesus was ministered to by angels. In addition, the Lord spoke to Joseph, Moses, Balaam, Samuel, Daniel and many others. Moreover, John the Baptist heard a voice from heaven. These mystical events happened almost every day during ancient times. In addition, these signs occupied a significant place in the life of the church in early Christianity and Judaism. Yet, there are very few wonders or signs recognized in the church today."

"Why would God offer signs for our faith then but not now? Couldn't the psychic experiences today be the same as the wonders and signs of the Bible, but not referred to as such?"

"Absolutely! And the difference between now and then

211

may only be a matter of semantics."

"Is Christianity the only religion with beliefs and secrets that can be interpreted as paranormal?"

"No. the Jewish religion also has references to prophecy and mysticism. In fact, Judaism was the first religion to embrace mysticism. Interest in the origins of man and the universe, evil and good, prophecy and the after-life, are all rooted in Judaism."

"Does Judaism then support the paranormal?"

"No. The secret, mystical part of Judaism called the Kabbalah is not available to all members. Kabbalists believe that the Bible is a guidebook that explains how to use the forces of the universe. According to the Kabbalah, there are profound passages in the Bible that refer to prophecy. Supposedly, there are ten psalms in Moses considered to be the hidden doorway to prophecy."

"Why is the Kabbalah not available to all people of the Jewish faith?"

"In order to study mysticism, a person must reach a mature age and have proper training and attitude. Kabbalists fear that an untrained person without spirituality or wisdom could use the information destructively."

"Then my quest to discover the answers to life and the meaning of prophecy is not an unattainable fantasy?"

"Absolutely not! You have had some very profound mystical experiences, so you shouldn't even question your journey. Soon, you will be able to let go of the last bit of your resistance to fully embrace it, by letting go of your strong religious views against it. Besides, mysticism has been a part of most major religions including Islam, Hinduism, Buddhism, Taoism and others."

"Couldn't paranormal experiences be modern signs of faith to strengthen our belief in God today?"

"Of course, they can be, but most religions don't agree with that viewpoint."

"Why not?"

"According to the religious perspective, the source of psychic information could be evil or it could be divine. And it is difficult for organized religion to discern divine guidance from a psychic's opinion. Therefore, they discourage paranormal exploration and dismiss paranormal experiences as nonsense."

"But why can't religious leaders discern the information? Aren't they supposed to be experts on God, evil and religious doctrine?"

"For centuries, religious leaders have interpreted and defined the concepts of evil and good, but only within the context of appropriate behavior for those who followed that religion. Therefore, there are no satisfactory definitions of good and evil that are universally adopted."

"If that's true, then how do we recognize in everyday life whether an experience or a person is inspired by an evil force or the divine? God and the devil have been depicted mostly as man-made icons defined by religion, and virtually no one has ever experienced either as a physical entity. Could the turmoil in our lives be a subtle evil force that we haven't recognized yet as such?"

"Yes, that's right. It's difficult to discern even for a psychic. That's why it's important to protect yourself when you meditate or receive psychic information, because we are all vulnerable to the interplay of forces between evil and good. So it's important to say a prayer of protection before meditating or receiving psychic information. In addition, it's difficult for people to discern whether the circumstances most people attract to them are evil or divinely inspired."

"What prayer do you say?"

213

"I often say some of the prayers I learned from my religion or I say the following words: *I am surrounded by God's light and nothing negative could ever penetrate it. I am always in God's loving protection. Wherever I am God is.*"

"Thanks. I will use that too. However, it bothers me that there is no definitive description of evil or even guidelines to help us decipher evil from good in our everyday life."

"It concerns me, too. Perhaps, your quest will uncover those guidelines to help us recognize such forces."

"I certainly hope so."

We ended our telephone conversation but it didn't end my search. I hungered for more answers, so I immediately looked into more research. Because somewhere buried deep in my mind and in the unknown there were still some elusive secrets to uncover.

Insights

❧ Although we mark time and measure it, no one can isolate time and pronounce a particular moment as the present or the future. Everything in life is in motion, including time. Therefore, our future depends on the choices and decisions we make that ultimately create our destiny.

❧ When a guide communicates directly with you, you will hear it as inner thoughts that flow without interruption in your mind. Sometimes there are whispered sounds that are audible, and sometimes the whispered voices just seem audible because of the continued cadence of thoughts. A numbing feeling can indicate your psychic ability is developing.

❧ There were no words in the vocabulary of ancient days to describe the mystical events recorded in the bible. Psychic experiences today could be the same wonders and signs recorded in the bible. They were not called psychic events because those words didn't exist at that time.

❧ According to some scientific research, there is a correlation between miracles in the church and the physical healing demonstrated in the laboratory by people with a mind-over-matter ability. These findings suggest that parapsychological experiences have religious implications.

THE PARANORMAL
IS NORMAL

The secrets, messages, memories, visions and coincidences all nudged me toward this moment. My journey thus far had been nothing less than enlightening. My confidence soared and my thirst for knowledge was quenched, at least for now. Therefore, the next step was for me to teach a course on the paranormal scheduled the next night at a local adult school. I didn't know what to expect, because I had never taught adults. However, my fears quieted just before I left for the class.

There were more than twenty-five students in my first class. Neither the students nor I knew exactly what to expect from each other. My students scrutinized me with curiosity and awe. And I looked at them wondering what could have prompted their interest in the paranormal.

While still gauging the students' reaction to me, I defined the course outline and had the students introduce themselves to the class. I observed a heightened sense of curiosity in my students, more than in most people. However, none of their introductory remarks revealed the reasons for their curiosity. Did they have personal reasons beyond the mundane for their interest in the paranormal? Did they have an experience like I had that set them in this direction? Or did they gravitate to the unknown purely for entertainment?

For now, I dismissed my curiosity to concentrate on the course content. I began the course by defining extra-sensory perception and by teaching the basic principles for psychic development. I also stressed that psychic ability is naturally inherent within all of us.

"Extra-sensory perception or ESP as it is commonly called is a way of knowing without knowing how you know it. It is the sensory information you receive from beyond the normal senses. Telepathy, clairvoyance and precognition are some of the components of ESP. And we will focus on understanding and developing all of them."

When I explained the procedures for developing psychic talent, there was a shift in the energy of the class. Instead of being open to change, the students were closed to the new concepts, despite their conscious intentions. In addition, there was a general reluctance to let go of inhibitions. I knew I had a problem, since the first steps toward any change are awareness and the willingness to change. My students, however, rejected the concepts without even trying to exhibit the behavior. If it hadn't been for my psychic sense, I wouldn't have been alerted to the problem. What could the reason be for their reluctant behavior? The students verbally expressed interest and desire, yet they were not receptive to the concepts.

Puzzled, I questioned myself for an answer. The word fear raced through my thoughts. I didn't portray a frightening presence, so I was confused by the message. I then tried to interpret the message again. Apparently, my students defined psychic talent as a power and they didn't know what to expect from that power. Therefore, I had to dispel their misconceptions about psychic talent before I could proceed with the course. So I asked the class if they had any questions for me.

A petite blonde girl in the back row timidly addressed me, "Can you read my thoughts?"

"No, I cannot." Jokingly, I added, "And I can't read your private thoughts either!"

The students in the class laughed and then relaxed. An older gentleman balding, with some brown hair, excitedly waved his hand, begging to be noticed. He asked, "Do you receive images of our future every time you look at us?".

"No. If I did, I would never be able to stand in a crowd of people, because the amount of information coming to me at one time would be confusing and overwhelming. So, I only enter the psychic mode when I give myself permission to do so. I have a set procedure which includes quieting myself in order to receive psychic impressions."

A student near the window shouted, "Is it frightening to have psychic talent?"

"No. It's not frightening unless your emotions are riddled with other fears. If you are a fearful person, then you more than likely will interpret the experience according to your perceptions."

I observed a girl who sat in the front row. Her face expressed concern as she asked, "Will I change as a person if I develop psychic ability?"

"You will not change in an overt way, but you will have a higher sense of perception and a greater understanding of life. And this newly acquired understanding could help you to make better decisions and thus create a more positive life."

There were no further questions so I took the opportunity to address the class with one more comment:

"The only difference between you and me is my psychic ability. My psychic gift is fully opened, while your psychic ability is still dormant. You may have spontaneous moments of psychic ability, but I can bring it to me at will. And that's the only difference between us."

The response of my students pleased me. All were in deep thought, and that is exactly the behavior I had hoped for before we started our question-and-answer session. The energy of the class was now open and receptive to learning. So I asked for a show of hands for my next question. "How many of you have ever had a psychic experience?"

Almost ninety percent of the students in my class indicated they had experienced at least one paranormal episode. And they were emotionally driven to attend the course to validate or to understand their experiences. At one time, all had been skeptical until they had an inexplicable experience.

Finally, I had my answer for their curiosity in the paranormal. They, too, had had a paranormal experience that set them on a path to further explore the unknown. Could the paranormal be a common experience for many others? If so, then these experiences could be the signs and wonders that could prove there is more than a physical, tangible world.

Next, I defined telepathy to the class for them to recognize some of the subtle differences in extra sensory perception.

"Telepathy is the awareness of information or emotion that exists in the mind of another person. It is a spontaneous transference of thought between two people that may, or may not, be physically present at the time of the communication. The phrases, 'You took the words right out of my mouth' or 'That's exactly what I was thinking' are examples of how you could feel if you experience a telepathic moment."

The definition of telepathy sparked a question from one of my students. A girl about thirty years old asked, "What is the vehicle of communication for extra-sensory perception?"

I answered, "During a telepathic episode, the avenue of communication is in the mind. The exchange of information between the two people occurs as if the two had some sort of wireless telephone communication system within their minds. The following experiences are real examples of telepathy. These examples will help you to recognize your own telepathic experiences."

Several years ago, Suzanne's daughter, Tracey, was hospitalized for an appendectomy. She was scheduled for discharge from the hospital four days after surgery. On the day of her scheduled discharge, Suzanne experienced a sudden feeling telling her something was wrong. She tried to visualize her daughter arriving home from the hospital that day, but instead she sensed a queasy feeling in the pit of her stomach. She just knew at some level there was a problem with her daughter. A short while later, Tracey's mother received a telephone call informing her that her daughter would not be discharged from the hospital that day as planned. Tracey had developed a temperature from an infection which had developed that morning. Tracey and her mom experienced a telepathic moment between the two of them.

In another experience, Ann and her husband had shopped all day, but there was a nagging feeling that haunted her, however, she didn't understand it. She had a fear that something had happened to her daughter Danielle. When Ann returned home, there was a telephone call from her daughter. Danielle called from the emergency room of the local hospital. She had cut her finger while at work, and she was now in the hospital waiting for stitches. Again, this was an example of a telepathic moment between a mother and her daughter.

In a telepathic episode, a person communicates a message to another person without using a spoken word or a sound. These episodes of telepathy can occur between two living people or between a living person and an unseen entity. It is necessary to have a sender and a receiver for a successful telepathic communication. The person who transmits the thought is called a sender. The person who receives and accepts the thought is called a receiver. Telepathy between family members like a mother and her child or husband and wife are more prevalent. Sometimes, the sender is not a living person but an unseen force, as in the following example.

While writing on her time card at the end of the day, Marie asked her co-worker the date. Her co-worker revealed the date as June twelfth. Marie became visibly upset without understanding why as she kept repeating the words, "It can't be June twelfth! It can't be June twelfth!"

Marie didn't understand her reaction until the early morning hours of the next day. At one o'clock in the morning, Marie received a telegram from the Commander of a United States Naval base. The telegram stated her brother had drowned at about the same time she had become upset over the June twelfth date. This unseen force or the spirit of her brother communicated to Marie that he had died, although she did not understand her emotions at the time.

I addressed my students for some of their experiences. "Has anyone here had a paranormal experience they think was telepathic?"

Samantha, a girl with long hair, about thirty years old,

raised her hand in an affirmative gesture and then began detailing her experience.

"A file on a college student had been missing for weeks in the registrar office of the school. For three weeks five people had tried to locate the file without any luck. The office workers searched the office as well as the filing cabinet. I walked into the room from another office in the building. As I approached the filing cabinet, I experienced extreme anxiety and then a strange pulsating, strong, tingling feeling ran down my right arm and into my fingers. I reached into the filing cabinet and pulled a file from the drawer. To everyone's surprise, the file was the one they were looking for. About a week later, I returned to that office. Again, there was a missing file. Jokingly, I opened the file drawer and reached into the files with my hand to pull a file randomly from the drawer. Again, I pulled the file that had been missing. After those two episodes, my co-workers teasingly labeled me a witch," Samantha explained.

"I knew this experience was more than coincidental but I was disturbed by my colleagues' reaction to these two episodes. Their reaction made me uncomfortable and I was unwilling to listen to my gut feeling after those experiences. Why do people label you weird or a witch if you experience something that is paranormal?" asked Samantha.

"Unfortunately, there is a tendency for society to mock or criticize what they don't understand. It is best for you to just ignore the comments and evolve into the unique person you are meant to be, with all of your talents developed, including extra-sensory perception."

Samantha's question triggered another student to respond. Alina, a slightly graying, middle-aged woman, shared her experience with the class.

"While walking to the train station after work one day, I noticed a person who reminded me of a college friend whom I had not seen in years. It was not my college friend, Janis, but the resemblance triggered thoughts of her. A few minutes later, as I turned the corner, I noticed Janis walking towards me. This time it was really her! We exchanged a pleasant conversation that day, but never saw each other again."

Alina continued, "In another instance I started thinking about my other college friend, Sharon. As I passed my old alma mater, I began to wonder if I would ever see Sharon again. The next morning as I waited for the train, someone tapped me on the shoulder. When I turned around, it was Sharon! We talked during the entire train ride to New York. Were these experiences just a coincidence or did I experience something paranormal?"

"No, they were not coincidences. You experienced paranormal episodes of extra-sensory perception that demonstrated telepathy. You received the thoughts of those old time friends and were in tune with them at that moment."

Another student gestured to me that she wanted to say something. Susan, a young girl about twenty-five years old, asked rather sheepishly if she could share her experience with me.

Susan explained, "I was a bit annoyed at Lorraine, my friend at work. I was scheduled to attend a computer course the following week on Monday. I had to cancel the course due to an on-site class scheduled at work. I knew that my support person, Lorraine, would not excuse me from the on-site class, so I started to think up an excuse not to be at work on Monday. I wanted to tell the boss that I had to attend a funeral on Monday. I thought it was odd to think of something like that so I dismissed the idea. When I went home that evening, my mother telephoned me with bad news. My mother told me that a close cousin had died at six in the morning. Two days later, I learned the funeral was on Monday."

Susan explained that she had fears ever since she had that experience. "Did I cause the death by my lying?"

"No. Of course not, you received telepathic information without knowing it. You thought of a funeral because someone or something telepathically tried to inform you about the death and funeral. You didn't recognize the thought as telepathic. Instead, you accepted the thought as the perfect excuse not to go to work without knowing in a few days it would be your future."

The telepathic experiences my students shared all had a common thread. In most cases, the person who received the message had suddenly focused their attention on another person. What distinguished the telepathic moment from an ordinary thought were the intensity and duration of the focus. The comments from the students who had the paranormal experience echoed the following statements: "I just couldn't stop thinking about the person no matter how hard I tried." Or, "My obsessive thoughts of that person grabbed my attention and wouldn't let me go!"

I observed other factors in the experiences that were telepathic. These types of experiences usually warned the person of an upcoming unpleasant event. In addition, the time span between the obsessive thoughts and the actual knowledge of the event was actually very short. Sometimes the message occurred within hours and almost always within forty-eight hours from the first moments of intense focus.

In each case, there was a sixth sense that forewarned of the event. Strong feelings between the two people seemed to be the common denominator that facilitated the psychic moment. What interested me was the surprise element each person exhibited when the telepathic moment was validated. All of them knew something had happened, but they just didn't know how it had happened to them.

According to my students, these psychic episodes were all spontaneous reactions to some unknown stimulus. They had no interest in the paranormal before these incidents occurred. Once it happened, however, their interest spurred them to seek more knowledge about the paranormal.

My students now had an understanding of telepathy, so I proceeded to explain clairvoyance to them. I was curious to see if my students had any clairvoyant experiences. Clairvoyant experiences are a little more difficult to experience than telepathy. Also, clairvoyant experiences could be precognitive glimpses into the future.

"Clairvoyance is a French term meaning 'clear seeing' and refers to the ability to see an occurrence that the physical eyes can not see. Clairvoyance sometimes occurs at great distances. For example, you can sit comfortably in your home in one state and describe a house or interior room of a house in another state. This practice is called remote viewing. A psychic uses his or her clairvoyant ability to see visual images from a distance in order to locate and describe a physical phenomenon," I announced.

"When a psychic sees spirits, spirit lights, shapes, faces, situations, colors or symbols that are not seen to the naked eye, the psychic uses the mind faculty of clairvoyance. Natural extensions of clairvoyance are the faces or images that appear inside your mind's eye before you fall asleep or the pictures you remember after awakening from a dream," I explained.

"Visions are strong impressions that can be seen with the eyes open or closed. The images in a vision represent information that is not physically present, which may help guide a person's life in some way."

"Precognition is the prediction of future events that can't be inferred from present knowledge. Surveys indicate that precognitive events occur more often than any other form of ESP. Dreams especially show precognitive results."

Trudy, a red-haired fifty-year-old, waved her hand persistently until I acknowledged her question. "I don't think I had the same type of experience as the examples that were shared. I had a completely different experience," Trudy stated.

"Can you tell us about it," I asked.

"I had constant thoughts of fire, but I couldn't determine why. I checked the light plugs, lamps and appliances in my house almost everyday. The thoughts intensified so much that I contacted my son to check the electrical outlets at his house. Then I started to have visions of a fire. After two weeks of this odd behavior, my husband, Jim, questioned me. I explained that I had a nagging, intense feeling about fire. However, Jim dismissed my feelings as nonsense."

Trudy continued, "On Christmas day, one week later, I received a telephone call from my niece, Judy. Judy informed me that her house had just burned to the ground, but everyone was saved. Although her husband was the fire chief, the firemen didn't arrive on time. Apparently, the volunteer firemen waited at the firehouse for the chief to arrive in order to dispatch the trucks to the fire. All my thoughts about fire ceased after that call."

Trudy then asked. "Could I have prevented the fire, if I had understood the dream represented an event that was going to happen?"

"If you had recognized where the fire was going to be before it happened, you could have possibly prevented the fire. However, you didn't have knowledge of that in the dream, so it was impossible for you to know before the event. You took the most-likely steps by checking your own home environment. When someone has a dream about fire, it is wise to be on alert that someone is trying to warn you about possible danger. However, without specific details it is impossible to pinpoint who should be warned."

Pat, a dark blonde woman about forty years old, gestured with her hand begging to be acknowledged. Pat confidently stated, "My experience has more of a religious tone to it, but I still feel it is appropriate to discuss as a paranormal event. My daughter's girlfriend, Sue, was told she had a lump in her breast. The doctor scheduled surgery and a biopsy. I prayed for my daughter's friend and visualized her lump shrinking and then disintegrating. After seeing it disintegrate I then visualized the lump and any possible cancer cells leaving the body. I did this for the two weeks before the scheduled surgery, several times a day. I also sent psychic energy to the affected area as I concentrated on the visualization. If the doctor said, "I don't believe it; I can't find it!", then I would know the prayers and visualization worked."

Pat continued, "On the day of the surgery my daughter called to tell me what the doctor said. The doctor told Sue "I cannot believe it, but there is no lump. I cannot find it." Therefore, he cancelled the surgery. I sobbed and thanked God for the healing. To this day Sue does not know what happened."

The number of students who had experiences demonstrated that extra-sensory perception is more normal than most people believe. As each student revealed a paranormal event, you could feel the whole class become more confident and willing to discuss their experiences. I was excited by the promise of more convincing information as another student had a vision she wanted to share with the class.

Karen, a college student, explained, "While driving my car, I had a vision of a person riding a bicycle on a darkened highway road. In the vision, I hit the person on the bicycle. The vision disturbed me enough that I began to pay careful attention to my driving. Not long after the vision, I encountered a person riding a bike in the slow lane of the dark highway. If I had not been paying attention to my driving, I would have hit the bicycle with my car. After the experience I concluded that "someone" warned me of the possible accident if I was not alert while driving my car."

Karen asked, "Do you think that was the meaning of it?"

"Yes, our guides are there to help us to avoid disaster. You were warned in the dream and you paid attention to the warning so you avoided the accident. Confirmation of that incident should now help you to continue to look for guidance."

Elisabeth, who had braided hair and sat in the back of the room, responded to the previous experience with another similar incident. "My experience really shocked me. I look at it as my wake-up call that there is an unseen guide directing life."

Elisabeth explained, "While planning my wedding, the priest suggested I contact the girl who was getting married on the same day as me to ask her to split the cost of the church flowers. When I contacted the girl's family, I learned the family were former parishioners of the town church I used to attend. The Coles now lived in the town that I had recently moved to and again attended the same parish. Several months later, I noticed the check I sent for the flowers was not cashed. I called to inquire if Mrs.Cole had received the check. I was then informed the check was her wedding present to Susan. To thank her for her generosity I bought a small thank you gift to mail to Mrs. Cole. While standing in line at a post office about twenty miles from my hometown, the next available clerk yelled "next!" I asked the clerk, 'What is the fastest way to deliver this package?' The very confused man behind the counter announced 'I can take it home with me!' After some explanations and verification of his name, Mr. Cole, the post office clerk took the package home to his wife without the need of a postal delivery."

"I sure like the way your guide saved you money!"

We all chuckled, amused by her unseen guidance. It was obvious her experience included direction from the other side.

Sharon asked to share her experience. From her demeanor, I realized this was going to be somber compared to the previous light-hearted experience. Sharon, who was no more than twenty-five, eagerly expressed her paranormal incident. I suspected she needed to be comforted.

"Several years ago while driving in my car I had a very strong feeling about my father that at first I did not understand. A thought popped into my head to indicate he was ill. Then I had a vision he was going to soon die. Confused and very upset by the vision I tried to force the thoughts from my mind. I reassured myself that he was just fine. He had no symptoms of illness so I dismissed the feelings as just my imagination. The next month, however, he was diagnosed with lung cancer. A year later he was hospitalized. While on my way to the hospital to visit him, I heard a voice telling me to go home. I noticed the time on the clock was 1:30 p.m. I decided to listen to the voice. I changed direction and went home instead of continuing on to the hospital. When I reached the front porch, my sister greeted me at the other side of the front door. My sister informed me that our father had just died. The time of death was listed as 1:30 p.m."

Sharon had one pressing question to ask me. Her eyes pleaded for an answer as she questioned, "Did my father direct me to go home because he was already deceased? And does that mean he communicated with me after he had died?"

"Yes, that is exactly what happened. Your father telepathically communicated that message to you after his death. The experience showed he was all right and could talk to you from his new spirit condition," I comforted.

Sharon looked relieved. Andy, an older man with a white thick of hair, waved his hand vigorously trying to get my attention. Andy commented, "I have repeatedly had very dramatic examples of what seem to be a guiding force. I don't know why I have these experiences, but I know at least one has saved my life!"

Andy explained, "For a week and a half every night I had the same dream. I dreamed that I was laid out in a coffin and everyone that viewed my body said, 'Too bad he didn't heed the warnings.' After a few nights, the repeated dreams caused me to fear going to sleep at night. After almost every night for two weeks the dreams finally stopped. A month later I had severe chest pains at work that would not stop. I called my wife to pick me up but was reminded that I had the only car. My wife secured a friend to drive her to my job and then transported me to the family doctor. The doctor found nothing wrong with me. The doctor asked what I wanted to do. I remembered the dream and simply told him I wanted to be admitted to the hospital."

Andy continued, "I was placed in the hallway of the hospital because there were no vacant rooms. After a few minutes in the hospital, I started to lapse into a state of semi-consciousness. I would describe my condition to be like that of falling into a black hole. I told my wife that I felt I was dying. So, I said good-bye to her. I could hear what was going on but could not feel anything as I slipped into a semi-conscious state. I heard the doctor tell my wife that he did not know what was wrong and it did not look as if I was going to live. Eventually, I woke up to discover I had been in a coma for five days. The doctor told me that I had a right collapsed lung that put pressure on my heart, which caused a heart attack. The doctor also said that if I had not been hospitalized at the time, I would have died."

"I am so glad you recognized and listened to the guidance you received in that dream. Repeated dreams always have significant meaning."

Two of my students questioned me about spirit communication and had an incident to share. Jackie revealed, "My grandparents moved in 1920 to the home I still lived in. My grandfather came home each day to eat his lunch with my grandmother. My grandmother had a fear of strangers, so my grandfather devised a special knock. It was two fast knocks and two slow knocks, so my grandmother would know it was he when he knocked on the door before she opened it. After he died, whenever anything happened to any family members, one or more family members in the house heard the same knock. When we heard the knock, our dog usually ran to the door, then suddenly and inexplicably turned away whining. Several people witnessed this knocking several times."

"Could these knocks be my grandfather communicating from the other side?"

"I most certainly believe the knocks are your grandfather trying to communicate. He chose the knocks because your grandmother understood what they meant. And he knew she would associate the knocks with him."

Gillian, who had ice-blue piercing eyes, raised her hand as she explained, "A few years ago, I broke up with a boy I had been dating seriously; I was very close to Vincent's parents. His parents had hoped we would marry. Several months later, I had a disturbing dream. Vincent's father appeared in my dream looking peaceful and happy to see me. He told me that it was all right that I had broken the relationship with his son, and he hoped I would have a happy marriage to the new guy I dated. When I awakened from the dream, I was visibly shaken. I tried to reach Vincent several times that day, but there was no answer. When he returned the call, Vincent informed me that his father had died during the night. To this day I believe his father communicated with me."

"Yes. Your experience is called a crisis apparition. It is common for a newly deceased person to visit loved ones by projecting a vision of his or herself to the still-living relatives in a dream or in a vision. These visions usually occur before the living relatives are informed of the death. In fact, I believe this may be the first behavior of a deceased person in the spirit world. They visit their still-living relatives to say good-bye."

The class became quiet and I could tell talking about spirits intimidated them. So I continued by pointing out the patterns in precognitive clairvoyant experiences.

"Precognitive clairvoyant experiences take a longer time to be validated than telepathic experiences. In fact, the experiences that involve the future have a time span longer than forty-eight hours before the vision is proved correct. Precognitive episodes have more unusual circumstances surrounding the predicted incident. Some precognitive experiences occur in the dream state as opposed to telepathy, which happens more often in the waking state."

"Are spirit encounters more unusual than the precognitive experiences?" Andy asked.

"Yes. Spirit encounters are more unusual, because we are psychically less open to them. People who have these encounters either see a vision of a spirit or become convinced a spirit communicated with them. In addition, spirit encounters almost always leave profound feelings of peace within the individuals who had them."

"So many of us in this class have had paranormal experiences. Doesn't that indicate our experiences have meaning?" Sharon asked.

"Yes, of course they do! Paranormal experiences demonstrate there is much more to life than what we already think or know. There is more to learn and to understand than just the tangible, physical world. These psychic incidents demonstrate there is a higher power that directs and guides our lives when we pay attention to the mental messages. Somehow, through the mind these psychic encounters forge a way for us to receive the thought message. The mind is not fully understood; we know there is a mind, but we cannot see it, nor do we have an explanation of how or why it works. Yet, we accept its complexities without ever doubting that it is real. Our reality is based on our perceptions. We believe in the existence of the mind because we experience a thought, a word or a feeling. And people will believe in the paranormal only when they have experienced a psychic moment that changes their perception."

"How does Science view extra-sensory perception?"

"Scientists usually pronounce ESP incidents as unfounded. They believe Psychic or ESP phenomena violates the basic principles of what is known about science and the world. Therefore, scientists do not give credence to personal stories. In fact, people who have had these experiences are sometimes thought to be emotionally unstable and even possibly crazy by scientists. In addition, scientists often explain such stories as coincidences, delusions, misunderstandings and wishful thinking."

"Doesn't it bother you to know that scientists could think you are crazy because of your psychic gift and beliefs?"

"Not since I've researched and analyzed science. At one time, I thought only science knew the truth about life. Now I know better. I no longer subscribe to the belief because I now believe that science isn't everything."

"What changed your belief?"

"Let me say a little something about science in general because it may change your view of science, also. Science tells us many things about the world we live in. It provides us with the knowledge we need to make our lives better, through the progress of technology. Many of us look up to scientists as those who have all the answers to our questions. Those who embark upon scientific exploration are individuals worthy of praise and are given a certain benefit of doubt by society. And this is rightfully so, considering the achievements that science has brought to us and how we can all agree on the answers. Although it does generate more questions than it answers, science is based on facts that lead to real knowledge."

Paranormal experiences are considered by many in the scientific community to be elusive and based upon feelings, experiences and opinions. These things are all subjective. What you experience is real and true to you and what I experience is real and true to me but it just isn't 'true' in the eyes of science.

"To believe that science has all the answers would be a mistake. To say that belief in the paranormal is based on mere opinion is also a mistake. Most people believe that if science is based on facts, then it must be cut and dry with no room for argument. A prediction is made, an experiment is performed and a new discovery is proven. In fact, this could not be further from the truth. Science, or truth, is much more complicated and subtle than that. It is interesting to know that the so-called facts that concern scientists are already interpreted facts. You can't directly see what is happening during most experiments. You have to infer the outcome from the things you can see using a theoretical interpretation."

"When an experiment is carried out, it gathers a certain kind of data, which is plotted on a graph. The graphed data only becomes interesting and significant when it is interpreted. The problem is, you have to know some science already in order to make the interpretation. In other words, you have to view what you are looking at from a chosen point of view. Once you choose that point of view, you are betting that things might turn out that way. This means that in order to get anywhere at all using science, experiment and theory – along with fact and interpretation – are always combined. What counts is not just what scientists see, but the way they see it. Therefore, science uses a mixture of fact and opinion. Science also relies on good judgement and informed opinion. To rely upon the mixture of fact and interpretation, to see the world through a chosen point of view, makes science more daring than most people realize. This process is not so unlike what I or others have used to try to understand a paranormal event or feeling. Belief in the paranormal requires faith in our feelings and perceptions. Faith to me is not a leap into what will become the wrong direction, but one that is right. The aim of my quest, like that of science, is to seek the belief about what is true."

"What does ESP suggest? It suggests that the scientific knowledge about the nature of the universe is incomplete. In fact, scientists have revealed that the majority of the matter within the universe is unknown. Psychic experiences also suggest that the capabilities and limitations of the human potential are also underestimated. Biologists now believe there is more to perception and the way we use our senses than we previously thought. Moreover, some paranormal incidents are often accompanied by profound feelings and meaning that have spiritual undertones. The bottom line to these experiences can simply be stated as: the paranormal is normal."

"Then all the answers to life are not found in science as most of us have believed?"

"That's right. Science uses a mixture of fact, good judgement, observation and informed opinion to validate hypotheses, which we later deem as scientific fact. If you were to analyze a paranormal incident, you would use observation and informed opinion to determine the validity of the experience. And these tools are similar to the tools of science."

That was my last statement before the class ended. As the students left the class, a majority of them thanked me for giving them some points with which to defend themselves from people who mock them for having such unusual experiences or beliefs. And I encouraged them to continue to believe in the paranormal. For the first time, I felt like an expert and I couldn't wait to let Anna know about the class. In addition, I was confident I had made the right decision. When the time was right, I knew my guides would provide signs for me to know where to take the next step.

Insights

❧ Once you are aware that you can access your higher consciousness, you must then be willing to change in order to open this avenue for your own personal experience. The biggest block to your development is fear. A fear of change or a fear of the unknown will cripple your ability to reach your psychic potential. In order to move forward in your development, you must let go of your fears.

❧ Having faith and trust in a higher power eliminates your need to fear the unknown. When you have faith and trust, you are protected. God is always around us, just waiting for us to ask for guidance. We are here under the rule of free will, so God cannot help us until we ask Him.

❧ You will not change as a person when you develop your psychic ability. You will still be you, but you will have a higher sense of perception and more understanding of life. Your newly-acquired skill and higher level of understanding will help you to make better decisions. Better decisions can then create a more positive life.

❧ A large percentage of the population has experienced unexplainable paranormal moments. Most of those who have had the experiences claim the experience changed their life. As a result, they conclude there is much more to life than the physical tangible world. You, too, have the potential to experience a psychic moment.

❧ The spontaneous transference of thought communicated between two people is defined as telepathy. Telepathy is considered a modality in extra-sensory perception and is the most frequently reported paranormal moment experienced. The phrase, "you took the words right out of my mouth," describes a telepathic moment.

ᥡ When you experience a telepathic moment, you suddenly focus your attention on another person. The intensity and duration of the focus of that attention distinguishes the telepathic moment from an ordinary thought. The time span from the obsessive thoughts to the actual knowledge of the event is characterized by a very short period. The event is often acknowledged within hours and almost always within forty-eight hours from the first moments of intense focus.

ᥡ When you see spirits, shapes, faces, situations, symbols and colors not seen by the naked eye, you are using the ESP faculty of clairvoyance. These visions can be seen with the eyes open or closed. When you witness a future event, you are experiencing the ESP faculty of precognition. A precognitive experience involves the future and has a time span longer than forty-eight hours before the vision proves correct. Precognition can also occur in the dream state.

ᥡ All the answers to life are not found in Science. Science uses a mixture of fact, observation, good judgement and informed opinion to validate hypotheses, which we may later deem as scientific fact. If you were to analyze a paranormal incident, you would use observation and informed opinion to determine the validity of the experience. These tools are similar to the tools of science. However, the paranormal will never be viewed the same way as science, until there is a scientific model that includes the experiences of people.

THE LAST SIGNS

A loud crashing sound in the middle of the night and other indistinguishable noises awakened me from a deep sleep. My heart pounded like the loud beat of a drum as I listened for other unusual noises. However, the only sounds I heard were the raindrops hitting against the windows in the front of the house. Could those other, frightening sounds have been nothing more than my imagination?

I searched for the source of the noise beyond the perimeters of the bedroom. When I glanced toward the doorway, I witnessed a shadow pass by the door and move across the wall. Hoping to glimpse it again, I bolted forward for a better look. This time I spotted an image in the corner of the room and panicked. Fear engulfed me and sweat beaded on my forehead when I thought it was an intruder. But when I recognized the image, I discovered it wasn't a person or even a shadow. Instead, it was a beautiful red rose. Suspended in mid-air amidst the darkness of the room just like a star in the night sky, the crimson-colored rose floated through the room.

I rubbed my eyes to check if I was dreaming or not, but when I opened them, the image was still there. Shocked, I just stared at the rose, expecting within a few seconds for it to dissipate. Instead, it hung eerily in the darkness as though something invisible held it suspended, seven feet above the floor.

As I scrutinized it, the rose seemed to move closer. Then twinkling lights surrounded it, completely illuminating the rose. The image looked so mystical it reminded me of a religious experience. In fact, a belief in my religious up-bringing offered a possible explanation for the image. When Saint Theresa answered a prayer, supposedly she manifested a rose, which preceded the miracle. Perhaps one of my prayers would soon be answered?

Some previous research on psychic powers offered me another possible interpretation for the image. Research on psychic phenomena indicates images suspended in mid-air, particularly images of flowers or geometric shapes, are often signs of developing mediumship. Thus, the vision could indicate mediumship tendencies and not signify my prayer had been answered. I studied the image and meditated for guidance, not taking my eyes off the rose. Unfortunately, it dissipated before I understood its purpose. A bit disappointed a short time later, I stopped analyzing the experience and went back to sleep.

The next morning when I telephoned Anna, her reaction to my teaching experience surprised me.

Enthusiastically, I commented, "I loved teaching the course on the paranormal and I can't wait until next week's class. My students were so curious and informative. In fact, a number of them revealed their own psychic experiences to the class. And those incredible experiences persuaded me psychic phenomenon isn't mysterious but rather a normal part of life."

She remarked, "Good! That's what the other side wanted you to conclude. Now what about the other experiences?"

"What do you mean? What other experiences?"

"You know. The one you had when you woke-up last night at 3 a.m."

"Oh my gosh. How do you know that? I didn't tell you!"

"No. you didn't, but I had a dream you experienced something strange last night. Then I had a vision of you staring at a rose. When I looked at the clock, it was 3 a.m."

"I did! I did! But how could you possibly know that?"

"Our guides must have communicated to us while we were in a dream state."

"What do you think it means?"

"Your guides probably wanted to introduce the next level of your psychic development to you. You will develop mediumship, but I don't think that's why I had the dream. I suspect there's a more significant meaning for it."

"Doesn't a rose symbolize something positive?"

"Yes, but it wouldn't be the reason our guides contacted both of us on the same evening. I think they're trying to warn us about something."

"Warn us? You mean about something bad?"

"Yes and no. I think we are being told to be alert so we can prevent a problem from developing."

"That's scary."

"No, it's not. Our guides are letting us know there could be a problem in the future, but they're trying to help us avert it, not frighten us. Our job is to pay attention to the signs."

"Is the warning for me or you?"

"It can be for either. However, I suspect it may be more for you than me, because you had the vision. I only had a dream of your vision. Nevertheless, our guides must want me to know because I am the substitute for the original plan. If you don't receive the guidance, I will. And then I will tell you. Therefore, you will still receive the guidance. We need to both watch for signs."

"Okay. I'll call if I sense anything."

We ended our conversation, but my analytical thoughts didn't stop. I focused on the possible reasons why my guides would need to warn me. I drove slower and more carefully for the next week, because images of accidents consumed my thoughts. However, nothing happened after three weeks, so I concluded our interpretation was incorrect.

Thus, I stopped worrying.

A few days later, there was a nagging vision. I ignored it, but it flashed again. This time I tried to decipher it. It looked like a whirling object, but I couldn't identify it. On the other hand, the speed of it held my attention. Again, the whirling object appeared in my vision, but this time an image of my son flashed in my mind. When fear welled-up inside me, I knew the warning involved my son. I suddenly became alert, open to any signs that might seem like guidance.

Meantime, I contemplated possible reasons for the vision. For several days my son had been working on the restoration of a 1965 mustang convertible in the house garage. But now I wondered if he was doing something on the car that could be dangerous? I dismissed the thought as quickly as I received it because I knew he was a mechanical engineer and quite capable of handling his restoration project. Therefore, I attributed my fear to nothing more than a mother's worry.

A few minutes later, my son came running from the garage and into the kitchen looking for a telephone book. He looked exasperated, which seemed odd to me.

"Are you doing something in the garage today that is dangerous?"

He stopped and in an exaggerated and slow manner asked me, "Why?"

When I told him my vision, he answered. "Yes. It could be dangerous."

Then he explained how a wrench had slipped and lodged between the engine and another part of the car. He had been mentally debating whether he could retrieve the wrench or not without it slipping further. He continued to tell me that if the wrench slipped while the spring was still compressed, the spring could dislodge and go swirling in the air.

"Could it cause serious injury if it hit a person?"

"Yes. The force from the pressure could cause the spring to act like a flying circular saw and be dangerous to anyone in its path."

"Can you do anything to make it safe?"

Before my son could answer the question my daughter interrupted our conversation. She had a frightening dream, which upset her. Teri Ann told us that someone in the dream died from an accident.

Jimmy and I just looked at each other and concluded we didn't need any more signs to act. He ordered the two of us out of the house, while he shut off the compressor. After he retrieved the wrench Jimmy addressed the two of us.

"Mom, I'm glad you told me your vision." And then he turned to Teri Ann and said with a sigh. "And I'm glad you told us about your dream. This could have been a dangerous situation for all of us."

"This must be what my guides warned me about."

"What do you mean?" asked the two of them.

After explaining details about how guides function in our lives, I called Anna and told her what had happened. "Do you think the other side tried to warn me about the danger in the garage? Could that be the reason our guides tried to contact us?"

"Yes. You avoided danger, which showed them you are sensitive enough to feel danger for those close to you. Sometimes, that's hard to do, but you received the vision and interpreted it correctly. In addition, your ability to receive psychic impressions became synchronized with your guides' ability to connect with you. Your guides have been waiting for this moment. Now your psychic ability will develop even further. And I think you will develop mediumship too."

"Will the mediumship happen right now?"

"No, it will happen in stages. Mediumship is just another level of psychic ability, so there is usually a progression toward it. You don't want mediumship to occur without previous psychic development. That could be dangerous"

"Why?"

"There is a fine line between living in reality and being out-of-touch with reality. Sometimes, developing psychic ability is too much for a person to handle mentally. Seeing the dead can be frightening without any preparation for it."

"Is there a connection between psychic ability and mental illness?" I asked.

"Yes. I am sure there are some people in mental institutions who are psychic. They probably opened their minds to the ability too fast and then couldn't shut the door. They are physically in this world, but function mentally in the spirit world."

"How do you maintain control of it?"

"Don't stay in a psychic mode twenty-four hours a day. And don't let spirits control you by listening and complying to all of their demands. Instead, the information should guide and not force you to do anything that could harm you or another person. In order to grow emotionally and spiritually, we have to make our own decisions. Therefore, it's important to develop a ritual to signify to our guides that we are ready to receive the psychic information. This ritual could include a prayer, a certain time of day, lighting a candle, meditating or entering into another form of relaxation. In other words, we should be able to receive the guidance and respond to it without feeling as though we are being told what to do. Sometimes, spirit guides become overzealous and want to parent us all the time. Knowing this fact can help us discern the information."

"Then the rose must have been a symbol of mediumship and not an answered prayer?"

"Yes and no. The rose served more than one purpose. It alerted you to wait for guidance. And it triggered you to associate it with a religious experience, which seems to be a pattern in your life. The other side recognized a long time ago that religious experiences always fascinated and made you more aware. Therefore, your guides use a religious symbol or experience whenever they need to capture your attention and not leave it to chance!"

"Do guides only alert psychics to danger?"

"Of course not!" Anna exclaimed. "Guides are there for everyone. It may seem as if people who are psychic are the only ones who receive guidance, but you know that's not true. Anyone, who looks for signs and recognizes them as such, is guided. Your students' experiences are excellent examples of that. But that doesn't mean the guides stop trying to reach those who aren't attentive or don't believe in guidance. It's an on-going process. The more sensitive and aware you become, the easier it is to recognize and act on the message. We operate here under free will. Therefore, we have to want the guidance, ask for it and then pay attention for it. Understanding this rule is one of the secrets of life."

"Does psychic ability have a greater purpose than we know?" I asked curiously.

"Yes. It's a gift God gave to everyone, but we have free will to choose whether to develop it or not. When we harness its power, we receive guidance to create a better life. Not all destinies are predetermined. We create and change our destiny every day by the decisions we make. Our emotions play a key role in attracting the circumstances of our lives that we call fate. On the other hand, God didn't intend for us to have lives peppered with suffering and endless challenges. Instead, we were given the power to transmute our problems by paying attention to the guidance we are given. By developing our natural psychic ability, we can change our lives for the better as well as discover our purpose. These are the tools God gave us to discover the secrets of life. We just have to choose to use them."

We ended our telephone conversation and once again it stimulated my mind. But I quickly stopped analyzing because my mind was overloaded with information. In retrospect, my analytical thoughts may have interfered with my ability to receive guidance. Unfortunately, a few weeks later, I had a car accident because I didn't perceive the warning accurately.

A freight train stalled on the railroad tracks near my house, which delayed the traffic in the area. Fearful of being late for a class, I turned my car around and headed down another street. I didn't want to wait to cross the tracks in the long line of stopped traffic. Instead, I followed another route toward my destination. However, an inner voice told me that I should've waited in the traffic, because that route was the shortest one to class. In addition, I had a queasy feeling about my decision to take a different route, but I attributed it to indigestion rather than guidance.

Before I realized those feelings were guidance I was in the middle of an intersection. A yellow car screeched from around the corner through the red light and headed straight for me. I slammed on my brakes, but it was too late. The car rammed into the passenger's side of my car. The jolt injured me and my first thoughts centered on that stalled train. While riding in the ambulance, over and over again I mumbled the same words. "I should've followed my gut feelings and waited for the train to clear the tracks."

The car accident landed me in the hospital in neck and back traction. The prognosis was good, but I had to stay in traction for three weeks. I couldn't imagine how I was going to endure three weeks in the hospital, but I tried to think positively. I reminded myself that doing nothing for three weeks would allow me to think and to meditate. And perhaps my guides would use this time to advance my spiritual growth. In fact, when I had that thought, I chuckled. There couldn't be a better time to get my attention than now. Strapped in traction for eight hours a day, I had nothing to do but listen.

The three weeks didn't pass quickly for me. I experienced a lot of vivid dreams that often awakened me. And there were out-of-body experiences to exotic places a number of times during my dream state. I discovered that meditating in the hospital was more productive than meditating at home, because there were no distractions or time restrictions to provide an excuse for me not to meditate. And that was a plus for my development. Even though some situations weren't pleasant, my hospital time proved more memorable than I expected.

This one afternoon I couldn't stop looking at my hospital roommate. Gertrude, an elderly woman, had just received good news. All her tests were negative so her doctor scheduled her hospital release for the next morning. Obviously elated, she telephoned her son to make plans for the next morning.

Although I shared a happy moment with Gertrude when she received that news, I just couldn't relax. An uncomfortable feeling tugged at me. Deep in the pit of my stomach a churning, nauseous feeling gripped me. Then I heard an inner voice tell me that she wasn't going home the next day because something terrible was going to happen to her. I tried to put those words out of my mind, but I couldn't. Why would I have such unpleasant thoughts?

I searched for a reason. Could I be reacting to a fear in me that manifested in my thoughts? Was I sad I wouldn't have her as a roommate or see her anymore? Nothing tangible explained my feelings.

As I tossed and turned trying to get comfortable, I glanced toward Gertrude's bed just to check on her. She seemed fine, but it didn't comfort me. When my glance became a stare, I worried she would sense my strange behavior. Yet, I couldn't stop obsessing over her nor could I sleep. Several hours elapsed but nothing changed. She seemed fine, but I still couldn't relax. This feeling of anxiety and my absurd thoughts annoyed me. In fact, I even had disparaging thoughts about psychic ability.

Then it happened. A trembling feeling suddenly filled my body. I looked at Gertrude, but she was fine. However, the fearful feeling wouldn't go away. When it intensified more than I could handle, I looked at Gertrude again. Gertrude's body jerked and stiffened and then went limp as she tried to talk to me.

I pulled the traction release, jumped out of bed and ran to

her. Gertrude struggled to speak, but she whispered to me to call her son. She pointed to a piece of paper on the table near the bed. When I read it, her son's number was on it.

Before I dialed the number I pushed the call button for a nurse. Gertrude struggled to speak again, but couldn't move her mouth or form her lips to speak. That's when I realized she was having a stroke. I panicked because a nurse had not yet responded to my call for help. So I pulled the emergency cord and screamed for a nurse, shouting it was an emergency.

While I waited for the medical emergency team to respond, an inner voice told me if I kept her calm, she would survive. Softly I stroked her hair and whispered, "Gertrude you will be okay. Just stay calm. Relax. You will be okay. Nothing will happen to you. Your son will be here shortly."

Her eyes stared into mine and a tear trickled down her cheek. Gertrude was still aware, but no longer struggled to speak. Finally, the medical team entered the room and I moved out of their way. While the doctors and nurses surrounded her bed, I called her son from my phone.

The next day there was a lot of activity in the room. Doctors, nurses and technicians assembled behind the closed curtain around Gertrude. I couldn't hear anything until the Neurologist pulled open the curtain.

"Are you Jane?" the doctor asked.

"Yes," I answered timidly .

He moved to the edge of my bed. I didn't know what he wanted, so I nervously waited for his next words.

He introduced himself as Dr. Cho, Gertrude's Neurologist, and then he commented. "You risked your own healing for Gertrude. And I want you to know that you saved Gertrude's life."

I didn't know how to respond.

251

He extended his hand to shake mine. "I am grateful you were so alert. Because of your actions Gertrude is alive and expected to make a full recovery."

Embarrassed by the compliment, I simply replied, "Thank you. I am grateful she is alive, too."

After he left the room I became euphoric because I was now grateful I had listened to the guidance. When I realized that psychic ability could avert danger or even save a life, I thanked God I had made the effort to develop my psychic ability.

There were moments Gertrude's eyes just sparkled when she saw me. And during the times I fed her when her family wasn't there, I could feel the bond between us, even though she couldn't speak. When she was discharged from the hospital ten days later, she had fully recovered with no signs of a stroke. And I gained a nickname from the ordeal. The nurses called me, "Florence Nightingale of the third floor!"

The accolades came fast and were soon forgotten, but the message I learned from the experience remained etched in my memory. If psychic ability could avert danger, then it had more value than most people believed. In fact, the experience with Gertrude convinced me it was an awesome power. If everyone has the potential to develop it, then psychic ability must have a purpose beyond the obvious.

Despite my previous reluctance to do readings, my opinion was swayed in the opposite direction. And I was suspicious it was the other side who pushed me in that direction. I needed to ponder everything again from the first psychic consultation to my own hospitalization. However, I didn't want to tell anyone I was thinking of offering psychic consultations, until I actually made the decision to do it.

Once I was released from the hospital, I went to the beach

for some solitude. It had been a long time since I had visited a beach. The sound of the surf crashing on the sand relaxed me. The cool, refreshing breeze cleared my thoughts and renewed my spirit. While walking along the beach and watching the ocean waves ebb and flow, I reflected on my life and then quietly asked God for a tangible sign. I wanted a sign to prove psychic talent was my purpose and the occupation God intended for me at this point in my life. A tangible sign would help me believe. Thus, I could accept it fully and never question it again. So I prayed and hoped for that sign.

Not far from the beach, I located an old museum on my way home. It was a small, quaint museum with a reputation for being haunted. I stopped there to peek into the windows and circle the building. However, I didn't expect it to be open so late in the day, but the lights were on and the door was open.

When I entered the more than 200-year-old building, a grayed-haired, eighty-year-old, pleasant-looking woman greeted me. She, as curator, instructed me on how to navigate the museum and learn its history by playing the recordings in each room. However, I explained to her that I was interested in the ghost history of the house and not the historical information. Her eyes twinkled and her demeanor showed delight as she obliged me.

Winnie, as she was known to the locals, revealed the various ghost sightings and experiences associated with the house, including tales of the local folklore. When she discovered I was psychic, she asked me if I would psychically sense for any ghost activity in an upstairs room of the house. There had been ghost activity reported that day. So I went up the stairs and into the room directly above us and sat quietly to feel for cold spots and to observe my psychic impressions.

After a few minutes in the room an ice-cold breeze enveloped me. In fact, it was so cold I could see my breath in front of me. Then I heard footsteps creak on the hallway floor, so I waited to see if someone visiting the museum had followed me upstairs. When I looked into the hallway, no one was there. I re-entered the room and quieted myself again. I closed my eyes to sense the room so I could receive impressions. When I re-opened them, a ball of light appeared near the ceiling and then floated to the other side of the room. A split-second later I had a vision. I saw a man in uniform standing near the window looking out towards the sea. The ghost of a sea captain stood in the room. When I gasped, the figure dissipated.

At first, the shock of seeing a ghost immobilized me. But I quickly regained my composure and ran down the steps to tell Winnie. When I reached the bottom of the staircase, Winnie and a priest were engaged in conversation. I didn't know how to react, because I wasn't sure I should let the priest know I was a psychic. I hesitated to approach them, but Winnie immediately invited me to join them. When I approached, she introduced me to Father Tyler. I had no intentions of revealing my experience until I was alone with her. However, Winnie didn't seem to mind talking about the ghosts inhabiting the museum with the priest still there.

Winnie blurted, "Did you feel any ghosts in the room?"

I hesitated, but she continued. "Father Tyler doesn't want to leave until he knows whether or not you experienced anything in the room."

I had no choice now but to answer. However, my thoughts ran wild trying to imagine why he wanted to know about my experiences. I finally answered in a shaky voice. "Yes, there is something in the room, and I believe it's a ghost"

Winnie and Father Tyler listened attentively while I explained my experience and described what I saw. The two of them looked at each other and then at me with startled expressions on their faces before either one commented.

"Do you mean you saw the spirit?" asked Father Tyler.

"Yes. He looked like a sea captain. He had a beard, wore a uniform and looked through a telescope in front of the window, which was pointed toward the ocean."

"Oh! That's wonderful! This house used to be an Inn where sea captains often stopped and docked their ships. They visited the Inn before they re-embarked on their journey back to the ocean."

From that moment on, the three of us engaged in conversation about ghosts, the paranormal and a psychic's ability to see the future. Two hours later, I was still engaged in this surprising discussion with Father Tyler.

We ended our conversation and I prepared to leave.

However, Father Tyler approached me, I thought, to say good-bye, but instead he made a request.

"Would you do a psychic reading for me?" asked Father Tyler.

How could I refuse a priest? Trapped by his request and trembling, I answered, "yes". I directed him to the picnic bench outside the museum. When I walked towards the museum back door, several questions raced through my mind. Why would a priest want a psychic reading? Could he have concerns about the future? Did I have to do a reading to overcome my own fear? Was the priest going to tell me my psychic ability was against our religion? Or did the other side arrange my first psychic reading to be for a priest in order to force me to do readings and give me assurance about my ability?

The walk from inside the museum to the outside seemed to go on forever. Scenes from history streamed across my mind with every step. I imagined what it must have been like to be led to a guillotine or to be burned at the stake for having these powers. To make matters worse, there was a replica of a guillotine displayed in the backyard of the museum. I couldn't look in its direction without my fear escalating into panic. In fact, I wanted to bolt from the museum's backyard to escape doing the psychic reading for the priest. However, I persuaded myself to stay calm because the encounter could have a hidden purpose. It could be a test or a sign from God.

Father Tyler sat across the table from me. I took his hand and closed my eyes to concentrate. Once I made the connection to my psychic mind, I proceeded with the reading.

Each time I verbalized the images of his future, he calmly nodded in an affirmative gesture. When I finished the reading, I asked him if he had any questions.

"Yes, I do. But I don't know how to ask you this."

"It's okay. You can ask me anything. I won't judge you."

"I live in a state of constant fear. And sometimes, I have thoughts of leaving the priesthood because of this overwhelming fear. I feel so mentally tortured that I have thoughts of ending my life. But I pray every day for God to lift this burden from me and to send me a sign, so I can continue my ministry."

Concerned, I asked, "Why are you so terrified?"

"I've battled the dark force, but the fear of it still torments me. You have no idea how horrible evil can be because it attacks more fiercely those who serve God than others. I am afraid I will have to face it again and not be able to overcome it next time. I am hesitant to ask you, but at the same time I need to know. Do you see the dark force taking control of me?"

I closed my eyes and waited for a psychic impression. At the same time, I wondered about evil and its power. Would I see evil when my eyes were closed? However, I didn't see an image of it. Instead, I saw a burst of red surrounded by the color green. Immediately, I understood the vision. The color red represented evil and the color green represented a healing power. Since the green surrounded the color red, it meant there would be a healing. I opened my eyes and then answered Father Tyler's question.

"You won the battle. I don't see you battling evil again. Now you just need to conquer your fear."

"Are you sure it won't attack me again?"

"Absolutely! I see your life in the future peaceful and joyful."

"Do you see me still a priest?"

"Yes. I had a vision of you old with gray hair and still a priest."

"That's a relief to know. I feel so much better."

"Now, can I ask you a question?"

"Yes Jane, of course."

"Did the dark force look like the man-made image of the devil?"

"No. You can't see it. If it looked like the man-made image of the devil, it would be easy to recognize and deal with. It's a subtle force that hides. And when you are vulnerable, it manipulates you. What makes the dark force dangerous, is the ability for it to hide or disguise itself. It tried to drive me out of the priesthood. That's what made me so frightened."

"How did you recognize the force?"

"I felt it through my emotions. I was in a perpetual state of confusion, which caused enormous turmoil. No matter how I tried there was no mental peace or joy. I felt fear, had no motivation, and sensed a heavy pressure on me at times. When I had moments of hatred toward others, I knew the cause. But by then

I had a cycle of problems I had to deal with, which was part of the battle. I even hated myself, but then I recognized why I had all of those feelings. It wasn't until I recognized the self-hatred and the turmoil in my life that I realized the dark force was lurking near me. But I still had a hard time letting go of my fear until I met you. Your vision of the future has comforted me and strengthened my faith."

"Then fear must be the emotion that allows the dark force to enter our lives?"

"Yes. I believe you're right." father Tyler replied. "When I had fear and couldn't let go of it, the fear became greater and then my life attracted more turmoil. It was like one vicious cycle. Once I let go of my fear, I felt the dark force release its grip on me."

"Fear must be the wedge the dark force uses to separate us from our faith in God. Only when we ask God for help, can God help us."

"Yes, that's true. My fear became so overwhelming I lost my faith and then I began to loathe myself. It became so destructive that I almost left the priesthood. But I asked God for help. I asked for the guidance I needed to fight the dark force surrounding me."

"That would have been terrible if you left the priesthood. That's what the dark force wanted you to do. If you had, then the dark force would've won."

"Yes. I know. It tried to possess me and that was the real battle. Those moments were the worst of my life. I had no control and it forced me to succumb to its power. I tried to fight, but I heard voices telling me what to do. There were impure thoughts, hatred, confusion and turmoil in all aspects of my life. It was a struggle. I knew the correct choices and behavior, but it didn't matter. During the struggle, my free will was taken from me. But

I didn't give up. I thought of God's love and negated the bad thoughts by transmuting them into good thoughts. Eventually, my thoughts were free and I felt feelings of self-love and love for others again. That's how I knew the dark force was gone, but it left its signature on me: fear."

"You don't have to worry about that battle, because your future doesn't show it. I don't see the dark force attacking you again."

"You have no idea how much you have helped me! I feel like an enormous weight has been lifted off my shoulders. And I have my full faith back, without fear. Thank you for the psychic reading."

"You are welcome. I am thrilled to have helped you."

Father Tyler turned toward the museum and started to walk away but then a few seconds later he turned abruptly to face me again.

"I have one more question to ask."

"Certainly, go ahead Father."

"Would you mind if I give you a hug?"

"Of course not!"

We embraced as he said good-bye and he blessed me with the sign of the cross.

He added one last comment before he left. "Thank you again. I have been praying to God for some help so I could release my fears and also for a sign telling me I should remain a priest. And I feel you are that sign. May God Bless you! I am convinced God sent you to me! This is the first time I have been to the museum. I was in the area searching for a way to relax, so I stopped to look at the ocean and saw the museum. I was emotionally pulled to visit it, which I thought was odd, but now I know why. My help from God was here."

I was too overwhelmed to say anything except to thank him for his compliment. I left the museum, but cried the whole time I drove home and replayed his comments in my mind. According to the priest, I was his sign from God. And according to me, the priest was my sign from God. The cliché, "God works in mysterious ways," seemed appropriate.

Father Tyler's words convinced me God wanted me to accept my psychic talent. So I prayed and addressed God aloud. "I don't know why I have been guided in this direction, but I am convinced this is what you want me to do. So I will stop resisting and make this my profession. Even though being a psychic consultant is not my choice of profession, I will offer readings and have faith that someday I will understand why you have chosen this for me."

I retired for the night feeling serene and peaceful. I had only one more hurdle. I had to tell Anna my decision and then decide whether to offer the readings in my home or secure an office.

I telephoned Anna and then visited her later that day. When I told her of my decision, she was thrilled.

"I told you your psychic ability had a purpose. Eventually, you will understand how and why your psychic ability is your destiny. Now that you are on track you will discover more."

"Do you think the message I received years ago in front of the statue of the Blessed Mother had anything to do with my being psychic?"

"No. I think being psychic will help you to receive the message again when the time is right. Somehow, your psychic ability is part of the plan. Eventually it will be revealed to you. And then you will know the message and be able to reveal it to others."

"Anna, do you know what's the greatest power of a prediction?"

"I think I do, but I would rather hear what you have to say about it."

"The greatest power of a prediction is its ability to create change. And I am proof a prediction can cause transformation. Before I experienced a psychic's prediction about my future I was an ordinary person with no hint of my purpose in life nor any knowledge of the secrets of life. But that's now changed and it began with a psychic's prediction. I am convinced that as a psychic we have a great power and an even greater responsibility for that power. We have the ability to help others when they can't hear the guidance for themselves. When more people learn to discern the voice of inner guidance from their own thoughts and wishes, they too will embrace the secret and discover their own truth."

INSIGHTS

🍂 When a person develops mediumship, there are signs that identify the up-coming ability. You will see images suspended in mid-air or hear voices when no one is present. You will notice an increase in lucid and precognitive dreams. And you will develop increased sensitivity, and might cry easily experiencing strong emotions.

🍂 Mediumship must be developed slowly and with some preparation. If you open the psychic door too quickly, it may not shut down completely and you could run the risk of developing mental problems. There is a fine line between reality and being out-of-touch with reality.

🍂 Spirits can be pushy. Once you open the door, they may try to take over your life. You should never allow a spirit to make a demand that takes away your free will. It is important to maintain control of your ability. Don't stay in a psychic mode 24 hours a day. Set a certain time during the day or a certain place in which you allow yourself to be open to spirit. Develop a routine that is your ritual when you are open to receive spirit. If you do, you will stay in control of your ability. Remember spirits are like children. They need discipline to develop properly.

🍂 Psychic ability could be a key for us to have a better life. God intended for us to stay connected, so we could be guided. However, we often ignore signs of guidance or dismiss them as coincidences. Psychic ability is a tool God gave us and the language spoken on the other side. Therefore, it offers a means of communication between the two worlds.

❧ Guides never stop trying to reach us. However, we have to want the guidance, ask for it, and then pay attention to it. Understanding this rule is one of the secrets of life, telling us how to create a better life. Either we make choices and act upon those choices or our lives are determined by chance, which we accept as our destiny.

❧ The effects of evil are felt through the turmoil and confusion it creates. It manipulates us through our emotions, yet remains hidden from view. Evil encourages fear, poor self-esteem and pro-motes self-hatred, impatience and the hatred of others. When we least expect it, evil can demean us and rob us of our free will. It stops us from moving forward and hinders our emotional and spiritual growth.

❧ Love is a positive force that encourages us to trust, to have faith and to believe in God's protection and unconditional love in us. Love inspires us to grow through our challenges and helps us to focus on the positive by encouraging optimism and trust. A positive force instills confidence, encourages self-love, love of God and love of others. Love enables us to become a more perfect soul through our choices, and not by an outside force.

EPILOGUE

There have been many changes in my life, since those very first psychic predictions about my destiny. Despite my initial skepticism about my supposed destiny, those predictions materialized and changed my life. Some changes were easy for me, while others were extremely hard to handle.

Just as Joseph predicted, my whole way of thinking and belief system changed. Claude was the first of many psychics to tell me I would be divorced. Even though I didn't believe in that prediction, my husband and I did, indeed, divorce.

Jim saw me on television and the letters NBC around me. Several years later, my first national television appearance was on NBC's *House Party with Steve Ducey*. Mexico was my travel destination on two occasions. The opportunity to travel there occurred unexpectedly and came in an unusual way, both times just as Alicia had predicted.

California seemed so distant from my thoughts when Alicia first mentioned it. However, California is now important to me. Several of my closest friends live there. All of those friendships developed after I became a professional psychic.

Anna said I would become prominently known for my psychic ability and so sensitive to spirit energy that I would communicate with them. There is a sizable media list to my credit, so I guess I have achieved a level of prominence for my psychic ability. Not only do I do individual consultations, but I also do ghost investigations and seances. In fact, I am extremely sensitive to spirit energy. When a spirit is present during a ghost investigation or séance, I have an unusual, visible, physical reaction to the spirit energy. This reaction helps me to locate the spirit or validate its presence.

Lori saw me riding in a fancy limousine as a result of my psychic ability. Fox Network News sent a limousine to bring me to their New York City studio for an interview in 2002. This could be what Lori had seen or it could be something yet to happen. Angela saw my name as an author of a book, which you are now holding in your hands.

Since Anna connected my psychic ability to God's work, I have discovered a part of what God wants me to do and this book's message helps me to fulfill that part of the plan. And I am confident I will know more of the plan, when the time is right.

APPENDIX

HOW TO JUMPSTART THE
PSYCHIC DEVELOPMENT PROCESS

Most people believe that if you do the psychic development exercises recommended by psychics, you will develop your ability. However, that isn't completely true. Developing psychic ability is not just a series of exercises. It is a process of emotional, spiritual and mental change that you must undergo to achieve your goal. This process takes time, dedication, patience, trust and practice. However, if you persevere, you will succeed, especially if you also strive to develop confidence and self-love. Both traits facilitate psychic development and are part of the process.

These suggestions and exercises are the first steps in the development process. You should not expect to become psychic with just these exercises. Instead, you should use these tips to begin the awakening process. The two most important words to remember are patience and self-trust. These two traits are the keys that will unlock the ability in you.

There are several basic skills necessary for you to master in order to develop the ability. Those skills are relaxation, awareness, observation, concentration, sensitivity and interpretation. Just like any other creative talent once the basic skills are developed, practice will enhance the ability.

The first and most important skill necessary for you to achieve is relaxation. Without the ability to relax, you can't master the other skills. You need to achieve a level of relaxation that you can do almost at will in order to receive guidance or psychic information on a regular basis. Unless you take time-out from the hectic pace in your life and quiet yourself enough to listen for guidance, you will never receive it. This is true even for a professional psychic. Therefore, learning how to relax is the first step in the process.

There are several techniques that you can use to learn how to relax. Deep Breathing, visualization, walking, meditation, hypnosis, and getting a hobby are a few of those modalities.

A. Deep Breathing: This is the fastest way to learn how to relax. Once you have mastered the deep breathing technique, you can use this skill over and over again to facilitate a state of mind conducive for receiving psychic information. Inhale and exhale slowly to a count of 5. Then repeat your deep breathing to 6, 7 and 8. This exercise will calm your body and your mind.

B. Walking: Exercise is one of the quickest ways to release stress and to relax. In fact, you are in a natural psychic state during and immediately following exercise. Take advantage of this natural psychic state and focus on a question you need guidance for and then listen for an answer. The answer is the first thought that pops into your mind.

C. Get hobbies: Take a course for fun. Try something creative like painting, ceramics, gardening or participating in a dramatic activity. Concentrating on a hobby reduces stress and also helps to develop that skill.

D. Use imagery or visualization: Pretend you are somewhere that you are particularly fond of visiting. Visualize a pleasant scene such as a beach or mountain scene. Or you can use another type of imagery for a different exercise. Become aware of the tension in your body by closing your eyes and observing the parts of your body that seem tense. Once you identify those areas, imagine a giant vacuum cleaner removing the stress. Not only do these exercises help you to relax but they are also helpful in developing the other necessary skills.

E. Take a shower or a bath: Water is very conducive to relaxation as well as for receiving psychic information. Stay 5 or 10 minutes longer in either. Silently ask yourself a question and then listen for the answer. The answer could pop-up or you could generate a new idea.

F. Meditate: Make yourself comfortable. Inhale and exhale. Then play some soothing music to help relax and put you in a slightly altered state of consciousness. While in this state, focus on a word and try to concentrate on that word. Let go of all other distracting thoughts. Try to focus on the word relax. Then silently repeat the word over and over again as you inhale and exhale. Try not to let distracting thoughts enter your mind. Stay focused on the word and let go of the memories of the day's activities, worries and problems. And as you do, notice the release of tension in your body and the calmness that you feel. Once you are in this relaxed state, pay attention to the thoughts that pop into your mind and analyze them for signs of guidance. Watch for any intuitive flashes of information that come into your mind and listen for sounds or words that could be guidance.

QUICK TIPS FOR DEVELOPING
THE OTHER SKILLS IN THE PROCESS

It is important for you to believe you can develop your ability. Without that belief you will never accomplish your goal. So let go of your preconceived ideas and start exploring your own truth. The following are some quick tips for you to practice everyday to help facilitate the process. Doing these exercises will increase your awareness and help you to develop better concentration skills.

A. To acquire the sixth sense, all of your other senses must be fully awakened. Try to expose your senses to a variety of stimuli. Take a walk and observe the beauty of nature. Take a walk in a park and notice the various types of trees, plants and flowers that are planted. Observe their various shapes, sizes and colors. Feel the texture of the leaves or flowers. Listen to the various sounds of nature and take a mental note of how you feel when you hear them. Try to smell the scents of the park and try to identify them. Continue to experience the park through all of your senses as much as you can. Do any of the sights, sounds, or smells trigger any memories? Keep a record of your observations and memories.

B. Practice making quick decisions. Try to select your choice of food from a menu within a certain time limit that you set. Shorten the time limit each time to help condition you to make quick decisions. Don't always plan your activities. Do some things spontaneously. Curb any tendency to procrastinate.

C. Write your to-do list and discipline yourself to accomplish one goal at a time. By focusing on a project or goal you are increasing your ability to concentrate. Concentration is an important skill for psychic development.

D. Let go of fear and preconceived ideas. Both are blocks to your development.

E. Cultivate positive traits such as confidence, self-trust, optimism, and other out-going personality traits. These are the traits that will help you to develop the ability. Have you ever seen a shy psychic? Most of them exhibit strong personalities.

F. Expose yourself to new things. Travel to new places. Read fiction if you usually read non-fiction books and vice versa. Go to a play or visit a museum. Attend an opera or take a course for fun. The goal is to stimulate your mind. Boredom affects your ability to awaken the gift. Even professional psychics do not function as accurately if they are bored.

G. Pretend you are already psychic and observe your feelings when you meet a new person. Do you feel comfortable with the person or do you feel repelled by the person? Try to form an impression of the person and write it down. Describe a person in terms of a particular flower and then write down why the person reminded you of that particular flower.

H. Walk into a room and sense the mood of the room. Do you get an empty feeling or engaged feeling? Do you feel sad, happy, excited, bored or some other feeling? Do this everytime you walk into a room. This exercise helps to expand your senses in order for you to perceive impressions more readily.

Hypno-Meditation For Your Psychic Development

Hypnosis played a very big part in my development. After I learned to meditate I needed to discipline myself more. I wanted to follow a process I could do automatically rather than have to consciously remind myself to do each time. So I made a hypnosis tape and played it frequently to program my mind to do what I wanted it to do. This hypno-meditation will relax you and gently program your mind to allow the psychic process to begin in you. The hypno-meditation will help to stretch the boundaries of your mind and jumpstart the development of your natural psychic ability.

Use this self-hypnosis script for your own guided hypno-meditation experience. Choose soft, relaxing music for the background. Get a tape recorder and read the script slowly, pausing at the breaks in the script as you tape record. Try to make your voice as melodious as you can. The hypnosis script is designed to create a deep level of relaxation as well as to stretch the boundaries of your mind. You will then program your mind to receive guidance from your higher self through this self-hypnosis technique. After you have read and recorded the script play the tape at least three times a week to begin developing your psychic ability. Eventually, you will enter the deeper levels of your mind through the repetition of this exercise. Remember that this technique is to start the process and everyone learns at a different rate and experiences a different level of success. It takes patience and perseverance. It took almost three years for me to experience the breakthrough with my guide. I hope you enjoy these first steps in the process and I wish you success in awakening the divine spark within you.

The Hypno-Meditation Script

Just allow yourself to sit as comfortably as you possibly can right now ... that's right ... just go ahead and adjust yourself to as comfortable a position as possible ... perhaps you may want to uncross your legs and put your feet flat on the floor so you can allow your circulation to flow freely … and when you feel comfortable, why not just close your eyes and allow yourself to enjoy these moments of quiet calm … and you begin to feel so good as you allow yourself to relax … and you finally let go of the tensions in your body …

Now I would like you to notice how much more comfortable you can feel by just taking one very big satisfying deep breath….Go ahead … take a big deep breath … that's fine … You may have already noticed how good it feels … And perhaps you can even feel the temperature of the air on your skin … And just how good you feel right now … As you continue to relax, focus your attention in on your body and allow these good feelings of relaxation and comfort to increase. Perhaps you are wondering where one breath begins and how the next one continues flowing in a soothing rhythmic cycle … the ebb and flow of your gentle breathing pattern.

Just begin to notice how your body feels so relaxed as you continue to drift … drift … brushing all tension aside … and perhaps your breathing pattern has changed since a few minutes ago. And maybe your head feels soothed and relaxed … you may have already noticed just how good breathing deeply and slowly feels, so why don't you take a few more deep breaths so that you can feel even more calm and peaceful … that's right … and you can even become aware of the warm pleasant feeling beginning in the area of your neck and shoulders … And as you continue to breathe naturally and rhythmically, you can experience this warm soothing feeling in all the muscles of your body … and you feel so good … so calm … so relaxed.

There is lots of time … so much time … time is slowing down … and you might even be able to sense just how much time is slowing down … and you can enjoy the luxury of not having to do anything ... lots of time ... so much time. And you can allow yourself the pleasure of experiencing the inner workings of your mind ... and every thought that you have can help you to go deeper and deeper into an altered state of consciousness ... And as you listen to your voice, you can feel so secure ... so comfortable ... so peaceful ... breathing so easily ... with each breath. Lots of time ... so much time ... and time seems to be slowing down more and more ... and you might even be able to hear the second hand on the clock ticking slowly ... ever so slowly ... and you can feel healing waves of deep relaxation flowing into every organ, every tissue, every cell of your body ... and as you feel the sensation of time slowing down you can feel so good ... so at ease ... absolutely calm ... thinking of everything and thinking of nothing ... as if you were in the middle of nowhere ... comfortably separated from your surroundings ... a mind in one place and a body in another place ... here but there ... now and then ... and isn't it wonderful to just drift along, listening and hearing about how comfortable you can be ... and when you experience the soothing feeling of relaxation, it is so easy for you to enter the deeper levels of your mind ... and you are here because you want to reach the psychic level of your mind ... and as you continue to feel so deeply relaxed, you feel so eager to allow yourself to experience your natural inherent psychic ability.

And breathing at a rate that feels so good ... and you can continue being gently lost in your thoughts ... as you feel so good ... so safe ... And you can allow yourself to continue to explore the conscious mind and unconscious mind ... strengthening the right brain hemisphere and then balancing both the left and right hemisphere for optimum ability ... and what a nice thing to know that you can be all alone with your thoughts ... allowing your thoughts to float between the conscious and unconscious mind ...

and you feel so secure, so clam, so peaceful to be alone deep within your subconscious mind and just a voice, my voice ... You can hear my voice ... and you can be there with my voice ... and my voice can be the voice of comfort ... relaxation ... the voice of encouragement ... the voice of motivation ... the voice of wisdom ... and guidance, or the voice of love ... whatever you need the voice to be ... it will be for you ...

As you listen to the sounds of your heartbeat, you become more and more aware of the ability of your unconscious mind to know exactly what is right for you ... And as you do you tap into your higher sense of perception, which is God-given to you ... And you start to notice how you are becoming more aware of images and sensory impressions ... Before long these images and sensory impressions become bits and pieces of psychic impressions that surface into your conscious mind.

You are in complete control ... there is something that you want ... it is here and it is now. And you are eager to explore ... and let's begin by comparing your mind to the surface of a quiet pond ... On the surface, everything looks peaceful and still ... but below there is great depth and much happening. You are beginning to tap into the psychic part of your mind ... At first the sensory impressions or feelings start to surface slowly ... and then more impressions surface ... until there are more ... and eventually you begin to recognize guidance in those bits of sensory impressions and feelings ...

Every moment of every day you remember and then forget so you can remember something else ... You can't remember everything all at once so you let some memories move gently back into your mind ... and somewhere back in your mind all of your memories are stored and some moment soon you choose to remember the things you want to remember ... and those memories surface so easily to the conscious mind ... And so enjoy a minute of clock time to let yourself drift back there to your memories ... And some of those memories help to further free the psychic part of the mind to be open to receive guidance for a better life.

And just like the ripples of water that surface on a quiet pond of water when a small pebble is thrown into the pond ... images ... thoughts and bits of extra-sensory information surfaces like the ripples on a pond to help guide you or to give you an answer to a question ...

Everyday you become more sensitive to your surroundings, in order for you to use this sensitivity to tune into your psychic ability. ... As time continues, you receive more and more information from the area of the brain that stores and controls your higher sensory perception ... the information enters at a pace that you can handle without it ever frightening you ... each day as you walk on the earth and feel the rays of the sun, you become more self-confident ... you look perfect ... you speak perfectly ... and you accept yourself more ... Each day you feel less self-conscious ... able to let go of guilt ... self-sabotage ... fear ... and all other destructive emotions that block your psychic ability ... to emerge a loving soul ... You feel your own self-love and you feel God's love ... To emerge from this deep altered state of relaxation more in tune with your higher sense of perception ... and able to retrieve the same guidance in the waking state ... Now just take a moment to enjoy this wonderful state of relaxation a little longer..... and when you are ready ... you will awaken by mentally counting backwards from 10 to 1 ... When you reach the number one, you will awaken and become wide-awake with a feeling of serenity and deep peace.

BIBLIOGRAPHY

Elliott, Rev. G. Maurice, *The Bible as Psychic History*. London, Great Britain: Rider and Company, 1959.

Hill, Dawn, *Reaching for the Other Side*. Australia: Pan Books, 1982.

Klimo, Jon, *Channeling: Investigations on Receiving Information from Paranormal Sources*. Los Angeles, California: Jeremy P. Tarcher, Inc., 1987.

Lombard Associates, Inc., *The Signet Handbook of Parapsychology*. New York, New York: New American Library, Inc., 1978.

Polkinghorne, John, *Quarks, Chaos and Christianity: Questions to Science and Religion*. New York, New York: The Crossword Publishing Company, 1997.

Sheinkin, M.D., David, *Path of the Kabbalah*. New York, New York: Paragon House, 1986.

Website: www.catholiconline.com. See information on Joan of Arc.

PSYCHIC REFERRAL:

Anna Lario
Denver, Colorado
(303) 639-9065

Anna has been a professional psychic for more than forty years and is the psychic referred to as the author's mentor in *Awakening the Mystic Gift*.

SUGGESTED READING:

Adrienne, Carol, *The Purpose of Your Life,* New York: 1997.

Banfield, Susan, *World Leaders, Past and Present – Joan of Arc*, Chelsea House Publications, 1988.

Blackaby, Henry T. & King, Claude V., *Experiencing God*, Nashville, Tennessee:Broadman & Holman, 1994.

Bristol, Claude M., *The Magic of Believing*, Pocket Books.

Hall, Manly P., *Invisible Records of Thought and Action*, Los Angeles, California: The Philosophical Research Society, Inc., 1990.

Hay, Louise, *The Power Is Within You*, Carson, California: Hay House, 1991.

Hitchcock, Mark, *The Complete Book of Bible Prophecy*, Tyndale, Wheaton, Illinois, 1999.

Hoffman, Enid, *Develop Your Psychic Skills*, Rockport, Ma: Pararesearch, Inc., 1981.

Garrett, Eileen, *Many Voices: The Autobiography of a Medium*, New York: Putnam, 1968.

Gawain, Shahti, *Living In the Light-A Guide to Personal and Planetary*

Transformation, San Rafael, California: Whatever Pub, Inc., 1990.

Keyes, Ken, *Handbook to Higher Consciousness,* Kentucky: Living Love Publications, 1972.

Keyes, Ken, *Power of Unconditional Love*, Coos Bay, Oregon: Love Line Books, 1990.

Morse, Melvin, M.D., *Where God Lives: The Science of the Paranormal and How Our Brains Are Linked To the Universe*, Harper Collins, New York, New York, 2000.

Nadel, Laurie; Haims, Judy; Stempson, Robert; *Sixth Sense*, New York, New York: Prentice Hall Press, 1990.

Roman, Sanaya and Packer, Duane, *Opening To Channel,* California: H.J.Kramer, Inc., 1987.

Ridall, Kathryn, Ph.d., *Channeling: How To Reach Out to Your Spirit Guides*, New York, New York: Bantam Books, 1988.

Rubin, M.D., Theodore Isaac, *Overcoming Indecisiveness*, New York, New York: Avon Books, 1985.   .

Sherman, Harold, *How to Make ESP Work For You*, New York: Ballatine Books, a division of Random House, 1964.   .

Viscott, M.D., David, *Risking*, New York: Pocketbooks, a division of Simon and Schuster, 1977.

Ward, Ph.D., Dan, *Reincarnation Is Making a Comeback*, Westchester, Pennsylvania: Whitford Press, 1990.

Wicker, Christine, *Lily Dale: The Story of the Town that Talks to the Dead*, Harper Collins, New York, New York, 2003.

Yott, Donald, *Man and Metaphysics*, Samuel Weiser, New York, New York, 1977.

Zukav, Gary, *The Seat of the Soul*, Fireside, New York, New York, 1990.

INTERNET RESOURCES

LABORATORY RESEARCH SITES:

http:// www.lfr.org ~ One of the world's leading parapsychologists, Dr.Edwin May, provides information about parapsychology.

http://www.psiresearch.org ~ Parapsychology information and tests by leading parapsychologist, Dr. Dean Radin.

Princeton Engineering and Anomalies Research (Pear Lab).

http://www.princeton.edu/~rdnelson/pear.html ~ One of the leading research labs.

University of Virginia Division of Personality Studies

http://www.healthsystem.virgina, edu/DOPS ~ This is the leading scientific research center for topics like reincarnation, out-of-body experiences, near-death experiences and other aspects of parapsychology.

SCIENTIFIC JOURNALS:
European Journal of Parapsychology
http://moebius.psy.ed.ac.uk/ejp.html One of the most important journals to read if you want to keep up with the latest developments in parapsychology.

Journal of Scientific Exploration
http://www.jse.com Scientific journal to read if you want to keep up with the latest developments in parapsychology.

ORGANIZATIONS:
American Society for Psychical Research
http://www.aspr.com The oldest organization in America for promoting research in parapsychology, has lectures in New York and publishes a journal.

Association for the Study of Dreams-
http://ASDreams.org The ASD holds a yearly conference on dreams.

Exceptional Human Experience
http://www.ehe.org The exceptional human experience studies the personal and transformative meaning at the core of all types of anomalous experiences. They list 335 on the website: mystical, encounter, psychical, healing, death-related, etc.

Institute of Noetic Sciences
http://www.noetic.org Promotes research and education in areas like alternative medicine, parapsychology, human potentials, creativity, etc.

International Association for Near Death Studies
http://www.iands.org/iands An organization that researches near death experiences and also has people who have experienced them.

Intuition Network
http://intuition.org

Spiritual Emergence Network
http://www.cpsh.org This organization tries to find professional help for those disturbed by an unusual experience, and turn such experiences into spiritual growth instead of pathologizing them.

HEALING RESOURCES:
Bereaved Parents of the USA, P.O. Box 95, Park Forest, Illinois 60466-0095.
http://www.bereavedparentsusa.org A self-help organization for bereaved parents, grandparents and siblings.

The Compassionate Friends (TCF), P.O. Box 3696, Oak Brook, Illinois 60522-3696. Telephone number is 630-990-0010. Self-help for the bereaved.
http://www.compassionatefriends.org.

281

http:// www.petloss.com

OTHER INTERESTING SITES:
New Dimensions Radio
http://www.newdimensions.org Weekly and sometimes even more often programs on various aspects of human potential. Shows are usually stimulating and enlightening.

The Next Dimension, Out of this World Talk Radio
http://www.outofthisworldradio.com Features interviews with leading authorities on mysticism, parapsychology and metaphysics. There is a toll free number 1-888-822-TALK for you to participate on the air. The show airs Saturday nights from 11 p.m. to 2 a.m. Pacific Time and can be assessed through the website.

Coast to CoastAM Radio Show.
http:// coasttocoastam.com Radio program pursuing the unexplained.

Association for Research and Enlightenment (A.R.E.), Inc.
http://www.are-cayce.com/index.htm The international headquarters of the work of Edgar Cayce, considered the most documented psychic of all time. Founded in 1931 to preserve, research, and make available insights from Cayce's information. A.R.E sponsors activities, services, and outreach throughout the world.

AquarianAge
http://www.aquarianage.org This is an online showcase of astrology and New Age studies built by the New Age community for the benefit of serious practitioners, students and the curious.

Esotericism Seti Team
http://esoterism.com/seti.html This site also conducts a scientific experiment that harnesses the power of hundreds of thousands of internet-connected computers in the search for extraterrestrial intelligence. You can participate by running a free program that downloads and analyzes radio telescope data.

Prophecies.US
http://www.prophecies.us This is a prediction registry site. The purpose of it is to record and validate predictions of the future that users of the site submit.

SpiritDaily
http://www.spiritdaily.com This site brings interesting spiritual news from every corner of the world and news of the prophecies from the many religious communities around the globe. Lots of interesting links.

www.guardians.net Contains reference info on ancient Egypt and up to date information on Egyptology events and museum sites.

ABOUT THE AUTHOR

Jane Doherty, a renowned psychic for more than 15 years, is the leading authority on psychic experiences. She provides individual guidance through private consultation and offers classes and workshops to those who are interested in discovering and developing their own psychic abilities. Widely recognized and respected for her extraordinary skill and sensitivity, she has been featured on *The Today Show, Fox Network News, CNN, Sightings, MSNBC Investigates, WB11* and numerous publications, including the *New York Times*. She has been named one of the top twenty psychics in *Woman's Own* magazine. Reuters news media has featured her in Australia, Austria, Germany, England, Russia and on a major Spanish television network, *Telemundo*.

Jane has also had the unique distinction of being an expert government witness on psychic phenomena during a U.S. Postal Service investigation of a major mail fraud case involving psychic claims. She is President Emeritus of the Jersey Society of Parapsychology, an organization started more than 30 years ago for the purpose of providing mainstream scientific research and support to this field. She has been written about in three books, including Dr. Hans Holzer's book, *The Psychic Yellow Pages: The Very Best*

Psychics, Card Readers, Mediums, Astrologers and Numerologists. Jane has also been heard on C-Net radio, Ground Zero radio broadcast from Oregon and on English radio broadcasts in Austria, as well as being featured in the *Industry Standard* magazine and *Woman's World* magazine.

Jane lives in New Jersey and publishes her own electronic newsletter, gives private consultations, teaches psychic development courses, conducts seances and ghost investigations. For more information regarding Jane Doherty and her seminars or seances, you can E-mail or write to her.

Jane Doherty
2325 Plainfield Avenue,
South Plainfield, New Jersey 07080
E-mail: janedoherty@comcast.net

Or visit her website at **http://www.janedoherty.com**

FREE CD/AUDIOTAPE
JUMPSTART THE PSYCHIC
DEVELOPMENT PROCESS

For those of you who would like to have a CD or audiotape of the hypno-meditation offered in this book – recorded by the author – you can request a free copy. This copy is a slightly longer version of the hypno-meditation offered in the book.

To order your free copy, just fill out the order form below. It's free with the purchase of *Awakening the Mystic Gift: The Surprising Truth About What It Means to be Psychic*.

Just send $2.95 for shipping and handling for one free CD or audiotape. Due to the overwhelming demand, you must send in the original form, and not a copy of it.

Awakening the Mystic Gift: The Surprising Truth About What It Means to be Psychic by Jane Doherty

Please send me a free copy of the hypno-meditation to jumpstart my psychic development process

Name:

Address: Apt.:

Town:

State:

Zip code:

Email:

Please make check payable to: Jane Doherty

Send to: **Jane Doherty**
2325 Plainfield Avenue
South Plainfield, New Jersey 07080
(Allow 4-6 weeks for delivery).

Please check one:

❑ Free CD

❑ Free Audio Tape

NOTES

As you read this book, you may experience new feelings, thoughts or dreams. Use these pages to make a note of your experiences including the date and time.

NOTES

NOTES